Winning *with Your* Stockbroker

Winning with Your Stockbroker

In Good Times and Bad

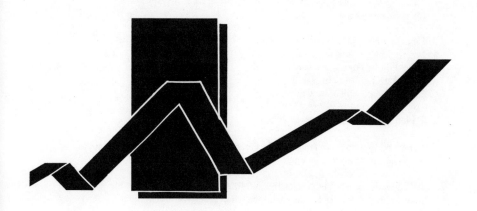

DAVID KOEHLER
& GENE WALDEN

Longman Financial Services Publishing
a division of Longman Financial Services Institute, Inc.

Executive Editor: Kathleen A. Welton
Project Editor: Roseann P. Costello
Copy Editor: Eugene Zucker
Interior Design: Edwin Harris
Cover Design: Salvatore Concialdi

© 1988 by Longman Group USA Inc.

Published by Longman Financial Services Publishing
a division of Longman Financial Services Institute, Inc.

Printed in the United States of America.

88 89 90 10 9 8 7 6 5 4 3 2 1

Library of Congress Cataloging-in-Publication Data

Koehler, David.
    Winning with your stockbroker in good times and bad.

    Includes index.
    1. Stockbrokers—United States. I. Walden, Gene.
II. Title.
HG4928.5.K64 1988   332.6'2'0973   88-602
ISBN 0-88462-740-3

Dedicated to the scores of investors and investment professionals who shared their experiences and insights and thus made this book possible.

D.K.

Also dedicated to Edith and James Walden, My Mother and Father.

G.W.

To Our Readers

Since the stock market crash on October 19, 1987, the rate of change in the securities industry has accelerated. E.F. Hutton, one of the country's oldest and most prestigious brokerage firms, is being acquired by Shearson Lehman Brothers. By the time you read this book other firms may have merged or been acquired.

The stock market itself has also become more volatile. Special commissions have been appointed by the President of the United States and the New York Stock Exchange to study the causes of the October 19th crash. These studies may result in further changes in the way securities are traded.

We hope this book will serve as a tool to help you assess the risks and rewards of all your investment decisions during this turbulent period in the market.

If you have experiences or philosophies (either as an investor or as a broker) that you would like to share, we'd like to hear from you with the idea of possibly using the material in subsequent editions of this book or in other works we will be compiling on the subject of investing. You may contact the authors, David Koehler and Gene Walden, by mail, c/o Longman Financial Services Institute, 9201 E. Bloomington Freeway, Minneapolis, MN, 55420.

ACKNOWLEDGMENTS _____

We would like to thank the many unnamed investors who shared their experiences and insights with us, as well as the many professionals listed below whose assistance and candid comments provided the foundation for this book.

Thomas J. Asher
Executive Vice President
Director of Sales and
  Marketing
The Robinson-Humphrey
  Company
Atlanta, Georgia

Adrian L. Banky
Executive Vice President
General Manager
Securities Industry
  Association
New York, New York

Joseph Baxter
Vice President
National Training Director
Smith Barney, Harris Upham
  & Company
New York, New York

Henry Basil
Senior Vice President,
  Investments
PaineWebber
Minneapolis, Minnesota

William Bergstrom
Financial Planner
IDS Financial Services
St. Paul, Minnesota

Rab Bertelsen
Vice President
Fidelity Investments
Boston, Massachusetts

William Blount
Senior Vice President,
  Investments
PaineWebber Inc.
Portland, Oregon
  (Named as one of the
  nation's top 10 brokers for
  1986 by Registered
  Representative magazine)

Betsy Buckley
Investment Executive
Dain Bosworth
Minneapolis, Minnesota

James Buehler
Account Executive
Roney & Company
Lansing, Minnesota

Donnis Casey
Vice President
Assistant Director of Training
  and Development
A. G. Edwards & Sons
St. Louis, Missouri

Phillip R. Clark
Senior Partner
Director: Branches and Sales
Roney & Company
Detroit, Michigan

Gary H. Cohen
Vice President
Branch Manager
E. F. Hutton & Company
Worcester, Massachusetts

Robert Cohn
Vice President
Training Manager
Drexel Burnham Lambert
New York, New York

Merrilee Cole
Training Consultant
Longman Financial Services
    Institute

Lory Dubbels
Registered Sales Assistant
Piper, Jaffray & Hopwood
Minneapolis, Minnesota

Robert Dunwoody   ·
President
Van Dusen & Company
Golden, Colorado

Ed Fleitman
Senior Vice President
Director of Retail Sales
Craig-Hallum
Minneapolis, Minnesota

C. D'Arcy Fox
Senior Vice President
Director of Training and
    Development
A. G. Edwards & Sons
St. Louis, Missouri

Ed Gerber
Director of Investor Relations
The St. Paul Companies
St. Paul, Minnesota

Dale Grubb
Account Executive
Shearson Lehman Brothers
    (Named one of the
    "Rookies of the Year" for
    1986 by *Registered*
    Representative magazine)
Seabring, Florida

Albert E. Heiam
First Vice President
Drexel Burnham Lambert
Minneapolis, Minnesota

Shawn Henley
Account Executive
Dean Witter Reynolds
Hayward, California

Lyn J. Hensle
Vice President
Director of Marketing
Morgan Olmstead, Kennedy
    & Gardner
Los Angeles, California

L. Scott Horrall
Financial Consultant
Thomson McKinnon
    Securities
Indianapolis, Indiana

M. Thomas Hudson
Vice President
Branch Manager
PaineWebber Inc.
Jacksonville, Florida

Mark Hulbert
Publisher
Hulbert Financial Digest
Washington, D.C.

Judy Johnson
Vice President
Divisional Manager
Advest, Inc.
Hartford, Connecticut

Lee Kopp
Senior Vice President
Investment Officer
Resident Manager
Dain Bosworth Inc.
Edina, Minnesota
  (Named as one of the
  nation's top 10 brokers for
  1986 by Registered
  Representative magazine)

Bill Koriath
Vice President, Investments
Prudential-Bache Securities
Indianapolis, Indiana

Dr. Robert Lefton
President
Psychological Associates
St. Louis, Missouri

Perrin Long
Analyst
Lipper Analytical Services
New York, New York

Norman R. Malo
Senior Vice President
National Marketing Director
Financial Service Corp.
Atlanta, Georgia

William McKinney
Vice President
IDS Financial Services
Minneapolis, Minnesota

Jack McTaggart
National Account Manager
Longman Financial Services
  Institute

Paul Neimann
Attorney
Moss & Barnett
Minneapolis, Minnesota

Allen Ruby
Attorney
San Jose, California

Charles Schwab
Chairman and CEO
Charles Schwab & Company
San Francisco, California

Lee Solot
Vice President
National Training Director
Kidder, Peabody & Company
New York, New York

Kathy Soule
Financial Consultant
Merrill Lynch, Pierce, Fenner
  & Smith
Minneapolis, Minnesota

John E. Sundeen
Vice President
Director of Compliance
Robert W. Baird & Company
Milwaukee, Wisconsin

David J. Thompson
Associate Vice President
Prudential-Bache Securities
Minneapolis, Minnesota

Donald M. Tidlund
Senior Vice President
E.F. Hutton
Minneapolis, Minnesota

James Vieburg
Managing Director
Piper, Jaffray & Hopwood
Minneapolis, Minnesota

David Waterbury
Senior Vice President,
  Investments
Dean Witter Reynolds
  (Named as one of 20
  "Brokers of the Year" in 1982
  by Registered Representative
  magazine)
Minneapolis, Minnesota

Marie Weiner
Attorney
Cotchett & Illston
Burlingame, California

Edward O. Wells
Staff writer
San Jose Mercury News

Kathy Welton
Executive Editor
Longman Financial Services
    Publishing
Chicago, Illinois

Bonnie Westbrook
*Director of the Office of
    Consumer and Information
    Services*
Securities and Exchange
    Commission
Washington, D.C.

Bill Wise
*First Vice President and
    Resident Manager*
Dean Witter Reynolds
Lancaster, Pennsylvania

Roy Zuckerberg
Director of Retail Sales
Goldman, Sachs & Company
New York, New York

Thanks also to:
George C. Anders
*New York News Editor of
    Markets
The Wall Street Journal*

CONTENTS

PART 1   Understanding the Business   1

CHAPTER ONE   By Any Other Name   3
Mutual Incentives? Taking Charge.

CHAPTER TWO   Life on the Inside   7
A Fine Line. Rejection. Beyond Prospecting. Paying Their Way.
Bridging the Gender Gap. A Day in the Life.

CHAPTER THREE   Earning Their Commissions: What a Broker
                Can Do for You   21
Earning Their Commissions. Fear and Greed. When to Sell.
Maneuvering the Twists of the Market. Analysts: Probing behind
the Scenes. Where Science Becomes Art. The Whole Package.

PART 2   The Selection Process   37

CHAPTER FOUR   What's out There: From Different Firms
                Come Different Services   39
Stage 1: Your Choice of Firms. The Big Nationals. Regional NYSE Firms.
NASD Firms. Penny Stock Firms. Institutional Firms.
Financial Planning Firms: *The Process. Finding a Financial Planner.* Dis-
count Brokers. Profiles of the Major National Firms.

CHAPTER FIVE   Making Your Final Choice   69

Stage 2: Determining Your Objectives: *Your Financial Status. Your Invest-
ment Attitude. Your Broker-Client Relationship.* Stage 3:
Seeking out Suspects: *Referrals. Investment Seminars. The Branch
Manager Approach.* Stage 4: The Interview: *The TAPES Approach.
Concluding the Interview. Follow-Up.* Ending the Search.

PART 3   Managing Your Relationship   89

CHAPTER SIX   How Your Broker Sells   91

Dealing with Rejection. Rounding up Suspects. Dialing for
Suspects: *The Product Approach. The Need Approach.*
Follow-Up: The 90-Second Sale. The 14/71 Rule. Incentives.
Responding to the Cold Call.

CHAPTER SEVEN   Broker's Pet   109

Rules for Becoming a Broker's Pet. Things to Avoid.

CHAPTER EIGHT   The Unscrupulous Broker   121

The Mind-Set of a Stockbroker. Crossing the Line.
*Misrepresentation. Unsuitable Recommendations. Churning.
Unauthorized Trades. Options and Commodities Violations.
Misappropriation. Increasing Abuse. The Other Side.*
Getting Relief.

CHAPTER NINE   When Things Go Awry   143

When to Fire Your Broker. Making the Switch.

PART 4   Getting the Most for Your Money   155

CHAPTER TEN   Buying at a Discount   157

Growth of Discounting. Pros and Cons. When to Use a
Discounter. Who Should Not Use a Discounter. Choosing a
Discount Broker. Commission-Free Stocks. Taking Charge.

CHAPTER ELEVEN   The Extras   171

Discounts. Margin Accounts. *Margin Calls.* Research. Financial
Planning Services. Discretionary Accounts. Broker Partnerships.
The Sales Assistant. Account and Monthly Statement. Special
Services.

CHAPTER TWELVE   Mutual Funds: The Fast Food of Investing   183
"We Do it all for You." "Have it Your Way." "Where's the Beef?"
"The Works." "Change Back for Your Dollar." The Best Funds
for Fast Times.

CHAPTER THIRTEEN   Investmentspeak   199
Cocktail Chatter. Gauging the Future. Reading an Annual Report.
Making Sense of the Financials. Dollar-Cost Averaging. Options
Trading. Program Trading. Reading *The Wall Street Journal.*
Kernels of Wisdom: *Advice. Informational Adages. Descriptive
Phrases.* Reading Your Statement. Following Your Investments.

CHAPTER FOURTEEN   The Final Exam: Rating Your Broker   221
1. Trust 2. Rapport 3. Service 4. Understanding
5. Investment Knowledge 6. Results 7. Extra Credit

APPENDIX   229
A Directory of the 100 Largest Brokerage Firms Based on Number
of Brokers. Contacting the SEC. Contacting Securities Industry
Organizations regarding an Arbitration

GLOSSARY   239

INDEX   253

PART 1

Understanding the Business

CHAPTER ONE

By Any Other Name

They are Wall Street's field force, its infantry, its entrée into America's abundant reserve of available investable assets. You may know them by any of a number of names. On the Street, they're known variously as "RRs," "reps" or "registered reps." PaineWebber calls them "investment executives." Merrill Lynch bills them as "financial consultants." Dean Witter, among others, lists them as "account executives" (though some prefer the more exacting "retail account executive" or "personal account executive"). But to the 25 million Americans who have occasion to use their services, these purveyors of stocks, bonds, mutual funds and the growing bounty of investment products still carry the same unpretentious designation: "stockbroker."

There are vast differences among the roughly 200,000 registered securities brokers in the United States. There are brokers who trade mainly in stocks or bonds, mainly in options or futures, or strictly in packaged investments—mutual funds, unit trusts, annuities and the like. There are brokers who cover the gamut and brokers who specialize within a specialty—dealing only in growth stocks, only in penny stocks, only in blue chips, only in government bonds, only in tax-exempts, only in partnerships. There are long-term traders, shorter-term traders, day traders. There are brokers who will knock themselves out to put you into a $2,000 IRA and brokers who will talk to no one with under $1 million in ready assets. Other important differences also exist—differences in style, in approach, in ability and integrity. "There are brokers," says Dain Bosworth branch manager Lee Kopp, "who are painfully honest, there are those who will tend to gloss over things, and there are others you wouldn't want to trust with your worst enemy." The trick is knowing how to choose among them.

"Most investors expect their broker to do three things for them," says Tom Hudson, manager of PaineWebber's Jacksonville, Florida, branch, "(1) tell them when to buy, (2) tell them when to sell and (3) tell them what is going on in the market."

The best brokers can do a reasonably good job of all three. One investor, the president of a young high-tech company, talks about his relationship with his broker. "My broker has made me a ton of money. He knows how to pick stocks, and he knows what he's talking about. Over the past three years, I've much better than doubled my money, and I've done it just by following his recommendations. When he says 'buy,' I buy; when he says 'sell,' I sell; and things have worked out very well. He's done everything I could expect of a broker."

MUTUAL INCENTIVES?

For many investors, a certain apprehension goes with dealing with brokers. Brokers, in essence, are salespeople, highly skilled at persuading investors to part with their money. Within the industry, some brokers are routinely honored as "top producers"—not because they produce big profits for their clients but because they produce big commissions for themselves. Brokers receive a commission on the sale of nearly every investment, regardless of how that investment performs. In fact, the crash of October 19, 1987, while a disaster for many investors (and a few brokerage firms); was a bonanza for many brokers who benefitted from the high volume of trading during and after Black Monday. "Brokers have a direct incentive for transactions and only an indirect incentive to make you money," says Mark Hulbert, publisher of the *Hulbert Financial Digest*, which rates investment newsletters. "Obviously, if you make money with those investments, you'll be happy and you'll keep investing with that broker. But for the broker, it's a derivative incentive."

Judy Johnson, a divisional manager with Advest, contends, however, that most brokers always try their best to put their clients into successful investments. "The vast majority of brokers are honorable and care about the people they're dealing with," says Johnson. "They have to. They build their business that way. What's in a client's best interest is also in the broker's best interest. So as a group, brokers are among the most honest people I've had the pleasure of dealing with. We conduct our business by word of mouth. Our word is our bond."

There is, however, a dark side to the investment profession. And while statistically, it's unlikely that you'll ever be the victim of deceitful investment practices, anyone who ventures into the market should be aware of the potential risks.

Pete Banaszak, the famed former running back of the Oakland Raiders, spent 13 bruising seasons in the National Football League, slashing through 250-pound defensive tackles. Now retired, Banaszak has found that life can be even more brutal in the investment market than on the football field. His financial advisor, say his attorneys, managed to do the one thing to Banaszak that years of crushing tackles never could: he brought him to tears.

Banaszak had invested most of his life savings through his financial advisor, Harry Stern, who managed a San Jose, California, investment firm called Technical Equities. Stern catered, as one attorney put it, "to groups that were notorious for having funds but not knowing how to manage them—doctors, dentists, professional athletes, widows and orphans." After some poor investments, apparent mismanagement and allegedly fraudulent practices, Stern's firm collapsed under bankruptcy in 1986, taking with it more than $100 million in client assets.

Banaszak's personal losses came to several hundred thousand dollars, wiping out almost all the money he had prudently put away during his days as a professional athlete. Yet Banaszak was considered fortunate compared to some of Stern's other clients. He still had a job, and he had plenty of productive years left to earn back part of the money he'd lost. Other clients, many of them retired or nearing retirement, were suddenly and unexpectedly faced with the prospect of living out their twilight years in poverty. "There are a lot of horror stories," says Marie Weiner, an attorney with the Burlingame, California, firm of Cotchett & Illston, which represents Banaszak and 170 other former clients of Stern and his associates. "One client, an elderly woman, has called me up crying that she doesn't have the money to buy groceries. Some of these people are really devastated."

Clients claim that even when Stern's firm was nearing collapse, they were kept in the dark and encouraged to pour more money into Technical Equities investments. They say that Stern and his associates urged them not only to invest all of their savings with Technical Equities but also to remortgage their homes and invest the equity. Some even invested their pension or profit-sharing plans with Stern. When Stern's company crumbled, everything the clients owned—their savings, their retirement income, the very roof over their heads—was swept away.

"I have many clients whose lifestyles have been dramatically altered," says San Jose attorney Allen Ruby, who represents more than 100 former clients of Stern and his associates, including Don Drysdale, former Los Angeles Dodgers pitching great. "Some clients went from substantial upper-middle-class affluence to being unable to make their house payments. We've also observed that many of the people damaged in this case have lost their health. The shock of it—the stress, the worry—has caused some very severe health problems for many of our clients."

TAKING CHARGE

Many of those investors might have been spared such heavy losses if they had followed what Ruby calls "the first rule of any investment text—diversity. Those people put all their eggs into Stern's basket—at his urging—and that's always risky," says Ruby. "There's nothing wrong with dealing exclusively with one investment advisor if that person is putting you into things that are truly diversified. In this case, however, it was all invested under the Technical Equities umbrella."

Adds Weiner: "You can't rely 100 percent on anyone. You need checks and balances. And you need to take the time to learn enough about investing so that you can monitor what these people are doing with your money."

In the pages that follow, you will learn how to find a broker or financial advisor who will keep your best interests at heart, how to deal effectively with that person and how to make informed decisions regarding all of your investments. You'll learn how brokers think, how they sell, how they gather information. You'll learn how to distinguish among brokerage firms and how to find a good firm that caters to your specific investment objectives. You'll learn how to evaluate your broker, what to watch out for and, if necessary, when to fire your broker. You'll also learn about discounting, about mutual funds and about some of the select services that brokerage firms offer.

If you're serious about your finances and about maintaining a comfortable standard of living throughout your life, you need a serious investment program. Investing is not something you try once, like the latest designer ice cream. It's not something you keep your eye on for a year or two, then tuck away in a file drawer. It is an ongoing, evolving process that requires pivotal decisions, year in and year out. If you're not prepared to make those decisions on your own, you need a professional who can keep you on course. You need a broker or financial advisor you can trust, someone you can work with, someone who will bring a cool professional perspective to the tempting array of investment options.

Before your search for the perfect broker begins in earnest, however, it's important that you understand what motivates brokers and what qualities successful brokers possess. The next chapter peers deep into the soul of the working stockbroker.

CHAPTER TWO

Life on the Inside

Brokerage houses tend to be imposing places. The major firms are located, by and large, in the finest, most prestigious office buildings in town. Venture into their corporate chambers and you are immediately taken by their conspicuous attention to style and elegance. The decor, whether in polished mahogany or contemporary chrome and glass, exudes wealth, power and prestige. And all by design. Brokerage companies, after all, are the commissaries of capitalism, the conduits between investor and entrepreneur. Money is their province, fortunes their promise. And they do their best to look the part.

This show of opulence, however, often ends with the reception area. Brokers toil out of sight of customers under conditions that are often chaotic and always tense. Some firms still assign brokers to "bull pens"—sprawling, crowded office rooms where work is conducted over the din of ringing phones, clicking keyboards and loud voices barking orders. But bull pens, increasingly, have been giving way to more refined arrangements. In some firms, workstations are divided into long rows of cubicles, offering brokers a bit more privacy. Other firms have gone a step further, providing private offices for all of their veteran brokers.

It is within the walls of these private quarters that the true nature of the stockbroker's life most graphically unfolds. The decor, to generalize, would be best described as "contemporary macho"—the kind of setting where mounted swordfish and bearskin rugs would fit in well. Artwork reflects affluence—oils of old ships, prints of foxes and hounds, photographs of expensive cars, plush golf scenes and yachts sailing into the sunset. Trophies and plaques are also big in brokers' offices. So are small sculptures—particularly of bronze bulls and bears.

But set against these trappings of prosperity are the implements of stress and toil: desktops cluttered with memos and reports, ashtrays filled with stale butts, coffee mugs half full, a copy of *The Wall Street Journal* rumpled, marked and clipped. Picture within this disheveled setting, the working broker: phone receiver wedged between chin and shoulder, fingers dancing frantically across the keys of the stock quote monitor. Stress and money. In no other profession are the two more intricately intertwined.

By almost all standards, it would be safe to say that successful brokers are aptly compensated for their troubles. On average, brokers earn about $70,000 a year. Newer brokers make somewhat less, and experienced brokers may make considerably more. Many earn between $100,000 and $1 million per year. Brokers may not all sail yachts, but it's not for lack of funds. These people can afford the best.

Which is not to say the money is easy. "We do make good money," says Don Tidlund of E. F. Hutton, "but we earn it. It's not a business you turn off when you go home at night." The hours, especially for newer brokers, can be grueling. "In my first year," says Scott Horrall, a broker with Thomson McKinnon, "I worked about 60 to 70 hours a week. I arrived at the office by 7:30 A.M., usually ate lunch at my desk and worked at the office until about 5:30 P.M. Then, after a quick workout, I would start in again at 6:30 and make another two hours of cold calls three nights a week. I would also come in on Saturdays and make cold calls from about 10:00 A.M. to 3:00 P.M. That was my first year. I'm now in my third year, and I still work about 60 hours a week."

In addition to the long hours, brokers must survive some formidable professional odds to succeed in the securities business. "We interview about 15 candidates for every one we hire," says Donnis Casey, vice president of A. G. Edwards. Generally, of every 100 people who set out to be brokers, less than ten are hired. Of every ten hired, seven make it through the first year, five survive the second year, and only four are still in the business after three years."

If you were to analyze a roomful of stockbrokers, on the surface it might appear that they have almost nothing in common. Some come to work in Brooks Brothers suits; others wear open-neck Hawaiian shirts. Some enter the business when they're 20; others enter it at 65 after retiring from another job. The average age of a new broker at most major firms is about 30 to 35 years old. "It makes sense to have some work experience and some business contacts when you come into this job," says Casey. Occupational backgrounds vary widely. "At one time, most brokers were former salespeople or accountants," says Casey. "Now we see a lot of former bankers, insurance agents, dentists, chemists—we've even had a retired brain surgeon join our firm."

The similarities among brokers, however, far outweigh the differences. Most of those who succeed in the business are cut from roughly the same psychological mold—they are ambitious, persistent, highly disciplined, confident, intelligent and unabashedly financially motivated.

"Successful brokers have to have a strong drive to be successful and to make money," says Dr. Robert Lefton, president of St. Louis–based Psychological Associates, a firm that assists in the testing and training of brokers for several major securities firms. "A good broker is willing to admit that he wants to make a lot of money without feeling any pangs of guilt." Many brokers readily agree with that assessment. "I have no pangs of guilt at all," says one young broker. "I would fall down dead on the ground if I didn't think I would be making at least $150,000 a year within the next three years."

"All brokers—at least the ones I've met—are driven by money," says Jim Buehler, a broker with Detroit-based Roney & Co. "We're in the business of money. We eat, drink, smell and breathe money. Everything we do here revolves around money—saving a buck, making a buck or doing something with a buck"

This fascination with money, contends Lee Solot, vice president and training director at Kidder, Peabody, actually works to the client's advantage. "If your broker is not interested in making money for himself, he probably is not going to do a very good job for you. Good brokers have big egos. Think of a broker as a fine violin. It must be fundamentally sound, but with a certain tension. The best relationship is a finely balanced act in which the broker wants to do well for himself and wants to do well for you."

To those ends, brokers are very ambitious, aggressive and fiercely competitive people. They see selling as a game—as a way to play out their competitive instincts. And they hate to lose. They do battle with themselves to try to increase their sales production. They do battle with others to try to be the top producer in the office. In a sense, they do battle with their customers to try to persuade them to invest their money. And, of course, they do battle with the market to try to keep their investments growing.

Brokerage firms tend to play on this competitive zeal to motivate their brokers to greater production. "That's why they measure performance every month," says Bill Koriath of Prudential-Bache's Indianapolis office. "That's why they measure office performance and regional performance and national performance, and that's why they have so many contests and giveaways." Some brokers, however, carry their competitiveness to an unhealthy extreme. "I've known a lot of young brokers who have problems with other people's success," says Koriath. "Their attitude is, 'if you're successful, you don't deserve it. Why you and not me?' Sometimes the worst thing a branch manager can do is brag about a broker doing a lot of production. Everybody will immediately hate the poor guy. He'll be a marked man."

A FINE LINE

Since brokers are in a business where uncertainty is the only constant, they must possess a high level of emotional stability. "It's a business that can eat you alive if you let it," says Betsy Buckley of Dain Bosworth.

"On the one hand," adds David Thompson of Prudential-Bache, "a broker must care about his clients, but at the same time he cannot lose sleep over the ups and downs of the market."

"A broker's job is a series of contradictions," says Dr. Lefton. "You need to be a person who really likes to deal with people, yet you're confined to a relatively small office for long periods of time. Also, securities firms want people who are very ambitious, very energetic and have a very strong need for achievement, yet a certain percentage of those people also tend to be very risk-oriented, which companies don't necessarily like. Firms also want people who are very organized and detail-oriented, yet the very qualities of a great stockbroker are often just the opposite—they're often disorganized and couldn't care less about details. The fact is most really good brokers are obsessed with relating to the customer, and it's very difficult to get them tuned into filling out forms and staying on top of details. The company, on one hand, is pushing them for production, but at the same time it's pushing them to do those other things. It can be very frustrating," adds Dr. Lefton. "When the broker's filling out these reports, he's saying to himself, 'I could be calling 10 customers instead of filling out these damn papers.' "

While brokers must work within the framework of their company, they essentially work for themselves. "I wanted a job where I could be my own boss and run my own business without putting up my own capital," says Thomson McKinnon's Horrall. "This is it."

Adds Buehler: "Being a broker is one of the last frontiers of being independent. I come and go as I please. I talk to who I want to talk to about what I want to when I want to. I don't report to anyone."

What other qualities must successful brokers possess? "They need a high level of intelligence," says Dr. Lefton. "To succeed in this business, you probably need an IQ of at least 110. We might make an exception for people who have a slightly lower IQ if they score incredibly high on ambition. What you don't want, though, is people with a modest IQ, unbelievably high ambition and questionable values. I call them 'klutzes with initiative.' They're like a runaway locomotive. You don't know what they're going to do."

Ironically, expertise in finance is in no way a prerequisite for success in the brokerage business. Sales ability is far more important—particularly in the early years. "You have to enjoy sales," says Dr. Lefton. The former door-to-door salesperson may do better selling investment products than the former economics professor. Brokers receive some training in financial matters, but generally they're expected to leave investment research to the analysts. "The training you have is geared primarily toward backroom operations, legal issues and sales," says Buehler. "But in terms of knowing whether to buy General Motors stock or Ford stock, no one tells you that in your initial training. You have to study the market and learn it on your own."

In time, the successful brokers develop skills in both sales and investing. "The successful broker today is a far cut above the broker of yesterday," says Al Heiam, a broker with Drexel Burnham. "They have to be conversant with bonds as well as investments in equities. They have to be aware of special products, and they have to continue to reeducate themselves. Look what has happened to long-term capital gains. There aren't any. Look what has happened to tax shelters. There aren't any. So what is the broker going to do for his clients for their retirement money? Brokers must continue to stay current on all these issues."

Investors' tastes have also changed. While stocks and bonds were once the lifeblood of the securities business, many investors are now more interested in packaged investments such as mutual funds, unit trusts and limited partnerships. As a result, stockbrokers have had to direct their efforts into new areas.

"At the major wire house firms—Merrill Lynch, E. F. Hutton, Paine-Webber, Prudential-Bache, Dean Witter, Shearson Lehman—the principal trend is for the salesmen to become nothing more than gatherers of assets, basically assets that are brought in-house and/or placed within a product that is managed in-house," says Perrin Long, an analyst with Lipper Analytical Services. "The average investor today has no interest in making money on his or her investments. Their primary concern is preservation of capital."

The Acid Test

How would you fare as a broker? Here are six questions Dr. Robert Lefton of Psychological Associates in St. Louis suggests you ask yourself if you want to evaluate whether you could make it as a broker.

1. Do you really enjoy selling?
2. Are you strongly disciplined and willing to take the time and effort to build up your business?
3. Do you react well to failure and rejection? "If your ego is fragile, this would be the wrong business for you," says Dr. Lefton.
4. Are you highly driven and self-motivated?
5. Do you have a strong need to make good money?
6. Do you want to be judged—and compensated—by your own performance? "Do you want to be evaluated by the marketplace, by what you produce?" asks Dr. Lefton. "It can be a cold, hard feedback."

If you answered no to any of the above questions, the chances are that you would not succeed as a stockbroker.

Adds Lee Kopp of Dain Bosworth: "There are very few true stock-brokers in the business today. When I started in the 1960s, stocks were about the only product we had to sell. Today the average broker is not a 'stockbroker'—he or she is a 'special products salesperson.' They're selling limited partnerships, insurance, mutual funds—everything but common stocks. The reason is, with common stocks it's very difficult to pick winners in this market and very easy to look like a loser to your clients when you suggest XYZ, and XYZ doesn't turn out. Out of the 500 or so salespeople at Dain Bosworth, there are probably only 25 people who might be called 'stockbrokers.' The other 475 are generalists. They can sell stock, and they will, but they do not specialize in stocks."

REJECTION

While intelligence, ambition and sales ability all play key roles in a broker's success, there is one other quality that a person absolutely must possess to make it in the business: thick skin.

To be a broker, you must subject yourself to a very high possibility of failure. When you apply for a job as a broker, the chances are at least nine out of ten that you'll be rejected. Even if you get the job, there's a 60 percent chance that you won't survive the first three years. And even if you do succeed, there's a 100 percent chance that you'll be subjected to a great deal of frustration and humiliation—that you will make mistakes, that you will misjudge the market, that people will hang up on you and that clients will verbally malign you. Stockbrokers put their egos on the line every day (every 90 seconds when they're making cold calls), and more often than not, their egos take a beating. Inability to withstand the constant rejection is the main reason so many young brokers leave the business.

"Most new brokers come into the job with a glorified image of what a broker does," says Buehler. "They think brokers spend their days at the country club playing golf, and they think people come to brokers all day and ask them to execute trades. They think it's going to be an easy way to make a lot of money. But being a broker requires a lot of work—and it's not the kind of work they want to do. They don't like prospecting—making 40 calls a day to people they don't know, and having 39 of them tell them to go to hell. They have a hard time dealing with that rejection."

"People are often attracted to this business for the wrong reasons," adds Tom Asher, director of retail sales and marketing at Atlanta-based Robinson-Humphrey. "From the outside, it appears to be a very glamorous profession—beautiful furnishings, Oriental rugs, money. When you go to cocktail parties, there are two kinds of professionals that people love to talk to: athletes and stockbrokers. The job has a lot of sex appeal. But behind the glamorous facade is a lot of hard work and frustration."

"People come into this business perceiving that it's a job in which you manage money," says Phil Clark, director of the branch office system at

Roney & Co., "in which you act as investment consultant, financial advisor, stock market genius, investment guru. And eventually, that is what you become. But in your early years, it's a job of sales—of selling people on the idea of using investments and other mediums to make more money. The career they select is not the career they get."

The hardest part of a new broker's job can be summarized in two words: *cold calls.* Cold calling, in short, means dialing phone numbers from prospect lists in search of new clients. It can be humiliating, agonizing and, at times, even nauseating. "It's the worst thing in the world for a broker," says Prudential's Koriath.

Brokers' prospects come from many sources—lists of doctors, lists of business owners, lists of homeowners, lists of Cadillac owners, lists of country club members, lists of former clients. Newer brokers spend half their life with prospect lists. Mornings, afternoons, evenings, even weekends, they dial. And dial. And dial. When Smith Barney says, "We make money the old-fashioned way; we earn it," you can bet that much of the money is earned by making cold calls.

"I would start out cold-calling early in the morning and call all day and into the evening—10 to 12 hours a day," says Dale Grubb of Shearson Lehman.

Typically, of every hundred calls, only one will eventually lead to a new account. What makes the high rate of rejections even worse is that sometimes those rejections can be quite biting. Cold callers must get used to being sworn at, insulted and hung up on—or "slam-dunked," as brokers say. Such outrage may seem a bit extreme until you understand the circumstances that might have precipitated it. For instance, consider the plight of a doctor with a new Cadillac who lives in a wealthy neighborhood and belongs to a country club. He would be on at least four prospect lists—and not just at one brokerage house but at every brokerage house in town. He could be forgiven for getting a little ruffled the fourth time his dinner is interrupted by a call from a broker selling bonds. Of course, the broker who makes the call doesn't know that. All he knows is that he's been rejected again.

David Waterbury, a leading broker with Dean Witter says it's not hard to spot brokers who've just hung up from a stinging call. "They'll get up and walk around a little bit and mumble to themselves," he says. One broker would stand up after a particularly bad call, brush himself off and mutter, 'She didn't touch me. She didn't touch me.' Then he'd walk over to the water fountain for a quick drink, gather the forces of his soul and return to his desk to begin dialing again."

"After a couple of bad calls," says Kathy Soule of Merrill Lynch, "there are mornings where you just sit there at your desk like a zombie. You can't pick up the phone, you can't do any paperwork, you cannot do anything. You just look at the wall or get up and get some coffee. It's really hard to get back on the positive track. You walk around, commiserate with some of the other brokers, and then you go back and start calling again."

Persistence and the ability to take rejection in stride are essential to success as a stockbroker. Someone so beaten down after ten rejections that he can't pick up the phone again simply won't survive. "You have to be extremely tenacious and extremely thick-skinned," says Buehler. "You have to get to the point where you don't care what people tell you on the phone—you can't let it affect you. You have to keep going in the face of a lot of setbacks." If the first 50 calls don't work, you have to be ready to try 50 more. Prospecting is a numbers game, and with persistence the numbers always favor the broker. "They're not paying us to listen to yeses all day," says Waterbury. "We're paid to listen to all the noes."

BEYOND PROSPECTING

If there's a silver lining to the business of cold calls, it's that for most brokers it ends after two or three years in the business. After that, most brokers acquire new clients through referrals from other clients.

Just the same, even the experienced brokers have their bad days. "The most frustrating part of being a stockbroker," says E. F. Hutton's Tidlund, "is that you can look like a total buffoon sometimes. The market does exactly what it wants to do and not what you think it should do." The inability of brokers to predict the unpredictable can make for some rocky relationships with clients. Anytime you're dealing with a subject as close to the heart as a client's life savings, emotions tend to be easily aroused. When brokers put clients into an investment that doesn't work out, they may be subject to criticism, second guessing and, at times, scathing verbal abuse from clients. "Every broker gets that," says Shearson's Grubb.

"It seems like you're only as good as the last time you made money for somebody," says Waterbury. If anyone should command the unfailing respect of his clients, it's Waterbury. He has impeccable credentials: a graduate of Yale, a senior vice president of Dean Witter, selected by *Registered Representative* magazine as one of the 20 "brokers of the year" in 1982, earns a six-figure income, active in church and charities and generally regarded as a solid citizen. Yet even Waterbury finds himself on the defensive from time to time. "I think the worst is when you recommend they sell a stock when it's at $22 and it goes on up to $28," he says. "People don't seem to forgive you for selling it at $22—even if they made a profit at that price."

Just as there are bad days in the brokerage business, there are also bad years. Those who were brokers during the bear market of 1973–74—when the Dow Jones Industrial Average dropped almost 50 percent, from 1051.69 to 577.59—still remember it vividly.

"The market went absolutely against you day after day, week after week, month after month for roughly a two-year period," recalls Dain Bosworth's Kopp. "It gets to be devastating. You walk in every day, and you walk slower and slower as you approach the office. It's a very difficult time, especially if your clients are on margin and you have to call them and ask them to put more money into their account, or else the margin department will sell out part of their position."

Drexel's Heiam remembers that market as "god-awful." Says Heiam: "Values you thought were there continued to decline. You weren't getting new clients, and because you felt bad about this entire event, you weren't doing much with the clients you did have. I hate to tell you what happened to my income. I had been earning over $100,000 a year, and it dropped to $17,000. At the bottom, I did a little church praying. I did a little talking with the wife. I think I did some resolving of my own. I said to myself, 'This is not of my doing. I did not contrive this. These things have happened before. In those times, what was the best solution? To buy, not to sell. Not to give up.' I made a determination that this was the bottom of the market. I just got all excited about buying values, and we did. And in 1975 and 1976, we came out of those doldrums, and things worked out very well."

It was a different atmosphere in October 1987 when the market plummeted nearly 1,000 points. Instead of a slow, painful two-year drought, the bulk of the market's decline occurred almost overnight. Most brokers who were around for both down markets said that the 1987 drop was preferable to the 1973–74 decline because it was over so much more quickly.

"My reaction to the 1987 crash," says Heiam, "was the same as everyone else's in the office—shock. We couldn't believe what we were seeing. I don't think anyone expected that. But it was probably preferable to the 1973–74 bear market because this one was over with in a hurry. The 1973–74 market was very draining, very eroding. It was like Chinese torture—drip, drip, drip, day after day, month after month, getting worse and worse and worse."

PAYING THEIR WAY

Securities firms make a major investment in each of the new brokers they bring on board. And they expect those brokers, over time, to make good on that investment by producing substantial sales figures. Those who don't won't last long in the business.

Typically, brokerage firms spend about $40,000 to $50,000 on first-year brokers for initial training and noncommissioned salaries. At most New York Stock Exchange member firms, new brokers are paid a salary for their first 4 months while they go through securities training and for their first 12 months on the job. The idea is to give them time to build a client base honestly and with some integrity rather than to put them into a sell-or-starve situation in which they might push some investments against their better judgment. But after the 16-month grace period, brokers must basically live or die on their commissions.

"Within three years," says an official of one brokerage firm, "brokers at most major firms are expected to be generating $200,000 to $300,000 a year in gross commissions. Anything less, and the broker's job could be in jeopardy. The problem with that, of course, is that if a broker is a little under quota one month, he might have a tendency to put his clients into products that have big payouts [commissions] rather than products that are right for those clients."

To generate $200,000 to $300,000 in commissions, a broker needs to handle $10 million to $30 million in investment buy and sell transactions each year (commission percentages vary depending on the product). This means that a broker must transact $40,000 to $120,000 in investment trades every working day to stay on track. Tom Hudson of PaineWebber points out the difficulty of maintaining that kind of pace. "Assume an investor comes to me with $5,000, which represents his total savings. Assume he invests it with me by buying 100 shares of a $50 stock. The commission on that trade comes to about $97. I would get about 30 percent of that. For the investor, that's his life savings, but for me, it's only $30. It takes an awful lot of those transactions to make a living."

The average gross commission for stock transactions is about 2 percent. For bonds it's 1 percent, and for front-load mutual funds it's about 3

Commission Payout to the Broker

Annual Gross Commissions Generated by the Broker	Percentage of Payout to the Broker
0 – $100,000	25%
$100,001 – $150,000	40%
$150,001 –$250,000	43%
$250,001 +	45%

This is the 1987 schedule for one of the 11 national New York Stock Exchange firms. The above percentages cover stock trades and other transactions such as options, in which the firm acts as an agent in effecting the transaction. At this firm the payout for limited partnerships and mutual funds is 45 percent, for principal transactions it is 40 percent and for insurance and annuity products the payout is 50 percent. This is a fairly typical payout schedule. Some firms are higher and some are lower. Note that the broker who grosses less than $100,000 per year receives a much smaller percentage of the commission than brokers who gross over $100,000. Most firms have determined that a broker must gross more than $100,000 in order to "pay for his or her desk" and cover expenses and share of overhead at the firm.

percent to about 8¹/₂ percent. Brokerage firms collect nothing on money market transactions, though they usually have a small administrative cushion built into the return rate.

Brokers are paid on a sliding scale that creeps up as their sales increase. Earn $100,000 in gross commissions, and you may receive 25 percent or less of the total. Bring in $250,000, and you're rewarded with 40 to 45 percent of the take.

The payout to the broker also varies depending on the size of the transaction. In fact, brokers may receive nothing at all for small orders on which the commission is $30 or less—which could explain why your broker may not greet with great warmth your order for 50 shares of a $10 stock.

BRIDGING THE GENDER GAP

Betsy Buckley's world is a cramped but efficient workstation on the second floor of Dain Bosworth's corporate headquarters building in downtown Minneapolis. Her desk is stacked with thick notebooks, work sheets, articles, newsletters, research reports and a scattering of notes and memos. She works nearly out of view between the two large computer terminals that occupy opposite corners of her desk. ("One," she says, gesturing left, "is the company's; the other is mine.") Although she is accustomed to more spacious quarters (at her last job she had two full-time secretaries and a large staff of employees), Buckley seems well suited to the surroundings. "I love chaos," she confides. "I'm at my best when things are going nuts."

Professional, articulate, engaging, Buckley represents a new breed in the securities business—the female broker. Until recently, the only brokerage jobs available to women, with few exceptions, were clerical positions—sales assistants, receptionists and back office help. But women are now assuming a growing presence in the profession. Of 54 brokers in Buckley's office, 8 are women. That figure is slightly below the national average, estimated to be around 20 percent.

Of the few women who landed jobs as brokers in the past, many had to do it through the back door. "They would take a job as a sales assistant and try to work up through the ranks," explains Merrilee Cole, a former sales assistant and broker at Piper Jaffray. "It was about the only way a woman could get a job at a brokerage firm."

Women have proven they belong in the business. Like their male counterparts, the successful women brokers tend to be ambitious, aggressive, disciplined, entrepreneurial, financially motivated and impatient with details.

Buckley, who entered the brokerage business in early 1986 after 15 years in the government and corporate ranks, is a prime example:

Details: "I hate administrative work," she says. "I absolutely despise it."

Competitiveness: "I've always been first at everything—valedictorian in high school, president of the student council, captain of the cheerleaders, president of my sorority in college."

Sales: "I love to sell. I'd sell anybody anything anytime—as long as it was something I believed in."

Money: "I'm not money-driven for money's sake but for what I can do with it. It's important that my children have a good education. I would like to have a home in Florida. I enjoy comfort. I give a lot to charities."

Independence: "This is a wonderful business in that you're really in charge of yourself. If you make it, it's because you do the work. It's my life, it's my show, and I do it my way."

Discipline: "I work about 70 hours a week at the office and another 15 or 20 hours at home."

Ambition: "I once read about a woman broker in Michigan who had five registered sales assistants. That's my strategy. I'll just take over the back half of the floor here. I have it all mapped out. When things get bad, I just sort of look over there and say, 'That's me.' "

Women brokers generally don't see their gender as an obstacle to success in the business. Merrill's Kathy Soule says she's had only one prospect cite her sex as a reason not to open an account. "The man was a general in the army. He said, 'Ma'am, I apologize for this, but I do a lot of cussin', and I don't want to be cussin' at you.' "

In fact, being female can sometimes be an advantage in attracting clients. "Sometimes it's easier for investors to open up to a woman and admit that they don't know anything about investing," says one woman brokerage house executive. "I have one male client who is a psychiatrist. On three separate occasions, I've tried to turn his account over to another broker because I don't have time to handle it. But he always refuses. He says, 'I don't want to admit to a man that I am a psychiatrist and I know nothing about finances. I don't want to let them know how dumb I am.' "

While women brokers share similar personality traits with male brokers, "effective female brokers operate completely different than men," contends one woman who has been involved in the securities industry for many years. "For instance, some clients look to a broker to be a mother figure. Some clients need a sister—they need a buddy, a friend. The really astute female will play the mother role for those who need a mother and the sister role for those who need a sister, and—treading on very thin ice here—there are some clients who need a 'lover.' That doesn't mean the broker would make love with the client," she adds, "but that she would relate in a way that would meet the client's needs in terms of being warm and compassionate."

A DAY IN THE LIFE

What's a typical day for a stockbroker? "There is no typical day," says Soule. "Every day it's something different." There are, however, certain routines that brokers try to follow, as this scenario of "a day in the life" portrays:

7:30 A.M.: Breakfast meeting with a client, prospect or "center of influence." (Attorneys, accountants or other professionals who may be in a position to refer clients to the broker are considered "centers of influence.")

8:30: Arrive at office. Go over new information from the firm and read *The Wall Street Journal.* Many firms also have morning briefing sessions to update brokers on the market. Thomson McKinnon, for instance, has a "Morning Equity Call," a conference call that originates in New York and goes to all 180 branches. Brokers are also handed stacks of reading material—memos, research reports, clippings and other information that they are expected to look through. "In a typical week," says Prudential's Thompson, "I get a stack of material about ten inches deep—and that would be conservative." Brokers might also check the Dow Jones wire service and their firm's internal wire for summaries of the previous day's events and late-breaking news. "I want to be knowledgeable," says Henry Basil of PaineWebber. "If a client says, 'Pabst is going to be bought out,' I want to know if that's a rumor or if there's some facts behind it."

9:00: Make calls to clients to solicit last-minute orders to be placed "at the opening."

9:30: Trading begins. The New York Stock Exchange opens at 9:30 A.M. EST (6:30 A.M. on the West Coast—which makes for a very early day for West Coast brokers) and stays open until 4:00 P.M. Brokers who deal in equities try to be available throughout the trading period so that they will always be accessible to clients who want to make trades. One PaineWebber broker makes a point of never leaving his desk while the market is open. He never takes vacations, he doesn't go to lunch, he doesn't even go to the rest room. His philosophy is that if the client needs to reach him, he should be at his desk to take the call.

Frequently, brokers watch how the market does for the first five to ten minutes to get a feel for the momentum of the day.

10:00: Call some key clients to update them on the market, report opening transactions and solicit more orders.

10:30: Newer brokers will be well into their morning round of cold calls by this time. ("I made about 200 outgoing dials in a typical day my first year," says Thomson McKinnon's Horrall.) Other brokers spend the time talking with existing clients or handling operational matters.

12:00 M. (noon): Lunchtime. Some brokers eat at their desks; others make it a point to get away. "I have to get away at lunch," says Soule. "You burn out fast enough as it is, so I don't just try to get out—I do get out. Nothing has ever been so urgent that my taking lunch has caused any problems."

1:00–4:00 P.M.: Back to work, making calls, making trades or solving operational problems.

4:00: Market closes. Brokers plan the next day's work, often jotting down a list of 20 or more clients or warm prospects to call about a specific investment idea. Then brokers often look through the latest stack of papers and reports that has materialized on their desk.

5:30: Meet with an important client or contact on the way home. To stay on good terms with their best clients or centers of influence, brokers try to schedule such in-person appointments as often as three evenings a week.

6:00: Dinner with the spouse or family.

7:00: Two to three nights a week, newer brokers may spend a couple of evening hours making cold calls. Veteran brokers may also spend some evening hours on the phone—especially if there's been a change in one of the investments they've recommended. "There have been times when I've had to call as many as 100 clients to tell them to get out of a given stock," says Waterbury. "If it's something that's really urgent, the night lasts a long time."

9:00: More time reading reports and such periodicals as *Forbes, Fortune, Business Week, Barron's, Money, Registered Rep* and *Investor's Daily.* "I also try to watch 'Business Report' and 'Moneyline' on television in case I missed anything during the day," says Basil. Most brokers also try to watch "Wall Street Week."

10:00: After everything else has been finished, some new brokers will spend a couple of evenings a week stuffing envelopes as part of a direct mail prospecting campaign.

So the days are long and hard and sometimes frustrating, but most established brokers wouldn't trade their job for any other. "If I weren't a psychologist," says Dr. Lefton, "I'd be a stockbroker. It's just a ball. It's one of the most fun jobs in the world."

"You have to have the personality for it," says Roney's Buehler. "I'm very success-oriented, very goal-oriented, very money-oriented. I knew that this type of business was the best way for me to meet my goal of making a lot of money. I'm in my mid-20s, and I already have a six-figure income, and I'm no brighter than anyone else. It's just that I'm very tenacious, and I got into a profession in which my efforts have a direct payoff."

Says Thompson: "I like everything about the job—especially the action. You sit here all day and watch the numbers change. It's kind of like continuous horse racing, but there's no winner because the race never stops."

CHAPTER THREE _____

Earning Their Commissions: What a Broker Can Do for You

Unless you're from Sunnyvale, California, the chances are that you've never heard of California Microwave. And until the summer of 1982, neither had most of the clients of Dain Bosworth broker Lee Kopp. But Kopp persuaded dozens of his best clients to invest heavily in the growing telecommunications company. When Kopp began to push the stock in August 1982, it was trading at about $10 a share. Within weeks, its price began to climb, quickly moving to $15 a share. "Some of my clients had already earned 50 percent on their investment," recalled Kopp, "and they started calling me to see if it was time to get out. I said I thought it still had potential at $15, but if they were uncomfortable at that price, they might want to sell a little and hold onto the rest."

Over the next eight months, the stock climbed to $20, then $25, then $30, and finally it reached a peak of $40 a share. Shortly thereafter, California Microwave succumbed to the same bear market that devastated the rest of the high-tech sector, eventually dropping to under $10 a share. But by the time the stock had started its decline, Kopp's clients had already sold out most of their position at extraordinary profits.

Helping clients stay one step ahead of the market may be a stockbroker's most important role. "In 90 percent of the cases," says Kopp, "people are dealing with me because they want my advice. They want to know what to buy, when to buy it and when to sell it."

At about the same time Kopp was recommending California Microwave, Henry Basil, a broker with PaineWebber, was encouraging some of his more affluent clients to put $50,000 into a research and development limited partnership for Genentech Corporation. If you're familiar with the biotech field, then by now you've undoubtedly heard a lot about Genentech. But in 1982, it was just another small, unproven high-technology company. Clients were understandably hesitant about risking $50,000 on such a speculative venture.

But on a visit to the south San Francisco-based company, Basil had learned about its plans to develop a human growth hormone, and he made it clear to his clients that he thought the company was worth the risk.

The handful of investors who followed Basil's advice and invested in the limited partnership were later compensated with 3,000 shares of Genentech stock, which by 1987 had split two for one and reached a high of about $63 a share. In just five years, their $50,000 investment had grown in value to about $380,000.

Providing clients with attractive investment opportunities that go beyond stocks, bonds and mutual funds is another service offered by brokers that individual investors would be unable to obtain on their own.

EARNING THEIR COMMISSIONS

When you use a full-service broker to execute your trades, you're generally charged about 2 percent for stocks, 1 percent for bonds and as high as 8½ percent for mutual funds. On a $10,000 stock transaction, for instance, you would pay about $200. What does that commission buy you besides a simple buy or sell execution?

For starters, it buys convenience. Many busy investors find that the time savings and convenience alone of using stockbrokers are worth the cost of their commissions. With the commission you pay a full-service broker, you have at your fingertips a personal financial consultant who advises you on how to allocate your assets, offers you fresh investment ideas and handles all of your transactions for you. That commission also buys you access to the entire world of investments—market research, investment products, financial expertise and timely recommendations.

Brokers serve in two principal capacities:

- As conduits between the client and the investment research department—providing clients with research reports and investment recommendations.
- As intermediaries between buyers and sellers. In addition to handling all of your normal securities transactions, your broker can offer you access to new stock issues, unit investment trusts, limited partnerships, mutual funds and a wide range of other investment alternatives.

But brokers can be much more than mere middlemen between investors and the market. At times, they're father confessors, lending a sympathetic ear to a client. They're friends, they're confidants, and occasionally they're therapists or psychologists. "Clients talk to me about whether they should buy a new car, or how they should finance it, or whether they should take out a home equity loan, whether they should buy more insurance, whether they should take a trip to Florida," says David Waterbury of Dean Witter. "Most of their questions are financially related, but that could cover a wide range of areas. They also have other needs. Their psychological needs are certainly every bit as important as their financial needs."

"It's such an emotional business," adds Kopp. "Some people need to be reassured periodically that it will work out over time. They want to call in during difficult times to have you tell them that it will be OK. It's during those rocky times that brokers really earn their commissions— even without executing a single trade—by encouraging clients to hold onto their position until the market turns around."

Waterbury recalls a bad stretch in 1987 when the market was down 150 points in three days. Clients were calling in, wondering whether it was time to sell out. Waterbury calmly tried to put things in perspective. "I told them that nothing goes in a straight line forever and that it was bound to turn back around," he says. "Then I reminded them of all the other times they had called with the same concerns and what happened subsequent to that. Sometimes you're right, sometimes you're not, but over the long term the stock market has gone up, not down, and anyone who has held on with decent securities has done well." The next day the market was up 30 points, and four months later it was up 400 points.

During the week of Black Monday, brokers put in long hours calling clients to offer advice and reassurance. "I just tried to offer some ideas on how to approach the situation from a logical, level-headed standpoint," says Scott Horrall of Thomson McKinnon. "I didn't want my clients to panic."

Adds Betsy Buckley of Dain Bosworth: "I just kept reminding my clients of our original strategy. Why did we buy the stock? We bought it with the intention of owning it for the long term. I said, 'We have good solid stocks, and if we hold onto them they're going to rebound and perform well over the long term.'"

Al Heiam of Drexel Burnham says he called all of his clients, discussed their options and offered his recommendations. "The majority of my clients followed my recommendations. They sold out a portion of their stocks on a rally, then waited for the next good buying opportunity before reinvesting in the market."

FEAR AND GREED

Emotion may be the individual investor's biggest enemy. The best investors, like the best gamblers, are cold and calculating—sometimes gutsy, sometimes cautious, but never emotional. "It takes a lot of inner strength, a lot of discipline and a lot of tenacity to make money in the market," says Kopp.

Of all the emotions that affect investors, fear and greed undoubtedly lead the list. Fear causes investors to sell too soon after making a quick profit, and greed causes them to hold onto a stock after it has reached a peak. Not satisfied with a reasonable profit, they hold out for bigger gains, only to see their tidy profit turn into a crushing loss.

Many investors who were heavily leveraged lost everything they owned during the Black Monday crash. They had built their fortunes through the bull market of the mid-1980s by buying stocks on margin (using their stock as collateral to buy more stock on credit). But instead of being satisfied with their gains, they yielded to greed and continued doubling up on their investments. "They would use their buying power from their gains to buy more stock on margin," explains Heiam. "That's a prescription for failure. The market can't keep going up forever. At some point it's going to come back and bite you, and in this case, it did that with many investors. I heard many, many stories of investors losing a million dollars or more in stocks or options during the week of Black Monday," Heiam added. "In fact, not only did they lose their entire investment, they owed money on top of that."

Emotion can hurt investors in other ways as well. Fear sometimes keeps investors out of the market when it is at its lowest level, and greed gets them into the market when it hits its highest peaks.

In the late 1970s, commercial real estate limited partnerships showed incredible gains—30, 40, even 50 percent per year—due in large part to rampant inflation. Hoping to capitalize on that market, investors began flocking en masse to real estate partnerships in the 1980s. But by then, inflation had abated and commercial real estate markets were becoming increasingly overbuilt. The consequences were devastating for many investors. In Houston, for instance, where commercial vacancy rates exceeded 25 percent in the mid-1980s, some building owners had to walk away from their mortgages, leaving their buildings to the bank. Many investors lost their entire investment. Others were asked to ante up more money to stave off bankruptcy.

TABLE 3-1   The Effects of Emotion on Investment Results

Fear	Prevents investors from buying when prices are depressed
	Causes investors to sell with a small profit
Greed	Causes investors to hold a stock while profits vanish
	Causes investors to buy when prices are at all-time highs

But while greed may get you into an investment at the wrong time, it can also keep you in an investment long after you should have sold it. A broker who was formerly with a major New York firm tells this story about one of his clients:

For almost ten years, this client had been accumulating shares of stock in Walt Disney Corporation, a firm that—like the magical Kingdom of Disney itself—seemed to be one long, happy fairy tale for its investors. Typically, the stock would go up and split, weather some temporary weakening in price, then go up and split again. At one point in the early 1970s, recalls the broker, Disney stock reached about $240 a share, then split two for one to trade at $120 a share. By February 1973, the client owned more than 4,000 shares of Disney stock valued at nearly half a million dollars. The broker, believing that the market had peaked, called the client to advise him to sell before his shares started declining in price. The client refused the recommendation, reasoning that to sell would mean paying $50,000 to $60,000 in capital gains tax. Besides, said the client, Disney had weathered stormy markets before and had always rebounded with another happy ending.

That very day, the market started dropping on its way to one of its biggest declines in history. The Disney stock quickly dropped 25 percent, to $90 a share. The broker again urged the client to sell. Again the client refused. The stock kept dropping. When it hit $80 a share, the broker called a third time, but the client still refused to get out of the stock. Two years later, when the stock had dropped all the way to $30 a share (and the client had lost more than $300,000), the client called the broker to ask whether he should sell the stock then. "At that price," recalls the broker, "I thought he would do just as well to hold onto it."

Letting go of a profitable stock is one of the toughest decisions an investor will face. "During that same period in February," recalls the broker, "I probably called 75 to 100 of my biggest clients to tell them all the same thing. And out of all those calls, I don't think I shook loose more than a few hundred shares."

Almost any experienced broker can relate a similar experience. Don Tidlund of E. F. Hutton remembers a client who had a position in Control Data when the stock was selling at $74 a share. "We thought it had gone about as high as it was going to go, but one of my clients wanted to squeeze one more dollar out of the stock, so he put in an order to sell at $75—a dollar above the current price. But the stock never did get to that extra point. It started falling, and ultimately dropped all the way to just over $20 a share."

Greed can also keep you out of the market when you should be investing heavily. In 1985, when the stock market began one of its greatest ascents, some investors refused to invest, reasoning that stocks had already gone too high. They felt that they had missed the bottom of the market and that anything they bought now represented an inflated price. Instead, they waited, expecting prices to return to previous lows. Alas, the market never retreated, and those investors who waited missed out on one of the biggest bull markets of the century. "You can't buy yesterday's prices," notes Waterbury.

"I've had guys who insisted on buying stock below the market," explains Tidlund. "The stock is selling at $30, and the client says, 'Let's try to buy it at $28 or $29.' Before you know it, though, the stock takes off and the client never owns it. Just by trying to get in a dollar or two under the market, he misses out on the stock's big gain."

Income-oriented investors can be subject to the same fatal reasoning. When corporate bond rates dropped from 15 percent to 12 percent in the mid-1980s, many investors refused to buy bonds because the rates seemed so low. Instead, they waited for the rates to move back up. But interest just kept edging down, and those who had the foresight to buy bonds at 12 percent made an outstanding return not only on the interest rates but also on the appreciation of their bond prices.

"If you sit and wait," says PaineWebber's Basil, "you'll wait forever. You have to look at your alternatives at the time."

That's where the objective, unemotional advice of a broker can be so important. It's the broker's job to defuse a client's feelings of fear and greed by presenting a realistic perspective on the market. When the stock market is moving up, it doesn't take a genius to pick a winning stock. What most individual investors need is a stockbroker who encourages them to get into the market when the market is moving. Your broker has no crystal ball, of course, and there are no concrete rules governing when to buy and when to sell. Stocks are fickle creatures that often defy common logic. But stockbrokers live with the market every day, and they receive information from research analysts and economists on a regular basis. Thus, although they can offer no guarantees, they are in a better position than the average investor to assess the mood of the market and make those crucial buy and sell timing decisions. That's what brokers are paid to do—to give opinions, to make tough decisions and to offer gutsy recommendations even when those recommendations may go against the grain of popular opinion.

As an investor, you're paying your broker to give you his or her opinion. Brokers are not expected to be right every time, but they are expected to be right most of the time. They are responsible for the results of their recommendations. If after following your broker's advice, you find that you're consistently losing money instead of making it, then it's time to get another broker.

WHEN TO SELL

Recommending what to buy is the easy part. The hard part for brokers is recommending what to sell and when to sell it.

For example, let's say you purchased 1,000 shares of stock in a company specializing in medical technology. Every time the price of that stock moves up or down, you face a new decision with three options:

1. Sell it to take a profit (or cut your losses).
2. Hold onto it with the hope of riding it higher.
3. Buy more of it to increase your position.

Your broker can help you make that decision by looking at such factors as the stock's price–earnings ratio, projected earnings and price patterns; the general condition of the stock's industry group, and the overall state of the market. That doesn't mean brokers always hit it exactly right; in most cases, they're happy to just come close. Says PaineWebber's Basil: "I always like to quote Bernard Baruch, who said, in effect, 'I always sold too soon, but if you always get out with a good profit, you should be satisfied.' " That's a rule more investors should heed. "The hardest thing for the broker," says Jim Vieburg, managing director of Piper, Jaffray & Hopwood, "is selling a stock at the right price, because as soon as you sell it, the client starts looking at the paper and following the price. If the price goes up, he gets upset." Remember, your broker's objective is to make you a profit—not to keep you in an investment to its highest uptick. You can never go broke making profits. The investors who stand to lose the most are those who are never satisfied, who always think a stock could go one tick higher. If you've made a profit on your investment and your broker says it's time to move on to something with a little better upward potential, take your broker's word for it, congratulate your broker on making you some money (which is what you're paying for), and don't look back. To expect anything more is unfair to your broker and unrealistic for you.

In other situations, your broker might advise you to hold onto a rising stock, citing this old securities adage: "Don't cut off the heads of your winners." If you have an investment that's moving up (whether it's a stock, a bond or a mutual fund), don't be swayed by emotion and sell it out for a quick profit. Investors who decided to sell Eastman Kodak or Cray Research after making an early profit may still regret their decision.

Your broker might also advise you to "cut your losses and let your winners run." This adage artfully addresses the emotions of both fear and greed. Prime example: You buy six stocks; three go up $3, and three go down $3. Fear says sell the three winners for a quick profit before they drop back, and greed says hold onto your losers until they rebound. So you sell your winners and use the proceeds to reinvest in four more stocks. Two go up, two go down. Once again, you sell the winners and hold the losers. On the books, you show a tidy little cash profit (which also happens to be fully taxable), but your investment portfolio is filled with losers. A good broker can help you avoid that situation by cutting through the emotion of the moment and persuading you to cut your losses—even if it hurts—and let your winners run.

But run how high? With few exceptions, stocks do not move up in a straight line year in and year out. After a period of steady gains, they tend to level off, or even to drop back a little. Some do more than drop—

they plunge. A broker who does his or her job correctly will have you out of those stocks before your gains become losses.

Al Heiam of Drexel Burnham talks about putting his clients into a $6 stock of a solar energy company that showed impressive earnings potential. But after making a surprise visit to the company's Pompano Beach, Florida, headquarters, Heiam suddenly had second thoughts about the stock. "I found the president of the company in overalls moving furniture," recalls Heiam, "which didn't bother me so much as the sales manager, who was eating a hero sandwich with onions dripping out of his mouth when he came through to shake my hand. Then when I saw the rest of the operation, I was convinced this thing was as phony as a $3 bill. It was built on hype. I didn't want to do too much while the stock price was rising," adds Heiam, "but underneath I knew it was a bad apple. Then a good friend of mine gave me the coup de grace when he raised questions about the legality of the reported earnings. That was enough for me. I said, 'I don't care what the price goes to, I'm getting out. I got my clients out between $30 and $36. The stock got as high as $39, and then it just plunged, and, of course, now it has been out of existence for some time."

MANEUVERING THE TWISTS OF THE MARKET

Inexperienced investors tend to be most vulnerable when the market is at one extreme or the other. When the market is low, they sell when they should be buying. What's worse, when the market is high, they buy when they should be selling. A broker who advises clients to use a little restraint in the heat of a rally can sometimes save his or her clients from major losses. When the market is up, yields are at their lowest and downside risk is at its highest. "If clients really want to buy a stock at a level I feel is too high," says Basil, "I recommend they put a stop order in to sell the stock automatically when it drops 15 percent below the price they paid for it. That way, they're not going to get burned too badly on the stock."

While investors are often all too willing to jump into a hot market, they typically sit out some slow markets when investment values are at their best. It's enormously difficult to get people to invest in stocks, for instance, when growth is flat, prices are low and Wall Street seems to have lost interest in the market. Yet it's at such times that yields are at their highest, downside risk is at its lowest and most stocks have nowhere to go but up. In 1974, when the market was at one of its most depressed levels in years, fearful investors refused to buy stocks even though many stocks were trading at bargain prices. General Telephone, for example, was selling at $16^{1/2}$ and paying a yield of 14 percent—at a time when bank deposits were paying 5 percent. Yet investors, succumbing to the pressures of fear, would have nothing to do with the stock market. Brokers who are successful at getting their clients into the market under such conditions will end up with some very satisfied clients when the market makes a comeback.

How do stockbrokers convince investment-shy clients to invest during a down market?

1. They have to be persuasive talkers.
2. They need some facts to back up their convictions.

"You have to have confidence in what you're selling," says Jim Buehler of Roney & Co., "and the ability to persuade the client to put some money into that investment."

Dain Bosworth's Kopp talks about one emerging high-tech stock he recommended that quickly moved up in price before getting caught in a bear market and tumbling down to about $10 a share. "The market had gone against me, but in my opinion the stock was even more attractive at $10 a share than it had been at the higher price." Convincing worried clients to keep buying, however, became tougher every time the stock made another downward tick. "At times like those," says Kopp," you give your clients all the facts at your disposal and you tell them that even though you can't predict when the market will turn, we know it will turn someday. If you have the confidence to buy the stock at times when no one else is willing or able to buy it, you will be rewarded in the long run. Eventually the stock recovered and moved back up to about $20 a share, and the clients who had stuck with me made a great deal of money."

Buehler had a similar experience with a stock he was recommending that ran into unexpected market turbulence. "The stock was Inertia Dynamics, which was selling at $9 a share when I first started recommending it," recalls Buehler. "They manufactured gas-powered hand-held trimmers and were a major supplier for Lawn-Boy and Black & Decker. Then they bought a new division that manufactured an exercise machine. We projected that the stock would go from $9 to $20, but the exercise machine turned out to be a flop and the stock dropped to $4 a share. Naturally my clients all wanted to sell out, but I told them I still felt it was a good stock, and a great buying opportunity at $4 a share. Some still sold, some held on, and some took my advice and bought more. Over the next three years, the stock went up and split and kept going up to the equivalent of $25 a share. Those who bought at $4 a share made $6 for every dollar they invested."

The job of a stockbroker is really part art, part science. The broker has to know his or her clients and to understand their goals and their investment thresholds. That's where the art comes in. But he or she also has to be in constant touch with the investment market. The broker's job is to pinpoint the best values in any given market. And that takes more than instinct. It takes facts, and it takes research. Prophesying the stock market has evolved into a genuine—if very inexact—science.

ANALYSTS: PROBING BEHIND THE SCENES

The main source of a stockbroker's "science" is the research department of his or her firm. The research department is the heart of a brokerage company. Large New York firms allocate $30 million or more a year for investment research. The largest firms may employ up to a hundred investment analysts plus research assistants to track the performances of several hundred publicly traded companies.

The top securities analysts are among the most revered people in the industry. They're frequently quoted in business journals and interviewed on TV. And they're very well paid. A salary of a quarter million dollars a year is not unusual for a successful analyst. In fact, the very top Wall Street analysts can make as much as $1 million a year in salary and performance bonuses.

The analyst's job, however, is not without its headaches. Being an analyst requires incredible dedication and long hours—often 12 to 14 hours a day. And analysts are under intense pressure to come through with accurate and timely recommendations. When an analyst makes a big mistake, the whole brokerage firm looks bad. Hundreds of brokers are set back, and thousands of their clients lose money. "One of our analysts came out from New York and said we should buy Digital Switch," says one broker. "I bought it in the 20s, and the stock fell to $7—during a bull market. That was very embarrassing." Analysts who make too many mistakes soon find themselves looking for a new line of work.

By and large, analysts are drawn from among the cream of the crop at the nation's most prestigious business schools. Those who make it as analysts must be tenacious investigators, pursuing every relevant fact regarding the companies they're assigned to analyze. Some analysts follow an entire market sector. Others may be limited to as few as half a dozen stocks. Their reputations—in fact their careers—depend on their ability to give good advice on those half dozen stocks.

To do their job effectively, analysts must not only evaluate the information a company freely releases, they must also look behind the scenes to dig up the information companies would rather not have revealed. Analysts pore tirelessly through balance sheets and earnings reports and grill corporate CEOs and CFOs the way Mike Wallace works over a Medicare violator. They often call a company's customers, its dealers, its distributors, its suppliers—even its competitors—to garner insight into the company's financial health and economic future.

As part of their research, analysts also rely heavily on computerized forecasting techniques to identify quarterly earnings trends and project future growth.

The research of analysts can be broken down into three major areas. They want to know:

1. *How the overall market is faring.* Research has shown that as much as 70 percent of the price movement of a typical stock is attribut-

---

Research Department Rankings

1 Merrill Lynch
2 First Boston
3 Drexel Burnham Lambert
   Goldman Sachs
5 Smith Barney, Harris Upham
6 PaineWebber
   Prudential-Bache Securities
8 Donaldson, Lufkin & Jenrette
9 Morgan Stanley
   Salomon Brothers
11 Kidder, Peabody
12 Dean Witter Reynolds
   E. F. Hutton
14 Wertheim Schroder
15 Shearson Lehman Brothers
16 Cowen
17 Montgomery Securities
18 Oppenheimer
19 Sanford C. Bernstein
   Cyrus J. Lawrence
21 Eberstadt Fleming
   L. F. Rothschild

Each year *Institutional Investor* magazine asks institutions to rank the research analysts who cover various industry groups in the stock market. The overall results are tallied and the individual analyst in each industry group who receives the most points is designated the First All-American Analyst in his industry group. Those analysts receiving the next highest number of points are designated the second team, third team and runnerup. When the firms are ranked according to their analysts achieving these rankings, the leading firms are shown above. The results are the 1987 rankings as published in the October 1987 issue of *Institutional Investor*. Since these are evaluations of institutional analysts, the results are necessarily skewed to the kinds of stocks that institutional investors buy—namely large capitalization stocks and reasonably well-known names.

Reprinted with permission from the October 1987 issue of *Institutional Investor.*

able to the movement of the stock market itself. If the market is moving up, it is very likely that any stock you pick will also go up. When the market tumbled nearly 1,000 points in October, 1987, all stocks were set back dramatically—even those with record earnings. The research department has done more than half of its job if it can determine in which direction the stock market is moving.

2. *How the individual sectors such as health care, retail, high tech or heavy manufacturing are doing within that market.* About 20 percent of the price movement of a stock is attributable to its industry group. If the steel industry is down, for instance, the chances are that all steel companies will be down. If interest rates are going through the roof, there's a good chance that nearly all savings and loans will be struggling.

3. *How the individual companies within those sectors are performing.* With rare exceptions, only about 10 percent of the price movement of a stock is based on the performance of the company that issued it.

That's why it's important to know, for instance, that the market is moving up and medical technology stocks are leading the pack. In that case, almost any medical stock you pick would have a good chance of performing well. On the other hand, if the overall market is flat, it's much more important to determine not only which industrial sector shows the strongest promise but also which companies within that sector show the best potential for growth.

FIGURE 3-1   Factors That Determine the Price Movement of a Stock

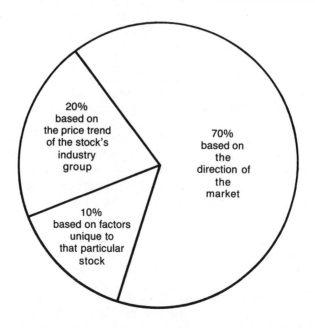

Every week, the research departments of most major brokerage firms come up with reams of research information for their brokers. In addition, many brokerage firms subscribe to other research services and closely follow the research reports of the other major brokerage houses. The brokerage firm of Thomson McKinnon, for instance, has its own research department and also subscribes to the research services of Donaldson Lufkin, an institutional securities firm with one of the top-rated research departments.

As a customer at a major brokerage firm, you are receiving the benefits of this multimillion-dollar research effort every time your broker offers you a recommendation.

WHERE SCIENCE BECOMES ART

But paring down the recommendations is no small task for your broker. From the stacks of growth charts, financial reports and research data, your broker must decide which investments are best for each of his or her clients. That's where science becomes art. The best brokers seem to possess an innate ability to translate this continuing stream of information into sound recommendations that apply specifically to the individual investment objectives of each of their clients.

What's their key to success in matching clients with appropriate investment recommendations? Listening—and not just for the obvious things; brokers must also read between the lines. "When an investor tells a broker he wants to maximize his return over the next two years, that may not be the whole story," says Adrian Banky, executive vice president of the Securities Industry Association. "That investor may be building up a nest egg to make a down payment on a house, and what he really wants is risk-averse investments." It's the broker's responsibility to flush out that information and put the client into the proper investment. "You've got to get underneath the clients' skin," says Dale Grubb of Shearson Lehman. "You've got to find out what they want, what their risk threshold is and what their investment objectives are."

In many cases, even the client hasn't decided exactly what he or she wants. When an investor says she wants income-producing investments, for instance, does she mean dividend-yielding stocks, a limited partnership with income, a bond or a bond mutual fund? Does she want taxable income or tax-exempt income? Does she want short-term notes, high-rated long-term bonds or junk bonds? And when an investor says she wants growth stocks, does she mean a $70 stock of an established company with a track record of steady growth or a $2 stock of a new software company that has the potential for rapid growth?

On the other hand, an investor might tell his broker, "I'd like to invest in some really sound, safe stocks—something like Automated Micro Systems." Generally speaking, "sound, safe stocks" means blue chips such as IBM, AT&T or General Electric—not Automated Micro Systems. The client is giving a mixed message, and it's up to the broker to uncover exactly what he means. A good broker will question clients carefully to determine their objectives and their threshold for risk. "I've got to know in English what it is they want," says Betsy Buckley of Dain Bosworth. "Only then can I help them translate it into investment language. You say you want 20 percent return every year? That's pretty aggressive. That means some years you're going to have a 10, 15, 20 percent loss. Are you going to be able to go to sleep at night under those circumstances?"

"A lot of times," says David Thompson of Prudential-Bache, "there's a big difference between what clients say their risk tolerance is and what it really is. You can really see this in a married couple. The husband will usually act macho: 'Oh sure, I can assume sizable risks.' But I try to read their nonverbal language—especially from the wife. If I see her fidgeting, I suspect they may be in over their heads. I also determine their investment objectives by looking at their investment history," adds Thompson. "What have they invested in previously? Leopards don't normally change their spots."

THE WHOLE PACKAGE

Stock and bond recommendations represent just a small part of the services that a broker can offer. Brokerage firms offer a wide range of investment products—mutual funds, mortgage-backed securities, index options and index futures, limited partnerships, asset management accounts, municipal bonds, unit investment trusts, annuities and life insurance products. Universal life, in fact, was created, not by an insurance company, but by the brokerage giant E. F. Hutton. And single premium deferred annuities were first successfully sold in large volume by Paine-Webber.

Brokers can also offer other important services. Eight hours a day, five days a week, brokers are plugged into an electronic network of information. They have access to a financial news wire that is constantly spinning out updates on interest rates, economic news and market information. Whether hostages are taken in Lebanon or oil is discovered off the shore of Louisiana, the stockbrokers in the United States are among the first to know about it. When news comes across the wire, the market trembles, pauses and decides on how to react. Your broker is aware of pertinent information regarding your stocks long before you are. He is your link to this vast and instantaneous network of information. "As a broker, you may not know what's going to happen," says Prudential's Koriath, "but you know what's going on right now. You have your hand on the pulse of the world."

Without a broker, you are largely dependent for your information on the quarterly reports of the stocks you own. One of your stocks could drop 20 percent overnight, and you might have no idea why. Maybe the company had a disappointing earnings report, maybe a merger attempt fell through, maybe a lawsuit was filed against the company, or maybe it was just a quirk in the market. Whatever the reason, your broker would be on top of it.

So for most serious stock market investors, the extra benefits of a full-service broker go well beyond merely executing trades. You get access to research reports, innovative new financial products and investment recommendations, and—most important—you get the assistance of a professional financial advisor whose career depends on keeping you in the black.

Stockbrokers must have the ability to be cool and dispassionate in a profession where pandemonium is the norm. "It's a real competitive business, it's a real emotional business, and it's a business where you have to exercise a great deal of discipline," explains Kopp. "The reason most people don't make money in the market is that they don't have the discipline."

It takes someone with nerves of steel to say "Sell" when the market is riding high or to say "Buy" when the market seems hopelessly depressed. Crowd hysteria plays an enormous role in the market. If you want to follow the crowd, you may not need a broker. But the investors who tend to do the best are those who know when to leave the crowd and move on to other investments. In some markets, it doesn't take brains to make money—it just takes guts. That's when it helps to have a broker who doesn't mind putting his or her convictions on the line—one who will say, essentially, "I don't care what your banker says. I don't care what your lawyer says or what your accountant says. This is my business, and I'm telling you to buy this stock now at this price." There's something very gutsy about that. If the broker is wrong, he or she risks being chastised or fired by the client. That's how brokers *really* earn their pay. With one well-timed piece of advice, your broker could make up for a lifetime of commissions.

Where do you find a broker who can consistently keep your investments ahead of the game? You can start by finding a good brokerage house. The choices are vast and varied, as the next chapter explains.

PART 2

The Selection Process

CHAPTER FOUR _____

What's Out There: From Different Firms Come Different Services

"Wanted: One stockbroker, name unknown."

It could be a case for Scotland Yard, but this one you'll have to solve yourself.

Your mission: Track down and engage "most wanted" securities broker, using any means possible.

Descriptive details on the suspect are sketchy:

Age: Unknown   Sex: Unknown

Race: Unknown   Height, weight: Unknown

Scars, birthmarks, tattoos: Unknown

Distinguishing characteristics: Affable, ethical, competent, dependable

Modus operandi: Lures unsuspecting investors into working relationship by promising reasonable returns; usually delivers

This is no ordinary investigation. Your livelihood, your future prosperity, your dreams of a comfortable retirement are all riding on this one. It deserves your very best shot.

But where do you begin? How do you cull from the thousands of potential suspects your own personal "Number One Most Wanted Broker"? Most investors use the "no-step approach." Pour yourself a pop. Turn on the TV. Read the paper. And wait. All you need is a telephone and a little patience, and sooner or later a broker will very likely call you.

As a familiar adage goes, "Securities are sold, not bought." Investors are not likely to buy a given investment of their own volition. They do so because a broker has called them and encouraged them to buy it. Likewise, most investors end up with a broker, not because they have sought out the broker but because the broker has sought them out. However, such arrangements often yield disappointing results because the fit—the underlying relationship between broker and client—just doesn't work.

"Too many investors are passive/aggressive in selecting a broker," says D'Arcy Fox of A. G. Edwards. "They're passive in that they let the broker select them rather than taking the initiative to select the broker. Then, when things don't work out, they suddenly become aggressive because they're unhappy with the relationship."

We recommend a more proactive approach: Visit some firms. Talk to some brokers. Probe. "Kick the tires," as Bob Dunwoody of Van Dusen & Co. explains. "Examine the warranty, and do any thing else you would do in any other relationship."

"Think of your investments as a business," advises Tom Hudson of PaineWebber. "If you were going to invest $50,000 in a fast-food chain, you'd do a pretty thorough job of researching it. You'd drive to the location, you'd interview people, you'd study the financial background. In other words, you'd do your homework. You should put that same kind of time and energy into researching the brokerage firm and the broker before you invest your money with them."

"Don't be in a hurry," suggests John Sundeen, compliance director, for Robert W. Baird & Co. in Milwaukee. "There are all types of brokers. Talk to several until you find one who is suitable for you. There's no point working with a broker you are not comfortable with."

We recommend a four-stage selection process:

1. Learn your options.
2. Determine your objectives.
3. Seek out suspects.
4. Interview the suspects and make your selection.

In this chapter, we'll focus on Stage 1—your options. What's out there? What types of services are available at the various securities firms?

STAGE 1: YOUR CHOICE OF FIRMS

From different brokerage firms come vastly different services. If it's the high-tech stocks of Silicon Valley that interest you most, you might select a regional NYSE broker that tracks growing California companies; Morgan Olmstead in Los Angeles is one such broker. If you live in the South, you might prefer Atlanta-based Robinson-Humphrey, which specializes in stocks of growing Southern firms. Every geographic area has its own regional NYSE firms.

If you're a wealthy investor with a taste for prestige and preferential treatment, you might prefer an account at one of the highbrow Wall Street institutional firms—for example, Morgan Stanley or Goldman Sachs. If you'd like to try your hand at small speculative start-up companies, you could deal with a penny stock firm such as Stuart-James in Denver. A number of smaller NASD member firms also specialize in small, local over-the-counter stocks and municipal bonds; these include Craig Hallum in Minneapolis, City Securities in Indianapolis and Williams Securities in Tampa.

If you feel you need an investment advisor who can help you assess your needs, determine your objectives and lay out a lifetime road map of investment strategies for you, a financial planner from a company such as IDS or Financial Services Corporation might be the way to go. On the other hand, if you make all of your buying and selling decisions yourself, your best bet might be a discount firm such as Charles Schwab or the brokerage arm of Fidelity Investments.

Most investors, however, open their first full-service account with a broker from one of the big national NYSE firms that gear their retail services to the investing masses throughout the United States.

THE BIG NATIONALS

Of the 77,000 brokers who work for New York Stock Exchange member companies, more than 70 percent are employed by one of the 11 largest retail firms. You're probably familiar with the names of the top 11— Merrill Lynch is the largest, followed by Dean Witter (owned by Sears), E. F. Hutton, Shearson Lehman, Prudential-Bache, PaineWebber, A. G. Edwards, Thomson McKinnon, Smith Barney, Kidder Peabody and Drexel Burnham.

Most of the national NYSE firms share a number of characteristics:

- *Packaged investments.* Most of the megafirms carry broad lines of packaged investments, including mutual funds, life insurance and annuities, unit investment trusts and limited partnerships. These firms are the leaders in introducing new products into the investment market. Merrill Lynch, for instance, claims to have more than 160 investment products.

- *Research capabilities.* The national firms are noted for their research capabilities. Their large staffs of analysts track hundreds of companies, including all of the better-known national companies, such as IBM, General Electric, Ford, GM and Digital Equipment, as well as a number of promising midsize companies. When you have a broker at a large national firm, you have a link to top research on the nation's—or the world's—most important companies. "The securities industry is in the information business," says Bob Cohn, training director of Drexel Burnham, "and information emanates first from a big Wall Street firm."

- *Influence.* These megafirms truly have the power to move markets. "The bigger your presence on Wall Street," says Cohn, "the more your firm and its opinion matters. When E. F. Hutton speaks, people really do listen. When the research department of a large firm likes a stock, and says so, it tends to move that stock."

- *Peace of mind.* Most of the top NYSE firms have been in business for generations, so if you deal with them, you don't have to worry about whether your investments are secure. These companies have deep pockets that enable them to weather difficult markets.
- *Strong reputations.* The big firms are very image-conscious—they have a national reputation to uphold. And while they're not immune to scandal (for example, the check-kiting and insider trading episodes of recent years), they generally do everything in their power to keep their business on the up and up. They have too much at stake to allow their images to deteriorate. They attempt to enforce strict, standardized controls, thus lending some assurance that your account will be handled in an aboveboard fashion. They make a point of maintaining strong compliance departments to see that everything is done strictly in accordance with the letter of the law.
- *Public education.* The megafirms put great emphasis on public consumer education. When listed options were first introduced on Wall Street, many of these firms distributed literature and sponsored lectures on options trading. When new tax legislation is enacted, these firms are often among the first to conduct community seminars explaining its intricacies.
- *Wide accessibility.* A key advantage in dealing with the major national firms is that they are *national.* They have branches throughout the United States. If you're an executive with a large corporation and you get transferred from time to time, you can be fairly confident that wherever you go, you'll be able to find a nearby branch office of almost any of the major NYSE companies.
- *Well-trained brokers.* As a general rule, major national companies tend to spend more time and money educating their brokers than do many of the smaller brokerage companies. When you deal with a major company, you can be fairly certain that your broker has gone through at least four intensive months of basic securities in-house training.

While the size and strength of the large national firms can work to your advantage, it can also lead to problems. Here are some possible disadvantages of working with a major national firm:

- *Feel like a number.* While your broker is likely to provide personalized service, others in the company may treat you more like an account number than a person. If you have a problem with your account, you may have to deal with an operations department in lower Manhattan that knows you only as account A-03957278.
- *Sales pressure.* Stockbrokers at the major NYSE firms are at times under great pressure to sell new proprietary packaged products introduced by the firm. Some of the major firms invest millions of dollars to create new mutual funds, unit trusts and limited partnerships, so they clearly have a commitment to see that those products are sold. As a

result, account executives may be pressured to meet sales quotas for the new products.

- *Turnover.* The turnover rate is somewhat higher at the major national firms than at some of the regional firms. This means that with the national firms the chances are greater that your broker could end up shipping out to another firm.
- *Split personality.* A handful of the major NYSE firms try to be both retail firm and institutional firm, and it's not always clear which type of client the firm feels is most important.
- *Recommendation limitations.* Because of their immense distribution power, the largest securities firms prohibit—or at least inhibit—their brokers from recommending the stocks of most of the smaller emerging growth companies. Says one broker who formerly worked for a large NYSE firm: "Most of the major firms have instituted rules prohibiting their research departments from recommending a stock unless it has at least 20 million shares 'of float.' The problem is, they have such huge buying power that if they recommend a smaller stock, they will dominate the market in that stock and create all kinds of internal problems. Unfortunately for clients of these larger firms, the economic growth in America today is in the smaller corporations—companies doing less than $20 million in sales. Those are the very companies that the very large securities firms cannot work with. They cannot underwrite a $3- to $5-million deal. And their research departments cannot recommend these stocks. So what you have at these major brokerage firms are stockbrokers—and therefore investors—who are virtually precluded from participating in the fastest-growing segment of the American market."

Most NYSE brokers are expected to recommend only stocks that are included in the company's "recommended" list. The smaller regional and local brokerage companies also have such lists, but they are more likely to allow their brokers to recommend stocks other than those recommended by the company. "For a broker at a major NYSE firm to recommend a stock to a client that isn't on the approved list," says Judy Johnson, a divisional manager with the regional firm Advest, "he has to go to a great deal of effort to get permission. He has to write up his reasons and send them to the home office for approval—which can take at least two weeks, if they approve it at all."

Johnson says that the same restrictions can apply to direct participation investments such as real estate limited partnerships. "They can't do a $10 million deal—it's too small," she says. "Of course, regional firms like ours can't do a $150 million deal like the nationals can do. But there are a lot more $10-, $20- and $30-million corporate finance and real estate deals to choose from than there are $100 million deals, so the regionals can be much more selective."

Doing Business with a Large National Retail Firm

Possible Advantages

- Excellent selection of investment products
- Influential research department providing coverage on hundreds of securities
- Stability—old established firm with large financial resources
- National network of branches to serve you wherever you go
- Image consciousness—strong emphasis on compliance with the rules
- Public education through informative seminars and brochures
- Well-trained brokers

Possible Disadvantages

- Vulnerability to operations problems—being treated like a number
- Emphasis on selling proprietary packaged products
- Quotas and other pressures for brokers to produce
- Higher turnover among brokers
- The "split personality" that comes from trying to be both a retail and an institutional firm
- Restrictions prohibiting the firm from underwriting or recommending companies unless they are "big enough"

REGIONAL NYSE FIRMS

Regional NYSE firms are similar in many ways to the major national NYSE firms. The main differences are that they are smaller, that their headquarters are located outside New York City, and that they tend to concentrate their research efforts primarily on companies within their own geographic area.

But like the national firms, the top regional firms are very concerned about their reputations. Many of them have been in business for generations and have become fixtures in their communities. Alex. Brown in Baltimore was founded before Thomas Jefferson became president. Sutro in San Francisco was founded in 1858, not long after the California gold rush began. So these firms don't concede anything in the way of prestige and tradition to the big nationals. But, because their focus is regional, they identify with the community in which they are located. Consequently they try very hard to maintain a positive image in that community.

Dealing with a regional firm also offers some other advantages:

- *Convenient locations.* Regional firms establish branch offices in areas that might not be served by a national firm. "In many of the smaller communities," says Advest's Johnson, "you'll have access to a broker that you wouldn't otherwise have."

- *Retail focus.* Unlike some of the major national firms, most of the regional NYSE firms concentrate almost exclusively on retail rather than institutional business. So if you have an account at a regional firm, you know you're number one with it.
- *Quality of service.* Regional firms offer more personalized service. "You will get better service from any of the good regional firms than you would get from the major New York–based national firms," says Perrin Long, an analyst with Lipper Analytical Services. "If you have a complaint, it will get settled more quickly because the office is headquartered in your general area. The people who work for those firms have the ability to work more closely together for the benefit of the firm as a whole, as opposed to a Merrill Lynch or some of the other major firms, where the account executives in the branch offices are nothing more than numbers in a computer."

"If a client needs help from his broker at a regional firm," adds Phil Clark, director of branch management and retail sales at Detroit-based Roney & Co., "the departments that provide that help are only a three-digit dial away from the account executive. So things can get done without going through a whole bureaucratic scheme."

If you are an active trader, you may get to know more of the people in the firm—the branch manager, some of the clerical staff and possibly some of the upper-management people. "One of the major advantages of a regional firm," says Clark, "is the short lines of communications from the top thinkers in the firm—the research analysts, product leaders and people who generate the investment ideas and investment products—to the sales force and from the sales force to the client. The short lines of communications put the account executive in a position to serve the client on an individualized, highly personalized basis."

In all fairness, however, it should be said that the larger regionals, like the national firms, have branch offices scattered throughout a wide area. Piper Jaffray, for instance, has about 50 offices throughout the North and Northwest. Advest has nearly 100 branch offices throughout the East and Northeast. While that hardly compares with the hundreds of offices of a Dean Witter or a Merrill Lynch, the brokers at the branch offices of the larger regionals as well as the major national firms can experience a sense of isolation from the home office.

- *Regional research.* Regional firms tend to focus on stocks from their own area of the country. "We identify with California," says Lyn Hensle, a vice president with Morgan, Olmstead of Los Angeles. "We will identify investment opportunities that might be overlooked by large national firms—for example, growing biogenetic companies or companies in Silicon Valley."

Tom Asher of Robinson-Humphrey in Atlanta says, "People who live in Atlanta like to own Southern companies. If you look at a pin map of stockholders, you generally find that they gravitate heavily around the home office of that firm." It's not just loyalty. These people are employees or customers of those companies, or they read about the companies in their hometown newspaper. "Individuals normally try to keep any business that they give to a vendor within their own locality," says Long. "You don't take your dry cleaning to St. Louis."

Just as investors develop an intimate interest in their hometown stocks, so too do the brokers and analysts of the regional firms. "People who live in Chicago or Minneapolis or Detroit or Cleveland—wherever you call home—will have special insights into those regional corporations that would be difficult for someone traveling in on an annual visit to have," says Clark. "We go to cocktail parties and to church with the people who make policy decisions at those companies."

Similarly, if you want to buy municipal bonds, it's a good bet that your regional brokerage firms will have a better selection of bonds from your home state than will the typical national NYSE firm.

- *Recommendation flexibility.* Unlike the brokers of national firms, who are generally encouraged to work strictly from recommended lists of companies with large capitalization, your regional broker has considerable flexibility in the stocks he or she can recommend. "At a regional firm, the broker has a great deal more latitude in searching out and recommending investment opportunities and in recommending smaller-capitalization companies with fewer shares outstanding," says Clark. "By contrast, at a national firm you can't tell 11,000 salespeople to buy a stock with a 400,000-share float even if that's the best investment possible. The hole just wouldn't be large enough for all of them to get through. For a broker at a national firm to get approval to sell a stock not on the recommended list is extremely cumbersome," adds Clark. "At a regional firm, approval to sell the stock is just three digits away. Instead of waiting two weeks for approval, you can get it in a few minutes—assuming that the stock meets the quality standard of the firm and the client."

- *Flexibility of national research.* While regional firms concentrate on regional stocks, most of them also subscribe to national research services—such as Donaldson Lufkin or Argus—to accommodate clients who are interested in information on the national blue-chip firms. "If, for some reason, that research is not in tune with what the sales force wants or what the public wants," says Clark, "guess what? We can hire another company to provide us with that research—in one hour. We can change overnight from Argus to Donaldson Lufkin. If one is not performing, we can leave. We can follow the best research. By contrast, it would take the major firms three to five years to turn their research departments around."

- *Mature brokers.* Regional firms tend to hire brokers who are somewhat older than those hired by the national firms. They look for individuals who are already established in the community and have a network of contacts. Brokers at regional firms are less likely to switch firms than are brokers at the big national firms.

Regional firms do, however have some drawbacks:

- *Less stability.* While most regional firms are profitable and financially solvent, the demands of the brokerage business over the past few years have created a need for greater capital resources, and that has put increased financial pressure on regional firms. As a result, some regional firms have had to look for other associations to obtain financing.

"There is more stability with a major national firm," says one securities industry executive. "While the number of brokers is growing, the number of firms has been contracting—due primarily to consolidations. The national firms have the capital they need to stay in business. When we run into the next bear market—and we will because that's just part of the economic cycle—there is some comfort in knowing you have the considerable financial stability of a major firm behind you."

- *Slower innovators.* Because they have less capital to draw on, regional firms can't keep up with the national firms in turning out innovative

---

Doing Business with a Regional NYSE Firm

Possible Advantages

- Convenient locations in smaller communities
- Image consciousness—have a strong reputation to maintain
- Retail focus
- High degree of personalized service
- Superior research on regional companies
- Good selection of regional municipal bonds
- Less turnover among brokers than in national NYSE firms
- Brokers given more latitude in recommending stocks than in national NYSE firms

Possible Disadvantages

- Less stable than national NYSE firms—more vulnerable to takeovers
- Less capital than national NYSE firms
- Fewer products than national NYSE firms
- Lack research expertise of national NYSE firms
- No offices in other parts of the country

new products. The regional firms, for instance, were among the last to provide asset management accounts.

- *Limited access.* If you relocate to a different part of the country, it is likely that your regional firm will not have an office there and that you will need to establish a new account with a different firm.

NASD FIRMS

Technically speaking, the principal difference between an NYSE firm and an NASD (National Association of Securities Dealers) firm is that an NYSE firm owns a seat on the New York Stock Exchange and an NASD firm doesn't. For you as a client, however, that difference will probably never matter, since your NASD firm can execute your transactions for you through an NYSE member.

A more significant difference is that NASD firms are more likely than NYSE firms to be local firms that specialize in local low-priced, over-the-counter stocks. Such stocks tend to be more speculative than most NYSE stocks. An NASD broker would probably recommend stocks that cost $5 to $15 a share, whereas a regional NYSE broker is more likely to recommend stocks in the $10 to $40 range and a national NYSE broker would generally recommend stocks selling at $30 and up.

If you're interested in trading in local over-the-counter stocks (especially if you're a businessperson with a local company and you deal regularly with other local companies), you might prefer an account with a local NASD firm. Such firms see themselves as serving a niche that is ignored by the larger brokerage houses. They serve the small company with sales of $20 million or less.

"We specialize in emerging growth companies—entrepreneurs who break away from the 3Ms and Honeywells and are starting their own companies," says Ed Fleitman, director of retail sales at Craig-Hallum in Minneapolis. "These are businesspeople who start out with their own money—which gets them through about a year. After that, we may help them out with a private placement, maybe raising half a million to a million dollars. Then when they're ready to go public, an over-the-counter firm like ours would probably also do the underwriting. The bigger firms all need bigger dollar amounts to justify the time and effort to do something with these smaller companies.

"So an investor has a chance with a company like ours to participate in small emerging companies at the very early stages," adds Fleitman. "That's our niche. We don't try to be everything to everybody. But if an investor wants a mutual fund or a Ginnie Mae or one of the bigger national stocks, we can offer that also. But we deal primarily in stocks we follow and research. They're usually the over-the-counter stocks—which may not always be all that small. Our brokers may make recommendations for larger firms."

The advantage of participating in a stock in its early stages is that if the stock does well, your gain can be far, far greater than would be possible with even the very best established firms. In 1977, for instance, Craig-Hallum brought St. Jude Medical public at $3.50 a share. A $10,000 investment in St. Jude Medical then was worth $610,000 ten years later. In 1972, Craig-Hallum brought Cardiac Pacemaker public. It was acquired by Eli Lilly in 1978 at 73 times its original cost. An initial $10,000 investment was worth $730,000 six years later.

"While some initial public offerings work out spectacularly well and multiply in value, others decline and result in large losses," says Fleitman. So with the rewards come significant risks. "You have to understand the risks," says Fleitman, "and you have to be prudent about how many dollars you put into those things—everyone has a different risk tolerance. But we think it's a place where people should have some of their money."

In addition to the greater risk of the stocks offered by smaller local firms, there are other possible disadvantages in working with such a firm:

- The smaller local firms are not innovators. They generally do not have their own lines of packaged products, though they can usually offer products developed elsewhere.
- The brokers of the smaller local firms generally have less training and experience than the brokers of the NYSE regional and national firms. This is not true of all NASD firms; some of these firms have exhaustive training programs for their new brokers. But at other NASD firms, a person can join the firm, take a two-week crash securities training course, pass the Series 7 licensing exam and be selling securities the very next day.

Doing Business with a
Local or NASD Firm

Possible Advantages

- Offers underwritings in aggressive local stocks
- Offers research and market making in aggressive local stocks

Possible Disadvantages

- Underwrites and recommends stocks that usually carry a high degree of risk
- Limited product line

PENNY STOCK FIRMS

Some firms position themselves as "penny stock" firms. This doesn't mean that their stocks sell for pennies. But these firms do follow the very low-priced stocks of under $5 a share.

While there is no hard-and-fast distinction between a local NASD firm and a penny stock firm (penny stock firms are NASD members), the penny stock firms tend to deal in riskier stocks than do the traditional local NASD firms.

The hub of penny stocks is Denver, the home of Stuart-James and Blinder-Robinson, two of the better-known penny stock firms. The obvious advantage of penny stocks is that if they do well, the profits for an investor can be enormous. But for every major success of the penny stock firms, there are many failures.

Among the other disadvantages of penny stock firms are that their research capabilities and their investment product line are quite limited. These firms rarely stray far from their penny stock specialty. By and large, brokers at the penny stock firms tend to have less training and experience than brokers at the major regional and national firms.

A final note: The sales practices of Blinder-Robinson, one of the leading penny stock companies, have been the subject of a number of complaints, investigations and charges by the Securities and Exchange Commission.

Doing Business with a
Penny Stock Firm

Possible Advantages

- Opportunities to make significant profits by investing in low-priced, speculative stocks

Possible Disadvantages

- Risk of significant losses from investing in low-priced, speculative stocks
- Limited research
- Limited product line
- Less training for the brokers

INSTITUTIONAL FIRMS

If it's white glove treatment you want, you might consider an institutional firm. But only those prepared to invest some serious money need apply. Institutional giants such as Salomon Brothers, Goldman Sachs,

Morgan Stanley, First Boston, Donaldson Lufkin, Oppenheimer, L. F. Rothschild and Bear Stearns cater only to the "high net worth" investor. As one firm puts it, "We serve the individual who wants to be treated like an institution." A handful of institutional firms might let you open an account for "as little as" $300,000, but others require far more. Salomon Brothers, which caters to the high end of this market, targets investors worth at least $50 million. (Not surprisingly, there are few takers, but the company reports that it now has at least 100 clients who meet its criteria.) Goldman Sachs has slightly more modest standards. "We're more interested in the guy who has a few million dollars—maybe $5 million—in the securities market, so his net worth may be $20 million," says Roy Zuckerberg, director of retail sales at Goldman Sachs.

Institutional firms, as the name implies, have traditionally catered to large institutions—banks, insurance companies, pension and profit sharing funds, mutual funds and other organizations that manage large pools of assets. They provide highly sophisticated investment research and advisory services for their brokerage customers. They also offer investment banking services, including securities underwriting, mergers and acquisitions.

While much has been made of the "institutionalization" of the stock market, individual investors still hold 80 percent of the common stock on the New York Stock Exchange. However, institutions dominate the trading—accounting for about two-thirds of the total trading volume. On days when the trading volume reaches 200 million shares, roughly 133 million of those shares are traded by institutions.

In the past few years, a growing number of institutional firms have begun opening their doors to individual investors. A few, such as Goldman Sachs, have been in the retail market on a limited basis for a number of years. "We've offered retail services for the high end of the market for about 40 years," says Zuckerberg, "although we've done it in a more organized fashion over the past 15 years. It's a new business for some of the other institutional firms."

If you opened an account with an institutional firm, the chances are that you would be assigned to a team of specialists. "Our average team is probably three in number," says Zuckerberg. "One would specialize perhaps in fixed-income investments, one would be equities, and the other would probably deal with options or futures. They would direct the account on a nondiscretionary basis. We take a complete asset allocation approach in which we get involved in special investments that might include real estate or cable television or small companies that are still privately held." Your team of institutional brokers would probably be paid a salary plus a bonus.

Brokers at institutional firms tend to be better educated than the typical broker at other retail firms. "About 95 percent of the people we've hired in the past 20 years are MBAs or attorneys," says Zuckerberg. "If you're going after the very best accounts, you have to have the very best people and the very best services."

There are some other advantages in dealing with an institutional firm. You might get discounts on trades—charges as low as 10 to 15 cents per share on large block trades. You would obtain access to excellent research. Institutional firms are noted for their outstanding research departments. And the research reports issued by institutional firms are far more detailed than those issued by retail firms. Instead of the usual two-to-four page reports that most retail clients receive, you'd probably receive the 20-to-30 page reports geared to the needs of the institutional client.

But there are also some drawbacks in dealing with an institutional firm.

You probably won't be able to deal face-to-face with your broker on a regular basis. Most institutional firms have only a handful of branch offices. (By comparison, Merrill Lynch has more than 500 U.S. offices, Dean Witter has almost 700, and Edward D. Jones has more than 1,100.)

If you prefer packaged investments, an institutional firm may not be of much help. Such firms rarely stray beyond stocks, bonds, partnerships and private placement investments (though some, such as Bear Sterns, have begun offering their own mutual funds).

The services of an institutional firm are geared to the "sophisticated" money manager. Those fact-packed 30-page research reports are highly technical. Unless you're an unusually sophisticated investor, you might be better served by the abbreviated two-to-four-page reports that retail firms put out.

And, in truth, if you have a million dollar account, you could probably get the red carpet treatment and discounts on large trades at almost any of the large retail firms.

Doing Business with an Institutional Firm

Possible Advantages

- Excellent research
- Sophisticated service
- Low commissions for large transactions

Possible Disadvantages

- Few offices, limiting opportunities for face-to-face relationships
- Research and other services not focused to needs of individual investor
- Narrow product line

But institutional firms do offer one thing that the Merrill Lynches and Dean Witters cannot offer—and that is snob appeal. If you've never heard of Donaldson Lufkin, L. F. Rothschild or Morgan Stanley, it's probably by design. You won't see them advertised during "Monday Night Football." They're not interested in reaching the mass market. They want to preserve that exclusive carriage trade mystique—which has a powerful appeal for some investors. There's a certain panache to telling your friends at the club that "my broker is Morgan Stanley."

FINANCIAL PLANNING FIRMS

Investors seem to have strong—and conflicting—convictions regarding financial planning. Some investors prefer a sound, methodical investment program, with clear objectives and long-term projections. And other investors would rather have their molars pulled than go through the financial planning process. They're not interested in having all of their personal financial information dissected, scrutinized and categorized by financial planning experts. They're not interested in estate planning, yearly budgets, cash flow analyses, long-term projections or regimented investment programs. They much prefer a more freewheeling approach, basing their investment decisions on existing conditions rather than some all-encompassing lifetime plan.

There is no "correct" approach. Investors can succeed or fail with a plan just as they can succeed or fail without one. But if you're the organized, meticulous type who likes to keep all of your financial affairs in order, a financial plan might be worth considering.

Where can you get a financial plan? Some brokerage firms, such as E. F. Hutton, are leaders in financial planning. But the bulk of it is done by specialty firms that deal almost exclusively in financial planning. IDS Financial Services is by far the largest. Financial Services Corporation and Integrated Resources are also well-known national financial planning firms. And every city has many independent financial planners and financial planning firms. While some of these firms do only the planning, most will also sell investment products to help you fulfill your plan.

"We attract the investor who is looking for one individual to handle all of his financial needs—his investments as well as his insurance, his estate planning and his tax planning," says Norman Malo, senior vice president of Financial Service Corporation. Adds Bill McKinney, a vice president with IDS: "We want to handle all of our clients' assets—their mortgage, their checking account, their lending needs, their life insurance, their homeowners' insurance, their IRA, their college education savings and all of their other financial needs."

Donnis Casey of the brokerage firm A. G. Edwards suggests that "the kind of investor who should use a financial planner is someone who is either not very sophisticated in financial matters or wants to plan for a goal. A typical stockbroker researches stocks and can maybe make you money that way. A financial planner is going to gather all the facts and sit down and help you decide what products to use."

Financial planning offers several key benefits:

- You get a complete diagnosis before you begin investing. A financial plan may uncover deficiencies in your investment program. If you need more life insurance, more disability insurance, more tax-exempt investments or a more diversified base of investments, those needs will be revealed in a financial plan.
- You will probably forge a close relationship with your financial planner. "We deal face-to-face," says McKinney. "We don't sell on the phone. We encourage clients to come to our offices. We try to develop long-term relationships."
- You will probably encounter less immediate sales pressure with a financial planner than you would with a stockbroker. "We are more oriented to getting assets under management," says Malo, "whereas the NYSE firms are probably more transaction-oriented." Adds McKinney: "The essential difference between an IDS rep and a typical stockbroker is the difference between a financial plan and a transaction. We want to gather the facts before we move into a transaction. For example, one of our reps, Britt Davis of Missoula, Montana, drove three hours to call on a prospective client. The client laid a check for $50,000 on the table and said, 'Invest it as you see fit.' Britt refused the check, offering first to do a financial plan to assess the man's needs. We don't shoot from the hip or grab the cash off the table."

Among the possible drawbacks of financial planning are:

- *Lack of checks and balances.* Some investors get very nervous at the thought of keeping all of their assets with one company. They would rather have their own insurance agent, their own accountant, their own tax planner, their own investment broker. Others, however, find great comfort in the convenience of the all-eggs-in-one-basket approach.
- *Up-front costs.* Instead of putting all of your money into investments, you'll pay an up-front fee of several hundred to several thousand dollars for your financial plan. But the fee generally amounts to a very small portion of your total assets. As a rule of thumb, you should spend no more than 1 percent of your total assets on a financial plan.
- *Extra effort.* Many investors don't want to go through the effort of tracking down all of their pertinent financial data and feel uncomfortable about laying it all out for a financial planner to see.
- *Limited shelf life.* While the promise of financial planning is that one solid comprehensive plan will serve as a road map throughout your entire lifetime of investing, the truth is that tax laws change, your income changes, your family circumstances change, your net assets change,

and your basic objectives change. Your lifetime plan of three years ago may already be outdated.

- *Lax regulations.* The financial planning industry is still experiencing growing pains. It is notoriously unregulated. Anyone can hang out a financial planning shingle and solicit business—no experience is necessary. While many independent planners are very professional and very conscientious, others are more interested in peddling financial products under the banner of financial planning than in offering meaningful financial planning.

The Process

Count on at least a two-hour interview with your financial planner to compile all of the information necessary to put together a comprehensive financial plan. You will be asked to bring in your tax returns, a record of all your investments, your life insurance policies, your will and any other pertinent information about income and expenses. "The financial planner wants to know everything about his client," says Malo. "He wants to know about his client's house—how much it's worth. He wants to know the client's monthly income and monthly expenses. He wants to know everything."

The financial planner will also question you at length about your financial objectives, your retirement goals and future expenses for your children's education. As McKinney puts it, "We believe in gathering facts and feelings—hopes, dreams and ambitions."

There are two broad types of financial plans:

- *Computer-aided plans.* All the information regarding the investor's current situation, risk threshold and long-term objectives is fed into a computer. The computer prints out a financial plan that addresses the investor's needs. The less expensive plans of this kind lack specifics. The more expensive the plan, the more closely it is tailored to the investor's individual needs. According to Malo, "Typically, our clients would receive a 15–30-page summary report which has been generated with the help of a computer. This report will provide an income statement, a balance sheet, a cash flow analysis, an insurance analysis, tax planning, retirement planning, estate planning and information on financing educational expenses. You can expect to pay in the range of $200 to $1,000 for this service. It is geared for the household earning $40,000 or more."
- *Comprehensive personalized plan.* For the very wealthy, a team of financial experts—perhaps including a financial planner, an estate specialist, an attorney, an insurance specialist, a tax specialist and an equities specialist— compiles a personalized plan that addresses the client's specific needs. It points out exactly how funds should be diversified, and it gives specific investment recommendations. The plan

would run 100 to 200 pages. The costs usually run about $8,000 to $10,000. Such a plan is appropriate for millionaires and highly paid executives and professionals.

Finding a Financial Planner

Before you choose a financial planner, we suggest that you interview financial planners in person at their office. Look at their track record with other customers, and ask some in-depth questions. Malo suggests asking the planner:

- How many clients do you have?
- What is the average performance for those clients?
- What is the worst case?
- What is the best case?
- Have you sold any programs (limited partnerships) that have gone bad? What percentage does this represent?
- What percentage of your business would you estimate comes from various product areas? Mutual funds, for example? Limited partnerships? What are other big areas of business for you?
- What is your background? What did you do before you entered the financial planning business? (Many planners are former brokers or insurance agents.) Why did you leave?
- What kind of support do you offer now? For example, how are you going to help me with tax problems? Do you have a tax attorney or accountant on your staff, or do you expect me to work with my own tax advisor?
- Do you recommend individual securities?

Doing Business with a
Financial Planning Firm

Possible Advantages

- One financial advisor to coordinate all of your financial affairs
- Strong, long-term relationship
- Less sales pressure
- Provides overview of financial needs

Possible Disadvantages

- Planners may lack expertise in the stock and bond markets
- All eggs in one basket
- Limited shelf life of plan
- Up-front fee
- Unregulated industry with potential for fraud and conflicts of interest

- How many of your clients look to you for total financial planning?
- What are your objectives for your business?
- Could you provide me with a sample plan? What would it cost?
- Can I talk to a couple of your clients to learn how they have fared with you?

By doing the interviews in person, you can get a good feeling for whether a financial planner is someone you would like to do business with—which is very important when you're establishing a long-term relationship. You should also learn about the firm the planner represents—its size, years in business and background. You should ask about the professional designations of the planner, says Malo. Is he or she a certified financial planner (CFP), a chartered financial planner (ChFP), a certified public accountant (CPA) or an attorney? And by asking the right questions, you can find out whether the planner is knowledgeable, experienced and adequately qualified to help you draft your personal investment road map.

DISCOUNT BROKERS

If you're an investor who makes all your own buying and selling decisions, you might want to open an account with a discount firm where you'll get lower prices for nearly all your trades. For a detailed look at discount firms, see Chapter 10, "Buying at a Discount."

PROFILES OF THE MAJOR NATIONAL FIRMS

While the national firms offer a type of service very different from that of their regional, local and institutional counterparts, the difference among the major NYSE firms themselves is far less obvious. "I think it's a blur," says Bob Dunwoody, president of Van Dusen Securities and the former marketing officer of one of the top 11 firms. "To tell you the truth, between PaineWebber, E. F. Hutton, Prudential-Bache and Merrill Lynch, I don't think there is a great difference. I think there were significant differences ten years ago. Brokers from different firms used to perceive themselves differently. But this is no longer so."

Adds Perrin Long of Lipper Analytical Services: "It's not going to make a bit of difference whether you use a Merrill broker, a Hutton broker, a Dean Witter broker or a Kidder, Peabody broker. It comes down to a question of, 'Is this broker meeting my needs?' Basically, no firm has better brokers than any other firm."

Lee Kopp of the regional giant Dain Bosworth says, "The real key is, when you walk into the office, is the branch manager tending to business, is his staff capable, and is the broker you're dealing with the kind of person you want to deal with? It doesn't matter what name is on the door."

With those cautions in mind, in the following pages we attempt to portray, in rough terms, the perceptions, tendencies and general characteristics of the top 11 national NYSE firms—in descending order of size. We also include the profile of Edward D. Jones, a unique "regional" retail firm that has more branch offices than any of the nationals.

Merrill Lynch, Pierce, Fenner & Smith, Inc.
One Liberty Plaza
165 Broadway
New York, NY 10080
(212) 637-7455

Merrill Lynch was founded by Charles Merrill, the founder of the Safeway supermarket chain. His policy was to achieve economies of scale through large volume. He originated the concept of selling stocks like groceries through a network of financial supermarkets.

Merrill Lynch has far more brokers than any of its competitors (13,000) and the third most domestic branch offices (531), and it ranks third in capital. Its corporate culture is sometimes characterized as a cross between IBM and the U.S. Marine Corps. In fact, through the years, a number of its top officers have been former marines.

The company prides itself on being number one not only in number of brokers but in number of clients as well. This is reflected in its various advertising themes—for example, "A breed apart" and, more recently, "To know no limits." It ranks near the top in underwritings, and it is perennially number one in the prestigious *Institutional Investor* rankings for its huge and highly respected research department. Until about 20 years ago, Merrill Lynch brokers were not allowed to sell mutual funds. All of that has changed. Now Merrill Lynch is number one in mutual funds, with $84 billion invested in its 40 funds.

Merrill Lynch has been a leader in product creation. Its Cash Management Account (which provides investors with checking services, credit cards and other benefits) is considered by many to be the most innovative financial product to have been introduced in recent years. The firm has 1.3 million customers enrolled in its CMA program.

Merrill Lynch achieved a goal that has eluded many other retail firms: it leveraged its enormous success as a retail firm to become a powerhouse in the institutional securities business as well. It is now also a strong force in the international securities business.

With its nationwide network of brokers and branch offices, Merrill Lynch provides convenience for people who move from city to city and want to keep their account with the same brokerage firm. One Merrill Lynch executive estimates that the firm has a branch office within 25 miles of 90 percent of the U.S. investing public.

Merrill Lynch is known for its ground floor offices. And as the largest national firm, it also enjoys wide name recognition. With its great size and visibility, Merrill Lynch offers something for nearly every investor and is particularly appealing to the investor who wants to deal with the biggest.

But Merrill's size has its drawbacks. The firm's service can be impersonal at times. As one broker put it, "If you have a mistake on your account, it seems to take forever to get it fixed. They cater to the bigger investors, and they want bigger producers." Merrill Lynch ranked near the bottom in service among major firms in a customer satisfaction survey conducted by *Financial World* magazine.

In recent years, Merrill's profits have sagged. Its profitability has gone from above average in the industry to below average. Critics say that the firm's huge and expensive staff has been a major drag on its profitability. In years past, Merrill Lynch was acknowledged as the best-run retail firm, but recently some chinks have appeared in its armor. In early 1987, during an unexpected swing in interest rates, the firm's mortgage bond trading department racked up more than $275 million in losses before management could react and cut its losses.

Merrill Lynch managers and brokers are known for operating "by the book." They cannot recommend a security unless it is on the Merrill Lynch approved list. Merrill Lynch brokers tend to see themselves as employees of the firm, and the firm tends to view its customers as customers of the firm who are being serviced by one of its brokers.

Ever the innovator, Merrill has instituted two new programs that may become industry standards in coming years. First, it has initiated the use of customer service representatives to handle smaller accounts. Unlike the more high-powered commissioned "financial consultants," these are salaried employees. This program remains controversial in the industry, and at this time it's still too early to say whether it will work out well for the small investor.

Second, Merrill Lynch has initiated a system of paying its brokers on the assets that they control in their accounts. This motivates brokers to accumulate assets (stocks, bonds, options and so forth) in a Merrill Lynch account rather than simply generate commissions. Other firms have adopted this program.

Merrill's stock is publicly traded on the New York Stock Exchange.

Dean Witter Reynolds, Inc.
130 Liberty Street
New York, NY 10006
(212) 524-2222

With its army of 7,735 brokers, Dean Witter Reynolds is the second largest brokerage firm in the country. Founded in 1923, the firm Dean Witter (a San Francisco–based firm) later merged with Reynolds (a New York–based firm). In 1981, Sears Roebuck acquired the firm and launched a major expansion program with strong financial backing from the parent company.

Dean Witter opened hundreds of branches in the Sears stores in shopping malls across the country. These branches have provided convenience by bringing investments to the mass market. This marketing strategy has been especially effective in giving Dean Witter access to the "hidden money" of the country. Most brokerage firms are effective at reaching executives who work for major corporations, but the hidden money is held by tradespeople, farmers and elderly people who have saved and accumulated substantial assets. These people are less likely to be contacted by most brokerage firms and are sometimes intimidated by the prospect of walking into a fancy brokerage office. They are perfectly at home in a Sears store, where they can visit with the Dean Witter brokers working there to talk about their money concerns.

Including the 308 Sears Financial Centers, Dean Witter ranks second in number of branch offices, with 679. It is a leader in packaging and selling investment products—especially various types of mutual funds.

In recent years, Dean Witter has been wrenched by a rift between a purely retail marketing strategy and an institutional emphasis. The rift has resulted in some internal dissension and in a number of departures from the institutional side. Although some firms have dropped out of the institutional race and focused purely on the individual investor, Dean Witter still seeks to be a major player in both the institutional business and the retail business. It has benefited greatly from Sear's ownership and support, but its relationship with Sears has also created some culture shifts as the influence exerted by the Sears management over this old-line brokerage firm has continued to increase.

E. F. Hutton & Co., Inc.*
31 West 52nd Street
New York, NY 10019
(212) 969-5300

With 6,700 account executives, E. F. Hutton, founded in 1904, is the third largest retail brokerage firm in the country. It has 404 offices and 1,300,000 customer accounts.

For years, E. F. Hutton was to Merrill Lynch what Avis was to Hertz— number two and climbing. However, E. F. Hutton's corporate approach was entirely different from that of Merrill Lynch. While Merrill Lynch stressed rigid organization, E. F. Hutton encouraged independence among its brokers, urging them to think of themselves as more or less entrepreneurs. For years, that approach helped attract some of the best and brightest brokers in the business to E. F. Hutton. But its lack of controls resulted in a sullying of this firm's once brilliant reputation. The most notable of Hutton's recent problems has been the 1985 "check-kiting scandal," in which some Hutton branch managers manipulated bank withdrawals and deposits to earn extra interest in the company account. The scandal involved a minority of Hutton's branches and virtually none of its brokers, but the publicity hurt. In 1986, E. F. Hutton lost millions of dollars in a bond program.

To its credit, E. F. Hutton has taken steps to rekindle its dimming image. In 1986, it appointed Robert P. Rittereiser as its president and chief executive officer. Ironically, Rittereiser was recruited from Merrill Lynch, Hutton's archrival. Rittereiser, formerly a top senior manager at Merrill Lynch, is widely respected for his administrative prowess. His appointment should herald a major change in Hutton's organizational structure. The Hutton management style can be expected to tighten considerably under his leadership.

Hutton's traditional strength has been its ability to generate innovative new financial products. The company invented universal life, and it was one of the early leaders in the sale of annuities and tax-advantaged products. It is far and away the leader in financial planning among NYSE companies with a variety of different financial plans to meet the needs of a wide range of individuals.

Within the securities business there has been a strong trend toward money management in the past several years, and in this sphere E. F. Hutton has again been a leader. It offers its own money management services, and its brokers also serve as advisors to help clients arrange for having their investments handled by one of several dozen approved outside money managements.

E. F. Hutton remains a very entrepreneurial firm. One industry source said that unlike Merrill Lynch, Hutton's management views its account executives as its clients (viewing its investors as the clients of those brokers). The firm had disappointing financial results in early 1987, and it continues to face a tough uphill battle to overcome the damage caused by the check-kiting scandal.

Through a flurry of mergers and acquisitions over the past ten years, E. F. Hutton has remained independent. It is traded on the NYSE.

*As this book was going to press the acquisition of E. F. Hutton & Co., Inc. by Shearson Lehman Brothers, Inc. had not been finalized. When completed, the combined firm is projected to have about 12,000 brokers, 700 branch offices and more than $5 billion in capital.

Shearson Lehman Brothers, Inc.
American Express Tower
World Financial Center
New York, NY 10285
(212) 298-2000

Shearson Lehman has emerged as the fourth largest retail brokerage firm on the strength of the enormous momentum of its sales force. It has 6,173 "financial consultants" in 332 branch offices, and its capital assets of $3 billion rank second only to those of Salomon Brothers.

The nucleus of the present firm was established in 1960, and the firm created at that time then grew by acquiring older, larger firms, including the venerable Lehman Brothers. In so doing, it became one of the six leaders in investment banking (Merrill Lynch is the only other retail firm in the Big Six).

Because the firm grew by hiring brokers from other firms or by acquiring other firms, the average age of its brokers is among the highest found in NYSE firms. Until relatively recently, the firm had no formal training program. Shearson Lehman is strong in commodities, and it is extremely well regarded in over-the-counter trading, where it makes markets in almost 3,000 different issues—perhaps twice the number of markets made by its nearest competitor.

Of all the recent brokerage house acquisitions, the acquisition of Shearson Lehman by American Express is considered to be the most successful. The backing of American Express has enabled Shearson Lehman to gain tremendous momentum in the securities industry. Industry insiders speak with almost universal respect for its salespeople and its cadre of tough, experienced branch managers.

The firm has something of an urban personality, and the brokers are often more aggressive in investment approach than their counterparts at other large retail firms. In 1987 Nippon Life, the largest life insurance company in Japan, bought a 10% interest in Shearson. Later in the year another block of stock was offered to the public, and now is traded on the New York Stock Exchange.

Prudential-Bache Securities, Inc.
One Seaport Plaza
199 Water Street
New York, NY 10292
(212) 214-1000

With 5,327 account executives, Prudential-Bache is the fifth largest retail securities firm. It is a full-service firm with 329 branches and 1.2 million accounts.

Prior to Prudential's acquisition of Bache in 1981, Bache was one of the least respected major brokerage firms on Wall Street. It was the leading brokerage firm in the Hunt brothers' ill-fated attempt to corner the silver market, until Prudential's friendly acquisition it had been the rumored takeover target of a hostile bid.

When the firm's fortunes continued to fall, Prudential moved swiftly to hire George Ball, then president of E. F. Hutton, as the Prudential-Bache CEO. Since then, Prudential-Bache "has been like a phoenix rising from the ashes," according to one NYSE broker.

Prudential-Bache draws large amounts of its business from such aggressive product areas as options and commodities. Like Shearson Lehman, it has traditional pockets of strength in the urban Northeast. Like other megafirms, it has developed a series of proprietary mutual funds that it sells very successfully through its brokers. Prudential's huge financial resources have enabled the firm to bring out a variety of products in quick succession. Prudential-Bache is committed to serving investors with high net worth, and its strategy for achieving this marketing position has been to develop and attract big producers on the theory that the big producers will bring in the big clients. Among the firm's strengths are a strong technical analysis research department for short-term trading and a strong international research effort with a focus on investments in Australia, Japan and Canada.

Despite the impressive progress of Prudential-Bache, a number of securities industry spokespersons remain unconvinced about the firm's leadership and direction. Like other major retail firms, Prudential-Bache continues to seek respect as a major institutional firm. The company is 100 percent owned by Prudential Insurance Company.

PaineWebber, Inc.
1285 Avenue of the Americas
New York, NY 10019
(212) 713-2000

With 4,500 brokers, PaineWebber ranks sixth among retail brokerage firms. It was founded in Boston in 1879, and it has a reputation as an old blue-blood, blue-chip firm. Over the years, it has grown by acquiring a number of regional firms. It has also acquired Blyth Eastman Dillon, a major investment banker, and Mitchell Hutchins, a leading institutional boutique. But its efforts to emerge as a world-class institutional firm or a top-rung investment banker have not yet come to fruition.

As a result, its strength continues to be its retail trade. As one broker put it, "They know what their business is—which is basically retail—and they've stuck with it." Others aren't so sure. They perceive PaineWebber to be engaged in the same tug-of-war between an institutional and a retail focus as many of the other Big Eleven.

PaineWebber has developed a particular strength in fixed-income securities, especially Ginnie Maes. It is also widely respected for its expertise in the asset allocation approach to portfolio management. That is, the firm tells its clients what percentage of their assets should be invested in cash, in fixed-income securities, in stocks and so forth. Recently, Paine-Webber developed a wide stable of proprietary mutual funds. Its competitors view it as a rather conservative firm with brokers who tend to be risk averse in their recommendations. PaineWebber remains one of the last of the independents (not owned by a large financial services company), and its stock is traded on the New York Stock Exchange.

A. G. Edwards & Sons, Inc.
One North Jefferson
St. Louis, MO 63103
(314) 289-3000

A. G. Edwards ranks seventh in size among the top brokerage firms, with 2,834 "investment brokers" and 298 offices. It was founded in 1887 in St. Louis, and it is the only one of the nation's 11 largest brokerage firms that is not based in New York. It views its off–Wall Street location as an advantage rather than a liability in that this gives it the ability to step back from the whirlwind of Wall Street activity and thus obtain a more objective perspective on the market. It intentionally opens offices in small communities rather than large metropolitan areas, being particularly strong in retirement communities. Its more urban-oriented New York competitors sometimes refer to it as a niche player because of its reluctance to compete head-on with the big firms in big cities.

The small-town culture of the company is reflected in its brokers, who tend to be more conservative than their Wall Street counterparts. A. G. Edwards has intentionally and repeatedly chosen to walk a path different from that of its competitors.

First, it does not develop its own investment products. It believes that this would represent a conflict of interest. Instead, it makes selections among the packaged products offered by various outside vendors, much as an independent insurance agent makes selections among the policies offered by various insurance companies.

Second, it has a purely retail focus. It has not sought to become a leader in the institutional field.

Third, in a business known for its sophisticated and expensive trappings, A. G. Edwards aims at being the "low overhead" firm. Its offices are often modest and sometimes downright dowdy. It serves hot dogs each week in its executive dining room.

Its competitors almost universally speak of A. G. Edwards with respect. "It is highly profitable," says one. "It is viewed as the hometown broker," says another. Perrin Long calls A. G. Edwards "the best managed" of the 11 largest brokerage firms. Long says: "Their philosophy is this: They believe the salesman should act as a broker between the customer and the firm, and they try to do as much of their business as possible on an agency basis. They do not have their own mutual funds; they are not a major market-maker in municipals or corporates or over-the-counter equities. Their primary concern is service, and generally in this business, service is defined as not screwing up in the back office. Their philosophy is that the salesman should get as close to his or her customers as possible on a personal basis and not on an arm's-length basis."

In keeping with its low-overhead approach, A. G. Edwards likes to use "producing" branch managers, generally appointing the top producer in each office to manage that office in his or her spare time. Although the firm has its million-dollar producers, the average Edwards broker generates less commissions than are generated by the top producers at the big New York firms. "There's less pressure on Edwards's salespeople to sell something than at the other full-line major national wirehouse firms," says Long.

A. G. Edwards was one of two brokerage firms named in the book *The 100 Best Companies in America to Work For.* (The other was the institutional firm Goldman Sachs.) Fiercely independent, it has declined a number of acquisition offers. Its stock trades on the New York Stock Exchange.

Thomson McKinnon Securities, Inc.
One New York Plaza
New York, NY 10004
(212) 482-7000

Thomson McKinnon was founded in 1885. It ranks eighth in size and has 2,383 brokers, including 134 institutional brokers. It has 181 offices and 470,000 customer accounts.

Thomson McKinnon is probably the least well known of the major NYSE companies. It does no national advertising, preferring to build its client base through acquisitions and its broker network. It acquired 11 brokerage firms in the 1970s, and it has acquired several more since. Its competitors refer to it respectfully as "the quiet company"—and less respectfully, as "old and stodgy."

"Thomson McKinnon is a very well run organization," says Long. "It is basically a national multiline firm with a very good record." Like A. G. Edwards, this firm has a strong retail focus. There are no tugs-of-war here. Thomson McKinnon has been particularly successful in the Midwest, where it has strong roots. It has its own research department, but it also has access to the highly respected research of Donaldson Lufkin. It is 23 percent owned by Hartford Accident and Indemnity Company.

Smith Barney, Harris Upham & Co., Inc.
1345 Avenue of the Americas
New York, NY 10105
(212) 698-6000

Smith Barney was founded in 1873. With 2,120 brokers, it ranks ninth overall. It has a branch network of 104 offices with 385,000 customer accounts.

Smith Barney is best known for its television advertising campaign that featured actor-director John Houseman. The slogan of that campaign—"We make money the old-fashioned way: we earn it"—has been one of the most well received and well remembered slogans on Wall Street. The image conveyed by the Houseman campaign is that of a stodgy-yet-reputable investment institution—which is half right and half wrong. Reputable, yes—in fact, some say the company is run by the compliance department: everything is done by the book. But stodgy it isn't. The company has pursued a very ambitious hiring and training program over the past ten years, and as a result its brokers' average age is among the lowest on Wall Street. The new brokers, however, are quickly taught to act and look like conservative Smith Barney representatives. The firm even has an arrangement with a New York tailor who sells handsome pinstripe suits to its newly hired brokers when they come to New York for their intensive training.

Like most of the large national firms, Smith Barney has focused much of its energy on creating a sales force of big producers. To that end, it has poured enormous resources into developing its municipal bond business and its tax-exempt unit investment trust business. Its efforts have paid off well. On a broker-by-broker basis, it is an industry leader in underwriting and selling those products. In the first half of 1987, it ranked second only to the huge Salomon Brothers in its volume of municipal bond underwritings.

Unlike most of the other major wire houses, Smith Barney does not want to get any bigger. Its directors have reasoned that by staying at its current size of about 2,000 brokers, it can better maintain its personality while offering high-quality investment services. In a survey of investors conducted by *Financial World* magazine, Smith Barney ranked number one among all the major firms in quality of customer service. That strategy, however, may change. In 1987, Smith Barney was acquired by Primerica Corporation (the former American Can), which owns a number of other financial service companies as well as the Musicland chain of record stores. The rationale for the acquisition was that Smith Barney needed more capital to continue to compete in the institutional arena—especially on the international scene.

Kidder, Peabody & Co., Inc.
10 Hanover Square
New York, NY 10005
(212) 510-3000

Kidder, Peabody ranks tenth in number of brokers, with 2,103. It has 72 offices, including 7 abroad. It was founded in 1865, making it the oldest of the Big Eleven.

Kidder, Peabody has a distinctive personality. Competitors describe it as "quiet and elite" or "white shoe and blue stocking." For years, it has been an institutional firm that gradually leveraged its reputation to win a growing share of the retail carriage trade. It caters primarily to institutional clients and investors with high net worth and has long distinguished itself from the large retail "wire houses" that serve a mass market. It prefers to compare itself to such investment banking giants as Goldman Sachs and First Boston. To bolster its position in the investment banking industry, Kidder, Peabody sold an 80 percent interest in the firm to General Electric in exchange for access to several hundred million dollars of additional capital.

Kidder's reputation was tarnished recently when it was implicated in an insider trading scandal involving Martin Siegel, a former executive of the firm. It paid $25 million to settle the government's allegations regarding insider trading and other securities violations. Partly as a result of these problems, General Electric replaced Kidder's chief executive officer, chief financial officer and chief strategic planner with its own people.

Kidder, Peabody is a very traditional firm, and it has continued to stress the traditional approach of investing in stocks and bonds as opposed to the newer packaged investments. This traditional approach has been supported by one of Wall Street's most respected research departments.

Kidder, Peabody tends to have large offices in major metropolitan areas. Its brokers are usually quite sophisticated, and their clientele retains some of the flavor of the old carriage trade. Like Smith Barney, Kidder, Peabody has made a commitment to remain at its present number of brokers. This may change under GE's ownership.

Drexel Burnham Lambert, Inc.
60 Broad Street
New York, NY 10004
(212) 480-6000

The 1,310 retail brokers of Drexel Burnham make it the nation's 11th largest retail brokerage firm. It also has 481 institutional brokers. (Although Bear Stearns has more brokers than Drexel Burnham, most of its brokers are institutional rather than retail brokers.) Drexel Burnham has 49 offices across the country and 350,000 customer accounts.

It is the most controversial of the Big Eleven. Its competitors tend to be both critical and envious of Drexel Burnham, which has enjoyed astonishing success in recent years through a tough, aggressive approach to the business. It tried for years without success to become an elite investment banker (like Salomon, Goldman Sachs, First Boston, Morgan Stanley, Merrill Lynch and Shearson Lehman), and when it failed at that, it created its own business—junk bonds. It invented the junk bond business, and this business put it on the map. The firm has underwritten billions of dollars in junk bonds during the past five years, fueling the biggest spree of hostile corporate takeovers in history. Its enormous profitability enabled it to hire away some of the best talent on Wall Street, including Martin Siegel, the leading takeover specialist, who was hired away from Kidder, Peabody. Siegel was reportedly earning $2 million a year at Kidder, Peabody before Drexel Burnham doubled the ante, luring him away for $4 million a year. (Siegel was later implicated in the Wall Street insider trading scandal.)

Drexel's retail brokers are perceived as younger than average, very aggressive and very sales-oriented. The standing of the firm's research department has continued to rise, and the department was ranked third among all brokerage firms in 1987 by *Institutional Investor*. Drexel Burnham is strong in commodities, which perhaps reinforces its image as an aggressive, risk-oriented firm. It has become a major force in all areas of investment banking, and thus its brokers have a rich array of underwritings to offer clients.

The Securities and Exchange Commission is continuing its much-publicized investigation of Drexel's possible involvement in the insider trading scandal. The outcome of that investigation and any potential litigation will have a great influence on the firm's future prospects. Drexel Burnham ranked dead last among the brokerage companies included in the 1987 *Financial World* quality of service survey.

Edward D. Jones & Co.
201 Progress Parkway
St. Louis, MO 63043
(314) 851-2000

Edward D. Jones ranks first among all brokerage firms in number of branch offices. With 1,115 branch offices, it has more than twice as many as Merrill Lynch. Although we have not categorized Edward D. Jones as one of the Big Eleven, it is a unique firm that warrants special mention.

Its competitors affectionately refer to Edward D. Jones as the "overall firm" because it is characterized by one-person offices in smaller communities like Pine Bluff, Arkansas, and Devil's Lake, North Dakota. It has a total of 1,169 retail brokers to staff its 1,115 offices. If you live in a major metropolitan area, you aren't likely to have an Edward D. Jones branch nearby. The firm prefers to locate its branches in communities with populations of 10,000 to 25,000 where it can be the "only game in town."

The success of Edward D. Jones has been nothing short of phenomenal. In the past six years, it has grown from 300 offices to its present 1,115. Part of its success may be a result of its investment philosophy. The firm insists that it avoids the "buy and sell" philosophy of its competitors, adopting instead a "buy and hold" approach in which its brokers are encouraged to identify long-term conservative investments that their clients can hold for long-term income and appreciation. In keeping with this philosophy, Edward D. Jones prohibits its brokers from doing business in certain aggressive short-term products, such as options and commodities. "Jones is a very excellent, well-managed company," says Lipper's Long. "The philosophy of the firm is, 'We don't want our customers to lose money,' so they're heavily into government bonds, certificates of deposit, municipal unit trusts and other conservative investments."

Since Jones's small-town brokers seek to cultivate a relaxing, folksy image with their neighbors and customers, their success—they now earn, on average, more than $100,000 a year—has been a source of some embarrassment for them.

CHAPTER FIVE _____

Making Your Final Choice

Now that you know what's out there (which brokers offer which services), it's time to redirect your investigation. Probe inward. Determine your expectations. And gather evidence. Put together a loose profile of your financial position. Only then can you arrive at a clear image of what you need in an investment advisor. Stage 2 lists ten key questions that are designed to help you extrapolate an accurate, revealing portrait of the investor within you.

STAGE 2: DETERMINING YOUR OBJECTIVES

The following questions not only will help you define your status and your goals as an investor; they will also be of great help to your broker in determining how to provide an appropriate level of service for you. The first five questions are designed to help you define your financial status; the next three will help identify your investment attitude, and the final two will help you determine what type of relationship you hope to establish with your broker.

Your Financial Status

1. How much money do you plan to invest with this broker at this time?

2. How much money do you expect to invest in the coming months or years? Do you anticipate a future windfall of cash—through business ventures, inheritance or other sources? If so, how much? The brokers you talk with will be very interested in this information.

3. What is your net worth? Determining your net worth is very simple. You merely subtract your total liabilities from your total assets.

To determine your total assets, add up the value of all your assets—the market value of your home and other real eastate, your savings, your checking account balance (if it exceeds your normal monthly expenses), your investments, the cash value of your life insurance, cars, IRA and so on.

To determine your total liabilities, add up your home mortgage, your car loans, and your other loans, including credit card balances.

Now subtract your total liabilities from your total assets, and that will give you your net worth.

4. What is your annual gross income? Determine that by adding up your salary, bonuses and commissions and any income you receive from investments or other sources.

5. What is your financial foundation? That would include such items as emergency funds, life insurance and special savings programs for retirement and for your children's education.

Your Investment Attitude

6. What is your attitude toward investment risk? Brokers call this your "risk threshold." Investors are generally categorized in one of three ways—"conservative," "moderate" or "aggressive."

Conservative investors take the path of least resistance and seek out low-risk investments designed to preserve their principal, such as certificates of deposit, government bonds, conservative mutual funds and safe dividend-yielding utility stocks. Generally, the closer an investor comes to retirement, the more conservative he or she becomes.

Moderate investors are willing to assume reasonable risks for reasonable returns. They may be interested in blue-chip stocks, corporate bonds, equity mutual funds and possibly a small investment in a real estate limited partnership.

Aggressive investors are willing to assume high risks for the potential of high returns. They may gamble a few thousand dollars on the stock of a speculative start-up company, in hopes of earning a substantial profit if the company survives and thrives. Investors who in 1977 put $10,000 into a tiny start-up computer company called Cray Research could have sold their holdings a decade later for $1.15 million. But for every Cray Research, there are countless other small companies that drop off the charts. Aggressive investors have to be psychologically prepared to take the big losses with the big gains.

Rate yourself conservative, moderate or aggressive.

7. What is your investment objective? What do you plan to do with the money you are investing? Is it for growth, income, tax savings or simply preservation of capital?

To determine your investment objective, decide specifically what you're going to need the money for. If you're trying to build up your assets so that you can start your own business, or move into a bigger house, or retire early, your objective is probably "growth." If you need interest or dividends from your investments to make ends meet, your objective is "income." If you're in a high tax bracket and you want to avoid paying further taxes on the money generated from your investments, your objective is "tax savings." If you're more interested in keeping what you have than in trying to substantially increase your wealth, then your objective is "preservation of capital."

8. What is your time horizon? The longer your time horizon, the more price volatility you can tolerate in an investment. If you're saving for a retirement that's 30 years down the road, you can tolerate a lot more volatility than if you're saving for a more immediate goal like the down payment on a house. Or perhaps you have no specific goal in mind other than to do something with the money you've accumulated—in which case time is not a factor.

Your Investment Profile

(You may wish to write these answers down on a separate sheet of paper to take with you when you meet with broker "suspects.")

1. I currently plan to invest $_____.
2. In the future, I expect to invest about $_____ per _____ (month or year).
   I also anticipate a windfall (from inheritance, etc.) of $_____.
3. My net worth is $_____.
4. My gross income is $_____.
5. My financial foundation consists of:
   Emergency cash fund: $_____
   Total life insurance face value: $_____
   Disability insurance: $_____ per month
   I plan to finance my retirement and my children's college education by _____
   _____
6. My attitude toward investment risk is _____ (conservative, moderate, or aggressive).
7. My primary investment objective is _____ (growth, income, tax savings or preservation of capital).
8. My time horizon for this particular investment is _____.
9. In my relationship with my broker, I want my role to be:
   _____
10. I want my broker's role to be: _____

Your Broker-Client Relationship

9. What role do you plan to play in your investment relationship with your broker? How active do you expect to be? Do you plan to make all your own buying and selling decisions, based on information you gather with the help of your broker? Do you expect to follow your investments on a daily basis? Or do you want as little involvement as possible, relying almost entirely on the recommendations of your broker?

10. What role do you want your broker to play? Do you want a broker who calls you regularly with fresh investment ideas, or do you basically want to be left alone? Do you want a broker who will closely monitor your account or one who will set your account aside for months at a time? Do you want a broker who will take charge and closely guide your investment program or one who will offer an occasional recommendation and then stand back and let you run the show? The role you want your broker to play is a key factor in determining which broker is right for you.

STAGE 3: SEEKING OUT SUSPECTS

Armed with your personal investment profile, you are now prepared to seek out appropriate suspects in your quest for the perfect broker.

How do you go about finding good suspects (besides waiting for the phone to ring)? Most investors seek referrals from acquaintances. Others attend investment seminars conducted by brokers. Still others decide on a brokerage firm or two, then try to meet with brokers at those firms. All three methods have their pros and cons, but if applied correctly, they can all work very effectively. However, you must be willing to shop around. Don't blindly sign up with the first broker you're referred to. Be prepared to interview more than one broker before making a decision. The money you will be investing is important to you—perhaps it's your life savings. You've probably worked very hard to accumulate it, and you owe it to yourself (and your family) to spend the time needed to find a broker who will help you invest it wisely.

Referrals

The common wisdom in the industry is that if you want to find a good broker, ask a friend. With a referral, you know that for whatever reason, the broker has made a positive impression on your friend. Presumably, the friend has made some money through the broker or has had a good relationship with the broker.

But there is one subtle yet significant flaw in relying on a referral. In the investment business, fit is all-important. The investment approach or the basic style of the broker who draws raves from your friend may not be right for you. Your friend may be perfectly at ease with speculative investments, but if your idea of a sound investment is a U.S. Treasury bond, his or her broker may be a poor fit for you.

In 1983, a 70-year-old widow whose investment objectives were safety and income was referred to a broker by a friend. Although her portfolio consisted of Ginnie Maes, grade A bonds and conservative utility stocks, the broker encouraged her to make progressively more aggressive investments. After some initial successes, he began to get even more aggressive. When he couldn't reach her by phone to get her approval, he would enter the orders anyway and tell her about them later. At first, the investments worked well for her. Then, without consulting her, the broker bought several thousand shares of a speculative stock. The stock started to decline in price, and seemed to drop further every day. The widow's portfolio quickly fell in value from $50,000 to $21,000. For her, the loss was devastating. She was retired and living on Social Security. That $21,000 was all she had left.

Clearly, the broker was at fault. His insistence on pursuing an aggressive investment strategy for a conservative investor and his policy of investing without prior approval were both violations of SEC regulations. But the more significant problem here was that the broker was a poor fit for the investor. The broker wanted to make aggressive investments to make the investor rich when all she wanted was safe, conservative income-oriented investments that would keep her from becoming poor. The result was disaster—and all because this woman had relied on the referral of a trusted friend.

Certainly, not all referrals lead to mismatches. A referral is usually a better way to find a good broker than a cold call. If a close friend strongly recommends his or her broker, you should by all means consider using that broker. In fact, you can increase your chances of success by following the advice of Tom Hudson, a 20-year veteran of the brokerage business. "Ask someone you respect who they do business with, then go talk to that broker. Tell the broker you were referred by so-and-so. There's a good chance so-and-so is a good customer of that broker, and he is going to be extra careful with you so that he doesn't lose your business and possibly the business of your friend as well."

And regardless of the strength of the referral, consider this broker only a "suspect" until you've taken the time to interview the broker to ascertain whether his or her investment approach coincides with your own.

Investment Seminars

Another way to find a good broker is through investment seminars. Such seminars are advertised periodically in the business section of the local newspaper. They tend to deal with a variety of subjects ("building wealth," "setting up trusts," "planning your children's college fund," "allocating your assets"), and they are typically conducted by a broker. Look for a seminar that is (a) being conducted by a broker from a firm you'd like to deal with, or *(b)* on a subject that coincides with your investment interests, or, ideally, *(c)* both of the above.

Investment seminars are usually conducted on a weeknight and last about 60 minutes, so they're geared to busy professionals. But in those 60 minutes, you can get an excellent opportunity to see your suspect in action and make your own evaluation. You may not need the full hour to make your decision. It may become very evident after the first five minutes that this broker is not right for you—for whatever reason. But at least you've had the opportunity to see the broker in person and to make your decision on that basis.

Pay particularly close attention to the broker's investment approach. If the broker spends the entire time talking about low-risk investments that are ideal for conserving capital and offsetting inflation, and that is what you want, he or she is probably the kind of broker you should consider using. On the other hand, if the broker talks about trading futures and options, using margin accounts and investing in high-risk, high-potential emerging growth stocks, then you can scratch him or her from your list.

Let's assume, though, that the broker meets your first two tests: (1) he or she seems like a competent, knowledgeable and personable professional with whom you believe you could build a good relationship; and (2) his or her approach to investing seems to coincide with your own. In that case, we suggest that you introduce yourself after the seminar is over and make some conversation with the broker. Your goal here is to get a little bit better idea of how well the broker handles a one-on-one situation. Ask such open-ended questions as "What do you think are really good investments at this time?" or "What percentage of my assets should be in stocks?" There is no one right answer to either question, but if the broker asks you thoughtful questions in turn and seems to know what he or she is talking about, then you should take the next step, which is to set up an appointment at the broker's office. That appointment will give you one more chance to evaluate this suspect before deciding whether to make him or her your broker.

Picking a Broker: The Investment Seminar Approach

1. Attend an investment seminar.
2. Evaluate the broker and his or her presentation.
3. If you like the broker, introduce yourself after the presentation and ask him or her several open-ended questions.
4. If you're comfortable with the broker's answers, set up a personal interview at his or her office.

Branch Manager Approach

A third common way in which investors find a broker is by calling a brokerage firm or walking in the door and asking to be assigned to a broker. This approach has some drawbacks, but these can be easily overcome by adding one simple but significant step to the process.

The main problem you face as a walk-in is that the receptionist will probably assign you automatically to the "broker of the day." More than likely, this broker is either a new broker or a less successful experienced broker who wants to get his or her fair share of walk-ins. Either way, the broker you end up with will probably be someone who is still learning the ropes. And even if that broker turns out to be surprisingly talented and resourceful, there's still no guarantee that his or her approach to investing will be compatible with yours.

Explains one NYSE branch manager: "Here we rotate the five newest people. Anyone who calls with questions about the market or might want to open an account is referred to one of these five brokers. To a certain extent," he adds, "the new brokers practice on new clients. Some brokers practice all their lives."

Unless you're willing to serve as practice fodder for some new and untested broker, the walk-in approach is not the best approach for you.

But by adding one key step, you can greatly increase your chances of walking into the firm of your choice and ending up with the broker who is ideal for you. That key step is to start out with a brief meeting with the branch manager.

After you've pared down your choices by deciding which two or three firms you would prefer to work with, call their offices. More than likely, a receptionist will answer your call:

Introduce yourself to the receptionist and ask for the name of the branch manager. Then ask the receptionist to connect you with the manager. For our example, we'll assume that the manager's name is Tom Davis.

When you speak with Davis, we suggest that you greet him by his first name. Don't call him "Mr. Davis"; call him "Tom." That's the way people in the brokerage business deal with each other. You don't want to come across as too deferential. By using the manager's first name, you are subtly establishing a relationship of reasonable equals. (Obviously you should not try to force the first-name issue if you're not comfortable with it. If you sense that you are much younger than the branch manager, or if you are a man and the branch manager is a woman, or vice versa, you may prefer to use last names. Use the first name only if you feel natural doing so.)

Then introduce yourself and explain a little bit about your circumstances. For example, you might say, "Hello, Tom, I'm Arnold Simms. I'm a new investor and I'm looking for a broker to handle my investments" (or "I'm an experienced investor, and I'm looking for a different broker," or I just inherited a substantial amount of money, and I'm looking for a good broker to handle my assets"). Then ask Davis whether you could set up a five-minute appointment with him in order to tell him a few more things about yourself so that he can recommend a broker who might be suitable for you.

We stress the five-minute appointment. Branch managers are always busy. In addition to running the branch office and supervising all the other brokers in the office, many of them have to handle several hundred clients of their own.

In your five-minute appointment, you should do two things:

1. Tell Davis what you want your money to do, how much experience you have in investing and how much money you plan to invest. For instance, you might say, "Tom, let me tell you something about myself. I'm interested in some long-term investments that can help finance my children's education and help me build up my net worth. I've never invested in the stock market, but I read *Money* magazine and many of my friends at the health club invest, so I know a fair amount about business and investments. I'd like to start my investment program with $10,000, and I'll probably be investing an additional $5,000 to $10,000 a year."

(If you are an attorney, an accountant or a financial officer with a corporation, make a point of mentioning that. As such, you would be more likely to get special care. Brokerage firms consider attorneys and financial professionals to be particularly valuable as clients because they tend to be centers of influence and excellent sources of future referrals.)

2. Ask Davis whether he can refer you to a broker who would be suitable based on your circumstances. And add, "This may not be the broker of the day." Mentioning the broker of the day alerts the branch manager to your awareness of normal brokerage house protocol and subtly indicates that if you wanted the broker of the day, you wouldn't have gone to the trouble of coming in to see the branch manager. We're not suggesting here that you flatly refuse to talk with the broker of the day. It's possible that the broker of the day would be exactly the broker for you. But if not, you've opened the door to other possibilities.

Also ask Davis about the firm and its philosophy. Try to glean from your meeting with him some insight into the ambience of this particular branch office. "The whole tone of the store depends on the branch manager," says Lee Solot of Kidder, Peabody. To prove his point, Solot talks about the time he visited two branch offices of his former firm in California. "They were located in the same state, about 50 miles apart, with similar constituencies, and obviously they were offices of the same firm. But they did a completely different business. One was heavily into listed stocks traded on the New York Stock Exchange, and the other was into over-the-counter stocks. I asked several brokers why. They wordlessly pointed to the branch manager."

Tom Asher of Robinson-Humphrey refers to the theory of "magnetic meatballism." "Meatballs attract each other," says Asher. "If a firm is unfortunate enough to have a meatball running a particular branch, it is just a matter of time before he has filled the office with meatballs." So size up the branch manager in your brief meeting, and you will be getting a good insight into the kind of firm and the type of broker you may be dealing with.

Asher adds one more caution: "If you display a lot of wealth, the manager may say, 'Don't worry, I'll handle your account myself.' I'd be a little wary because if the manager becomes your broker and you ever have a problem with your account, who can you turn to for help?"

The chances are that once you've communicated your investment position to Davis, he will refer you to a broker in his office and will probably introduce you to the broker. At that point, you and the broker will probably walk over to the broker's desk to discuss your needs in a little further detail.

This is where you have to take charge of the conversation. You tell the broker basically the same things you told the branch manager—with a few twists: "I'm looking for a broker. I've selected your firm as a suitable firm for my needs. I just spoke to Tom Davis, and he recommended you." (Be sure to mention the branch manager by name. Don't just say you stopped by the office, because then the broker will automatically think of you as a walk-in. When you mention the branch manager by name, for all the broker knows, you may be the branch manager's next-door neighbor, or his nephew, or his tennis partner.)

STAGE 4: THE INTERVIEW

Whether you've selected your suspect through a referral, through a seminar or through a branch manager, the follow-up interview you conduct with that broker will be pretty much the same. If at all possible, conduct the interview in person. This is your money, and if you're going to feel comfortable entrusting it with a new broker, it's best to meet that person face-to-face. Throughout the process, you should maintain control of the interview. You're in charge. And when the final decision is made, it will be your decision based on your very specific preferences and investment objectives—not on the luck of the draw.

One benefit of this proactive screening approach is that it will have a lasting effect on your broker. The broker will be aware that you are in control of your life—and in control of your investment program. While honored by your choice, he or she will also be aware that if things don't work out, you could just as easily go out and find another broker.

Another benefit is that your initial interview will give you the opportunity to express your expectations and to have those expectations confirmed before you set up the relationship. If you want your broker to call you with "sell" recommendations as well as "buy" recommendations, get the broker to agree to that ahead of time. If you want research updates on all the stocks in your portfolio, make sure the broker is willing to commit to that. And while the broker may not normally deal on that basis, he or she will make an exception in your case because that's the way the relationship was set up.

To begin your interview with the broker, you might say, "I'd like to give you a little background about my investment interests and then ask you some questions about your approach and how you work with your clients. OK?"

By setting the stage that way, you've put yourself in charge of the situation. You've said, "This is what I'm going to do. I'm going to tell you some things about myself, and then I'm going to ask you some questions." The broker becomes a captive audience.

Then you offer a brief description of your background and investment objectives (as in our earlier example with the branch manager). After that, you say, "Now let me ask you some questions."

The broker may say, "Sure I'd be glad to answer your questions, but first let me ask you a few questions." There's nothing wrong with that. It's only fair that you respond. The broker may ask questions like these: "When you say 'long-term investments,' exactly what do you mean?" or "When you read *Money* magazine, what kinds of articles interest you the most?" The broker will be trying to get a little more detail about your basic needs and investment preferences.

Profile of the First Time Investor		
	1985	1983
Median Age of First Time Investors	34	34
Median Household Income of First Time Investors	$34,900	$30,000
Portfolio Value of First Time Investors	$2,200	$2,200
Value of Stock Transactions in Past Year	$3,810	$2,260

Source: New York Stock Exchange, Inc. "Shareownership 1985"

"For new accounts," says Dale Grubb of Shearson Lehman, "I like to ask about their objectives: 'Do you want to increase your retirement fund, your wealth, your income or decrease your taxes?' I ask them how much of their total investment dollars they want allocated to growth and how much to income—and is that taxable or tax-free income? Then I ask about their income, real estate holdings, debts, retirement account and tax bracket. We also get into types of investments—CDs (when are they coming due?), stock holdings, bond holdings, mutual funds, unit trusts, etc."

With your ten-question investment checklist, you will be prepared to answer almost every question the broker might ask. But do not volunteer more information at this point. It is far better to see whether the broker asks for it.

When you do get a chance to ask the broker your questions, try to do it as casually and cordially as possible. Obviously, if you have a quarter million dollars or more to invest, most brokers would be willing to jump through rings of fire to respond to your questions. But if you're a typical new investor with $5,000 to $10,000, the broker could become very resentful if you come across like Edward R. Murrow. Try to commit your questions to memory before you go into the interview. Walking in with a yellow legal pad full of notes is no way to start a long, compatible business relationship.

The TAPES Approach

One good way to memorize your questions is by using what we call the "TAPES" approach (think of "ticker tapes"). Each letter of TAPES stands for a key element of each of the five topics you should cover. Here are the questions we recommend:

(T) *Types of investors.* With what types of investors do you work best?

(A) *Approach.* Tell me something about your investment approach. (You might add, "In your experience, what sort of investment approach works best for most people?")

(P) *Products.* What investment products do you specialize in? Can you describe an investment that worked out especially well for your clients?

(E) *Experience.* Can you tell me something about your experience in the securities business?

(S) *Service.* Assuming that we start working together, what kind of service can I reasonably expect from you?

As you can see, all of these questions are open-ended, offering the broker the widest possible latitude in formulating an answer. By the time you've covered all five areas, you should have a fairly good understanding of the broker's experience, competence, approach and attitude.

TAPES Approach

*T*ypes of investors
*A*pproach
*P*roducts
*E*xperience
*S*ervice

The response to the first question on "types of investors" may be that the broker covers the gamut, or works mostly with conservative investors, or works mainly with traders and commodities investors—in which case you may decide right then that this is not the broker for you. (But that would not be very likely if the broker was referred to you by the branch manager.)

To the question on "approach," what you're angling for is the broker's basic philosophy. Again, the broker could give you any number of answers. Here is one possibility: "I find that most people want to double their money as quickly as possible, and that's why I like to trade options." And here is another: "I find that most people are interested in maintaining their present wealth and using their investments to offset inflation, and that's why I like to invest in conservative stocks, bonds and mutual funds." Such answers should give you some insight into whether the broker's philosophy jibes with yours. In order to get your business, the broker may slant his or her answers somewhat to fit your needs. If you sense such hedging, you may wish to return to the subject later.

The question on "products" will serve to define the broker's philosophy even further. Here the broker gives examples of favorite investments and tells about results that have been achieved for other clients. Obviously, you may have justifiable second thoughts about the ability of a broker who can't come up with any good examples of investments that have worked well.

"Brokers tend to have specialties," says Bob Dunwoody of Van Dusen & Co. "It might be covered option writing or municipal bonds or something else. You need to get a feel for the broker and the broker's bias."

The question on "experience" could be very revealing. The investment profession is incredibly complex. It takes years to learn the business inside out. As Dain Bosworth broker Lee Kopp puts it, "When we start out in this business, it's amazing how little we really know even though we've gone through a four-month intensive training program. We really are babes in the woods. There's so much to learn. What a painful path to get to where you feel fairly comfortable with your knowledge."

However, a broker's experience should not be the deciding factor in making your selection. "Do you want a broker who is in the first month out of the chute?" asks Betsy Buckley of Dain Bosworth. "If they're approaching you with something that's appropriately conservative, like a municipal bond or a blue-chip stock with a good yield, yes, I absolutely would do business with them. But if they're talking to you about the latest initial public offering, I don't think so, because they're not even going to know how to fill out the forms."

While the experienced broker has greater knowledge of the market, the newer broker can also offer distinct advantages to the investor. "There's no retraining in the brokerage business," says Joe Baxter, training director for Smith Barney. "What the older broker has is a greater breadth of experience to bring to the table. But he may not be as up-to-date in terms of new products that have been added since he came through training. The newer broker, despite a lack of market sense, is probably more aware of the new alternative investments—mutual funds, limited partnerships and the other packaged investments."

Adds Asher: "It's like a doctor. Some people prefer a new doctor because he has the latest techniques and he has more time to spend with you. An experienced broker may not even talk to you, and if he does, he'll probably do it very quickly because he doesn't have time for you. A younger broker probably has more time to devote to your account, and he's probably more up-to-date on all the latest money management techniques and investment products."

Kathy Soule, a newer broker with Merrill Lynch, says, "I have the time to devote. I'm fresher, and I know more about the new products. If you want personal attention from your broker, I would recommend you work with someone who is starting out in the business."

Soule talks about one veteran broker with 3,000 to 4,000 accounts who left the firm, leaving her with some of his old accounts. "I called them, introduced myself and told them my intention was to learn how I could help them. They were thrilled to have a broker who was willing to take time to talk to them. I had a few calls where I said, 'So-and-so has left,' and they said, 'Thank God.' A lot of these clients had a lot of money that had been sitting in money market funds for several years earning only five percent, and they weren't aware that the money had never been reinvested. They would tell me that every time they called this broker, their calls were not returned. He never had time to talk to them about their statements; he never had time to talk to them about their investments. On many occasions, the customers would tell me, 'I really appreciate that you've taken the time to talk with me and bring me up-to-date.' And it's not a lot of time—it's five minutes."

Newer brokers tend to take a somewhat different investment approach than older brokers. "All brokers start out as money raisers," says David Thompson of Prudential-Bache. "I know I did. You have to rely on your firm." The newer brokers follow the firm's research, and they sell packaged products to accumulate assets in their accounts.

Kidder's Solot points out another distinction. "At Kidder, many new brokers are afraid of losing money for their customers, so they tend to be more conservative than experienced brokers, and they sell a lot of fixed-

TABLE 5-1   Advantages of Dealing with *Experienced* Broker versus *Newer* Broker

Experienced	Newer
Knows more about stocks and bonds	Knows more about new, packaged investments
Knows more about the "market" — its cycles and psychology	Has more time to answer questions and service your account

income investments and mutual funds until they become comfortable with equities."

The final question on "service" will give you one more indication of what you can expect from this broker. He or she may say, "When I see an investment that I think will be of interest to you, I'll give you a call." That's the minimum you should expect. What you might also hope for here is that the broker will promise to keep you posted on how your investments are doing and to recommend when you should sell your investments. Some brokers also offer annual or semiannual reviews of your investment portfolio to make sure your investments still conform to your needs and objectives.

What have you gained from asking these questions? You've gained two things:

1. You've acquired some factual information. You now know whether this broker likes to deal in the kinds of investments that would be suitable for you. That's a critical point. If you want to invest in stocks, you don't want a broker who thinks that the stock market is no place for the small investor. As PaineWebber's Hudson puts it, "If you want to trade commodities, don't do business with a regular stockbroker. Find a specialist in commodities. The same goes for investing strictly in municipal bonds. Find a specialist in bonds."

2. You've learned whether you have rapport with this broker. Do you feel that you're both on the same wavelength? Does the broker respond in terms you can understand? "Look for a broker you can be comfortable with," says Al Heiam of Drexel Burnham. "He might be a real whiz kid, but if I can't get along with him, maybe I should forgo the opportunity." You need a broker who can converse with you freely and openly and who is not going to overwhelm you with the obscure jargon and technical terms of the investment business.

Once you've asked your questions and listened to the broker's answers, it's time to make at least a preliminary decision. If you're absolutely convinced that you don't want to do business with this broker, you simply stand up and say, "I appreciate your time. I don't think I would be a good client for you. It sounds like we have somewhat different investment approaches. Thanks. Good to talk with you." Then you excuse yourself and go on to the next firm. If that sounds unnecessarily blunt, it's important to understand that brokers are very busy, very impatient people. Naturally they may feel a twinge of rejection when you turn them down, but for them, it's all in a day's work. If you've made up your mind, the broker would by all means, prefer to hear about it right away rather than waste time in making follow-up phone calls to you later.

However, this may not be a decision you will want to make immediately. You may prefer to go home and let the matter percolate in your mind for some time before you reach your decision. And meanwhile, feel free to interview other brokers.

If you feel that this broker may be the broker for you, then say, "What else can I tell you about myself and my financial needs?" The broker may ask you about your family situation, your tax bracket, your risk threshold, other investments you've made and how much contact you would like to have with your broker. Again, your ten-question checklist may come in handy here.

If you're a new, fairly modest investor (one with less than $25,000 to invest), that should conclude the interview, and you can excuse yourself and let the broker get back to work. But if you have $25,000 or more to invest, you should ask the broker whether you can ask a few more questions. The chances are that if you've got that kind of money to invest, the broker will be happy to spend a little more time with you. Now if the broker doesn't have the time to do so, then you've got a judgment on your hands. Are you going to want a broker who cannot spend an extra five minutes with you to establish an initial relationship? Your decision, of course, should depend on the circumstances. If it's lunchtime and two people are waiting for the broker to leave, his or her reluctance to go on with the interview is understandable. But in most cases, if you have $25,000 or more to invest, the broker will find the time to take your questions. Here's what you should ask:

- "I understand that brokers give away accounts that they feel uncomfortable with. What kinds of accounts do you give away?" This question will tell the broker that you know the business. The broker's answer may be of little value, but then again it may be very illuminating. The broker may say, for instance, "I find that if someone wants to trade stocks several times a week, I just don't have the time, so I try to refer such accounts to other brokers." The broker's answer to this question will increase your insight into his or her investment approach.
- "I understand that one of the hardest things in the investment business is giving sell recommendations. If I bought some stocks from you, what could I expect from you in terms of telling me when to sell the stock?"
- "What did you do before you were a broker?" This question gives the broker an opportunity to elaborate on his or her background—if, indeed, the broker has credentials worth talking about. On the other

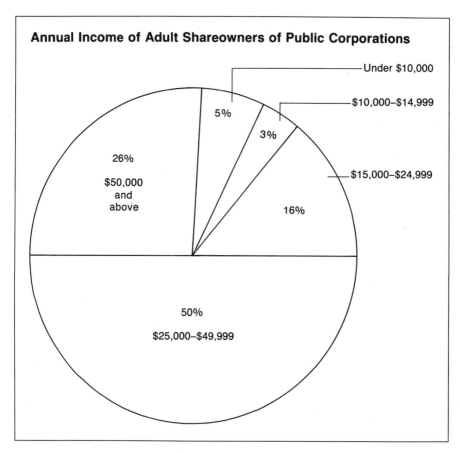

Annual Income of Adult Shareowners of Public Corporations

Under $10,000

$10,000–$14,999

5%

3%

26%

$50,000
and
above

$15,000–$24,999

16%

50%

$25,000–$49,999

Source: New York Stock Exchange, Inc. "Shareownership 1985"

hand, if he or she fried burgers at McDonald's before becoming a broker, that's also worth knowing.

- "Can you tell me something about the training you've received?" (An experienced broker should be asked, "What kind of continuing training do you receive?") This question will enable you to gain some insight not only into the broker's training but also into the broker's attitude toward that training. The broker might say, sarcastically, "I went through the basic crash course," or he or she might answer the question very seriously and say something to this effect: "One of the reasons I joined this firm was because of its excellent training program."
- "What do you feel is a fair way for me to evelute you?" The broker's answer to this question will give you an excellent point of reference. The broker might say, "I think you should do as well as the Standard &

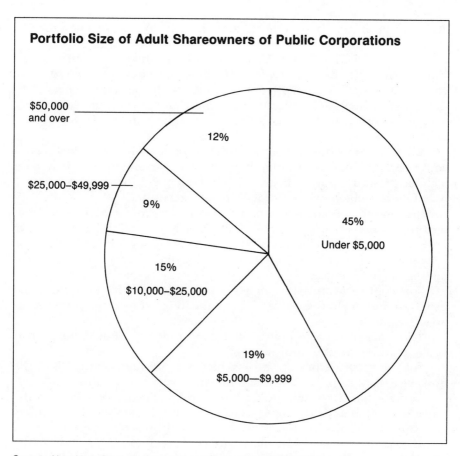

Portfolio Size of Adult Shareowners of Public Corporations

$50,000 and over — 12%

$25,000–$49,999 — 9%

$10,000–$25,000 — 15%

Under $5,000 — 45%

$5,000—$9,999 — 19%

Source: New York Stock Exchange, Inc. "Shareownership 1985"

Poor's 500. And if you don't do that well, then I think you have every right to look for another broker." You can certainly take a broker who says that at his or her word. Or the broker might say, "My objective is to bring you peace of mind, and you're ultimately the judge of that."

All of these questions are very open-ended, and there are no right or wrong answers to them. The benefits you derive from asking them are that they give you an opportunity to get a rich response from the broker and to evaluate that response.

D'Arcy Fox of A. G. Edwards recommends that you request a brochure on the firm and a description of its brokerage account. "Ask what services are offered with the account. Ask what access you will have to the broker. Ask who you should call with problems. Ask how you should deal with problems—with a note? a phone call? When is a good time to phone?"

Drexel's Heiam suggests, "Ask him about mistakes. Get him to talk about them. Then ask him to describe some successes. Ask him to show you some sample accounts from his book with the names covered to show exactly how they have done. A potentially big account should ask the names of several of the broker's clients that he could phone for a referral."

Adds Asher: "Look at their recommended stock list. Are they names you recognize like Coca-Cola, IBM, Kodak, or are they little-known high-tech issues? That will give you a better idea of their investment orientation—which may be exactly what you want."

Prudential's Thompson would take an even bolder approach. "Ask the broker how much he earns. Find out if he is successful. Long term, the only way a broker can be successful is to make money for his clients. So if he is successful, you have a pretty good idea that he knows how to make money for his clients."

Some of these approaches may not be comfortable for you, and some may be annoying to the broker. You be the judge of how far you want to press the questioning.

There are also some points of interest that you should note when you're talking with the broker:

Sales assistant. Does the broker have an assistant nearby? Is it the broker's assistant, or is the assistant shared with several other brokers?

Office setup. Does the broker have a private office or a desk in the midst of a big bull pen? (Some firms give every broker an office; others give offices to only the top producers.) "Look around," says Asher. "I would want it to have a professional atmosphere. I don't know how to describe that, but I'd know it if I saw it."

Working attire. Are the brokers at this firm too casual or too formal for your tastes?

Once again, there are no rights or wrongs here; these are just other matters that you should consider in making your final decision.

Concluding the Interview

If you're satisfied with the broker's responses, what should your next step be? That depends on how much you have to invest.

If you have a modest amount, we suggest that you seek no further interviews. Thank the broker for having seen you, and ask the broker to give you a call when he or she has an investment suitable for you.

If you have $25,000 or more to invest, you should interview a couple more brokers. But go ahead and ask this broker to call when he or she has a suitable investment for you. If you find a broker you like better in subsequent interviews, you can explain that to the first broker when he or she calls you back. But if you don't find a broker you like better, by keeping the lines of communication open, you've started out your relationship with this broker on a positive note.

Follow-Up

If you were referred to the broker by the branch manager, after your session with the broker you should follow up by writing a note to the branch manager: "Dear Tom, Thanks for your help. I enjoyed meeting Joan Smith. Thanks for referring her to me. I think I will enjoy working with her."

Why do you do this? You do it, of course, as a professional courtesy. But you also do it to place your role in the mind of the branch manager. The branch manager can be a valuable resource for you—even if you never directly need his assistance. The chances are that after your meeting with the broker, the branch manager will stop by the broker's desk to find out how the interview went. He may even follow up weeks later to find out how your investments are working out—which should motivate your broker to work even harder on your account.

On the other hand, if you choose not to use the broker the branch manager recommended, we still suggest that as a professional courtesy you write a note to him: "Dear Tom, Thanks for your interest. I talked with Sam Cook. I concluded that I need a broker with a different investment approach."

The branch manager may call you back to recommend a different broker, or he may just file the note away. But at least you've made a positive impression on him, and if you ever have occasion to use that brokerage firm again, he should view you in a favorable light.

Picking a Broker:
Branch Manager Approach

1. Select two or three firms.
2. Phone the office of one of these firms; ask the receptionist for the name of the branch manager, and ask to be connected with the branch manager.
3. Request a brief appointment with the branch manager.
4. Tell the branch manager about your investment interests, and ask the branch manager to refer you to a broker.
5. Tell the broker about your investment interests.
6. Answer the broker's additional questions, using your ten-question checklist.
7. Ask the broker questions, using the TAPES approach.
8. Decide whether to ask the broker follow-up questions or to terminate the interview.

ENDING THE SEARCH

When should your search end? As we've mentioned, if you have a modest amount to invest and your interviewing has led you to a broker you feel comfortable with, then by all means use that person as your broker. There's little point in spending any more of your time (or other brokers' time) in continuing your search.

On the other hand, if you have more than $25,000 to invest, you should interview at least three brokers before making your final choice—even if you're completely satisfied with the first broker you interview. Why? It's possible that you'll find a broker you like even better. Or maybe you'll find that the first broker is indeed better than the other brokers you end up interviewing. Or maybe, if you're like some investors, you'll find different strengths with different brokers. You may decide that you need two brokers—one, for instance, for bonds and another for speculative stocks or options. In any case, by conducting those extra interviews, you've expanded the possibilities and probably strengthened your confidence in the first broker.

The proactive approach to finding a broker has its disadvantages, especially for busy professionals. It's time-consuming, and it's somewhat discomforting if you have to tell a broker that you don't want to use his or her services. But you probably worked long and hard for your money, and it's worth a little extra time and effort to find a broker who can do a competent job of putting that money to work for you.

PART 3

Managing Your
Relationship

How Your Broker Sells

It's four o'clock; another business day is winding down. You're at your desk, poring over the latest trayful of interoffice memos, when suddenly your phone rings. From the other end of the line comes the voice of a young woman: "Hello," she says. "This is Andrea Tolbert. I'm the assistant to Thomas James, who is a vice president with Cromberg Securities. We're calling from New York. Can you hold for Mr. James, please?" Click.

And there you sit, waiting for Mr. James and wondering why he's calling you.

This scenario is played out thousands of times every business day. Originally developed by Lehman Brothers (now a part of Shearson Lehman), it's a sales technique often referred to as the "New York approach," because a number of New York–based brokers use it to tap the investor market outside the New York area. It's one of several finely honed prospecting techniques that brokers use to fetch new clients.

Survival in the securities business is tied, in large part, to the broker's ability to amass a wide base of clients. Most brokers shoot for 200 to 500 clients; top brokers may have well over a thousand. Once brokers have an established clientele, if they are personable, provide good service and do a reasonably good job of handling their clients' investments, they can expect to build their business through referrals from their current clients. The tough part, though, is establishing the client base in the first place. That's why new brokers get as much training in sales as they do in investments. And most of that sales training is devoted to cultivating the cold call prospect—which brings us back to your call from Mr. James.

Let's imagine now that you're still on the line, on hold, listening to the soft music through the receiver and becoming more than a little restless waiting for Mr. James to get to the phone. Just the same, you keep holding, and as you hold, your curiosity builds. Why, you keep asking yourself, is a vice president of a big New York securities firm calling you at your Midwestern office?

Finally, Mr. James comes to the phone. "Hello," he says. "Thank you for holding. I was tied up with another call. The reason I'm calling is I'm a vice president with Cromberg Securities in New York and I specialize in takeover opportunities. My firm has special research on companies we feel are likely takeover candidates. We deal only with affluent investors who are willing to take above-average risks for above-average opportunities. Let me ask you, please, do you ever invest in securities?"

If your answer is no, there's a good chance that Mr. James will say "Thank you very much" and hang up the phone. If you say yes, he'll pursue a carefully scripted line of questioning. Your conversation may proceed as follows:

Mr. James: Can you tell me something about your investment objectives?

You: I like to buy stocks and watch them grow.

Mr. James: Can you tell me about some of the investments you've made in the past.

You: I bought some Seagate, and that did well. I bought some Mercury Datamax, and that fell off the charts. I bought Diamondhead Motors, and that moved up 25 percent the first three months.

Mr. James: I see. May I ask you this: When you buy stocks, how many shares do you tend to buy at a time? Are we talking 500 shares, 1,000 shares?

The conversation reaches another pivotal stage here. If you say you're a small investor and you buy 50 to 100 shares at a time, Mr. James will probably end the conversation. If you say you buy in blocks of 500 or more, he'll continue with his pitch. In most cases, his goal will be to get you to agree to have him call you back when he finds an investment opportunity that he believes would be suitable for you.

For the most part, brokers are looking for "suspects" (as prospects are known in the securities industry) with the means and the proper attitude to be active investors. Brokers seek to "qualify" suspects by probing for four key criteria:

1. *Capital.* Standards for this criterion vary by broker. Some brokers prospect for investors with at least $50,000 in investable assets. Others, particularly newer brokers, set their sights much lower. "I'm not really going for the big ticket," says Kathy Soule of Merrill Lynch. "I've opened a lot of accounts through IRAs." In general, brokers are looking for individuals with household incomes of at least $50,000 and current investable assets of at least $10,000. The $10,000 minimum, however, is by no means hard and fast. "No potential client is too small for a phone call," says David Thompson of Prudential-Bache. "I had one account who had invested his life savings with me—$5,000. Then he referred another investor to me who opened up a $1 million account."

FIGURE 6–1   The Two-Step New York Approach

Sales Assistant: "Will you hold?"

Broker: Qualifies you

---

2. *Attitude.* The broker is trying to assess his or her chances of doing business with the prospect. Attitude is often the most difficult criterion to evaluate.

3. *Experience.* Some veteran brokers prefer not to deal with inexperienced investors because it takes too much time to educate them. "I don't enjoy the hand-holding process you sometimes have to go through with new investors," says one such broker. Other veteran brokers welcome inexperienced investors. One of them is Bill Koriath of Prudential-Bache—even though he already has more than 2,000 clients. "Those investors are my bread and butter," he says. "Two thousand clients may sound like a lot, but most of those clients are good for maybe one trade a year."

4. *Objectives and risk threshold.* Does the investor want current income, long-term growth or something else? How much risk is the investor willing to assume? "I have to diagnose the need, and when I have something that I think fits the bill, test it out on you," says Betsy Buckley of Dain Bosworth. "If that's not what you want, fine. I'll come back later with something else, and I've probably learned a little more about you that's going to help me be more effective in the future."

**Four Criteria That Brokers Use
To Qualify Prospects.**

1. Capital
2. Attitude toward investing
3. Experience as an investor
4. Objectives and risk threshold

By using the four key criteria, brokers can usually identify qualified prospects fairly quickly. The real difficulty comes in converting those prospects to clients.

DEALING WITH REJECTION

Even with the most innovative sales techniques, building up a sizable clientele of active investors can be a long, grueling process. "For every 100 dials, I usually contact the decision maker about 25 times," says Scott Horrall, a broker with Thomson McKinnon's Indianapolis branch. "Of those 25 contacts, about 10 become prospects for follow-up calls and one eventually becomes an account."

With a failure rate typically as high as 99 percent, it's small wonder that brokers have to come up with inventive ways to keep themselves motivated. Some firms encourage brokers to put a stack of dollar bills on one side of the desk and then to move one of them across the desk every time they hang up from a cold call—in essence, paying themselves as they go. "Power dialing" is another popular technique. Glued to the phone, brokers dial numbers in rapid succession. They often call for two hours or 100 dials—whichever comes first—without setting down the receiver. Two brokers at Dean Witter's Hayward, California, office power-dialed for 15 consecutive hours on March 26, 1987, each recording what they believe to be a record of 1,069 dials. The brokers, Shawn Henley and Kim Bradford (Bradford later moved to Merrill Lynch), each reached about 110 interested prospects (of whom 15 to 20 ultimately opened an account). "The only time we set the receiver down," says Henley, "was to go to the rest room or eat lunch. We started at 6:00 A.M., calling business owners we thought might be in at that time, and called until nine o'clock that evening." In a normal day, says Henley, he will cold-call for two to three hours, making about 300 dials in all. At most firms, brokers are encouraged to make 200 to 300 dials a day (though, in reality, few brokers are able to maintain that pace day in and day out). "It's awfully difficult," says Soule. "I think 50 to 100 dials is more common."

"There's a real stigma attached to calling up people you don't know and asking them for money," says Jim Buehler of Roney & Co. "You have to be extremely disciplined. And the rejection can be devastating. For every success, you get 99 rejections. To pysch yourself up, you have to go at cold-calling from a standpoint of controlled arrogance. My attitude is, 'I'm calling to do them a favor. If, for one reason or another, they're not in a position to take advantage of my help, it's their loss.' When I call someone who says they don't have any money, for instance, I'll say, 'I'm a good broker, but I can't help people who don't have money. Thank you.' Then I hang up on them—rather than to wait for them to hang up on me. That's the attitude you have to have in this business in order to keep from being depressed all the time from the constant rejection."

One tool that a few brokers use to blunt the force of rejection is a "computerized lead generation system." This might be characterized as an answering machine in reverse. It automatically dials numbers from a prospect list, gives presentations, asks questions, records answers and enters the names of prospects who show interest. It is programmed to dis-

---

FIGURE 6-2   Cold Calling Success Ratio Is 1 Percent

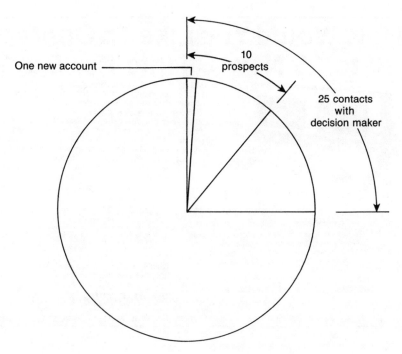

One new account

10 prospects

25 contacts with decision maker

*Out of a total of 100 calls

---

connect on busy signals, operator intercepts and even on answering machines. But best of all, no matter how many times people hang up on it, the computer registers no "call reluctance." It just keeps dialing for dollars. Although automatic calling machines have been effective for many brokers, they are unpopular with some consumers, who in a few states are pressing to have their use regulated.

The New York cold-calling approach, described earlier, is another means that brokers use to shield themselves from the rigors of rejection. Cold call specialists (who are usually either unemployed actors or recent college graduates trying to work their way into the securities business) initiate the calls instead of the broker. In some cases, the cold caller's role ends when the prospect answers the phone—as in our earlier example. In other cases the cold callers try to qualify the prospect. They may ask prospects about their investment objectives, their financial resources and their willingness to invest. Only after the cold caller has qualified the prospect will the broker pick up the phone and talk to the prospect.

FIGURE 6–3   Advertisement for an Automatic Calling Machine

Reprinted by permission of Comtel Broadcasting Corp. 1987.

FIGURE 6–4   The Qualifier Approach

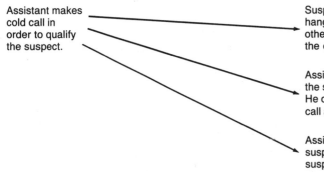

Assistant makes cold call in order to qualify the suspect.

Suspect may hang up or otherwise reject the caller.

Assistant may learn that the suspect is not qualified. He or she then terminates the call and makes another call.

Assistant qualifies the suspect and turns the suspect over to the broker.

ROUNDING UP SUSPECTS

One way for brokers to increase their odds of turning suspects into clients is to start out with a strong prospect list. By using a good source, brokers can virtually assure themselves of reaching suspects who meet the first criterion of suitability—adequate capital. And they can often determine from such a source whether the suspects meet the second criterion—that is, demonstrate a positive attitude toward investing. Coming up with good lists is a well-refined science in itself. Brokers turn to a number of sources to identify potential clients:

- *Rented lists.* Brokers often rent lists of names from list brokers. One of the country's largest is Best Mailing Lists and Printing Corporation in New York, which sells 50,000 different mailing lists with 82 million names. The names are sold by the thousand at a rate of $30 to $60 per thousand. You are probably on a number of these lists. There are lists of dentists and doctors, of course. There are lists of personal computer owners, disc jockeys, economics professors, car buffs, Jewish contributors, foreign diplomats, tax shelter investors (an expensive list), corporation presidents, yacht owners, aircraft owners, America's wealthiest farmers, individuals on the *Social Register* by state (there are only four in South Dakota), women bankers, air balloon owners and portfolio managers. There are lists of political contributors, lists of new homeowners, even lists of stockbrokers. Among the more popular lists for brokers are subscription lists to business publications such as *Fortune, Business Week, Money, Barron's, Forbes, The Wall Street Journal* and *Investor's Daily*. Some of the best lists are also the most difficult to come by (membership lists of exclusive country clubs, alumni lists of social fraternities, directories of company employees), but resourceful brokers often manage to find a way to come up with such lists.
- *Neighborhood cross-reference directories.* Brokers can be reasonably sure that the residents of affluent neighborhoods (whether the neighborhood is Scarsdale, Shaker Heights or Beverly Hills) have the means to be active investors.
- *Newspapers.* The business section of most newspapers carries lists of executive promotions. If you're promoted to executive vice president of your company, there's a good chance that you'll receive some prospecting calls from stockbrokers.
- *Obituaries.* With death often comes hefty life insurance payments and legacies. The survivors sometimes find that they have more money than they've ever had before and that they need a financial advisor to help them invest it.
- *Advertisements.* Brokers or brokerage firms sometimes place ads in newspapers to attract the attention of prospective investors. Such an ad might read, "Are you interested in getting a higher income on your investments? Mail in the attached coupon, and we'll send you our *free*

brochure 'Getting More for Your Investment Dollars.' " (Direct mail campaigns by brokerage firms often make similar offers.) Readers who respond to the ad by calling in or returning a coupon will indeed receive the free brochure, as advertised, but they will also receive a prospecting call from a broker.

- *Investment seminars.* You've probably seen investment seminars advertised in the newspapers, or perhaps you've received a written invitation to such a seminar in the mail. Seminars of this kind may cover a wide range of themes. When new tax laws are introduced, brokers routinely conduct seminars on such topics as . . . "reducing your tax liability under the new tax laws." . . . Some seminars are geared to a specific investment. When AT&T was going through divestiture, E. F. Hutton brokers conducted seminars on how the breakup would affect AT&T stockholders. Broad-ranging themes are also common, such as "applied strategies for building wealth" or "laying the groundwork for a prosperous retirement." Seminars are usually conducted on weekday evenings, and they may consist of either one session or a short series of sessions, one night a week for two or three weeks. Either way, the aim is the same—to attract large groups of potential investors and to try to make a positive impression on those prospects. Brokers follow up seminars by either phoning or interviewing those who sign attendance registers, and try to convert them into clients. Seminars have proven to be a very effective way to open new accounts. In fact, Bill McKinney of IDS Financial Services says that his firm's financial planners add to their clientele by conducting about 10,000 seminars a year.

- *Door-to-door.* Some brokers prefer to cold-call in person rather than on the phone. "When I was prospecting," recalls Henry Basil of Paine-Webber, "I'd go visit different office buildings near my home in Minneapolis and hand out cards and talk to people. They were all very flattered to have a broker stop by and visit them. I would spend some time talking to them about the problems they had had with their accounts, and if they thought I could do a better job; before long they would open up an account with me. In the process, I learned from their past mistakes (and so did they), so we could avoid those mistakes in the future."

Roney & Co.'s Buehler took a similar approach. "I would take a stack of business cards and go to all the stores in downtown Lansing and get to know everyone by name. It didn't work out right away, but within a year or two it sure paid off. People would get upset with their present broker, and that's when they would remember me." Buehler, who is in his 20s, explains, "The one thing you have going for you as a young broker is that everybody loves these Horatio Alger guys—particularly the older businessmen. You need to show a lot of enthusiasm and ambition. I told them that I was new in the business and I would really work hard for them. That really appealed to them."

While door-to-door (business-to-business) prospecting tends to work fairly well in metropolitan areas, it is probably more effective in smaller communities. Some brokers stake out a geographic territory—maybe a three-county area—and call on businesses on the main streets of the towns in that territory on a regular basis. Residents of smaller towns tend to be very cautious, and they're not likely to turn their money over to a new broker the first time they meet the broker. But brokers can win their trust by returning regularly, having coffee in the local cafe' and by generally getting to know the people in that community.

DIALING FOR SUSPECTS

Of all the prospecting techniques, by far the most common is cold-calling by phone. In addition to the New York approach, there are two other classic telephone techniques—the "product approach" and the "need approach."

The Product Approach

With the product approach, the broker weaves his or her pitch around a certain stock or an investment product. Normally, brokers prefer a reasonably safe, reasonably well known product that offers some income. The product might be a local municipal bond or tax-exempt mutual fund, a local utility stock or a blue-chip stock of a local corporation. "You can always become more aggressive later," says Horrall of Thomson McKinnon, "but if you start with an aggressive investment, you might turn off the suspect and never get a second chance."

"On my prospecting calls," says Merrill Lynch's Soule, "I've been offering a no-load, no-redemption fee government bond mutual fund that's totally liquid. Prospects really like it because the fund involves no fees to buy or sell. The advantages for the broker are that you get the assets in under management and you gain their trust. My objective at this stage is not commissions. It may sound sappy, but I really do want to do what's best for them. I don't want to take their money and lose it for them. My objective is to help them out."

The typical product approach goes something like this:

"Mr. Smith, I'm Tom Mathews with ABC Securities. The reason I'm calling is that our firm is doing an underwriting of Northern States Power common stock. The stock is selling at two points above its low for the year; it's yielding 8 percent, it's a good, solid, safe stock that will provide you with a very generous income, and over the years we could see increases in that dividend. Would you be interested in this investment opportunity?"

The chances are that the prospect will say no. In fact, says Soule, "sometimes I would prefer that they say no because that's when I can find out what their real objectives are." When the prospect says no, the broker will typically respond by asking, "Well, what do you invest in?" The conversation that follows might go something like this:

Prospect: Well, frankly I'm in a fairly high tax bracket and I generally invest in municipal bonds.

Broker: I see. Can you tell me a little more about the types of bonds you invest in. What kind of quality do you look for? Do you buy A-rated or the lower-grade bonds?

Prospect: I stick with A-rated.

Broker: What kind of maturity do you look for?

Prospect: I try to buy bonds with no more than ten years' maturity.

Broker: Do you buy unit investment trusts?

Prospect: No, I like to buy individual bonds.

Broker: If you don't mind my asking, Mr. Smith, what size lots of bonds do you buy at a time?

(With this question, the broker is trying to determine whether the individual has the assets to be a good prospect. Sometimes brokers are even blunter. Dale Grubb of Shearson Lehman says, "I would ask, 'Mr. Smith, would you have at least $10,000 to invest in the right opportunity right now?' If not, I would find out if he had a CD coming due or expected to have money to invest later. Then I would call him back at that time.")

Prospect: I tend to buy bonds in lots of 10 to 25 at a time.

Broker: Well, thank you, Mr. Smith. I don't want to take any more of your time now, but here's what I would suggest. When we see a bond that looks like it would be attractive for you, may I give you a call and tell you about it?

Prospect: Uh, actually, I have a broker already.

Broker: I understand that. I'm glad to hear that. But I'd just like the opportunity to earn your business. You've been helpful to me here, Mr. Smith, and I'd like to give you a call. That would be all right, wouldn't it?

Prospect: Well, if you really want to.

That's the first step in the product approach. The aim is to have a starting point to open a discussion with the prospect. "I try to keep the calls as brief as possible—about 30 seconds a call," says Dean Witter's Henley. "That's about as long as folks on the other end are going to give you before they lose interest and hang up. If they're interested in what I'm selling, I'll mail out some information to them and then follow up with another phone call in a week or two." Brokers don't really expect to sell anything on their first call—though that occasionally happens. They simply want to establish a basis for conversation. And through that conversation, they hope to qualify the prospect as a likely investor and to get some specific information on the types of investments that the prospect prefers. "The thing that surprises me the most," says Soule, "is the amount of information people give you on the first call."

FIGURE 6–5   The Product Approach

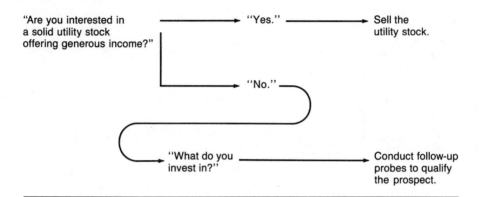

The Need Approach

A more difficult approach is the need approach. "I would never talk about a product," says Grubb, "only about the idea of investing. I would ask prospects if they would like to increase their income or decrease their taxes."

A typical conversation using the need approach would go something like this:

Broker: Mr. Smith, I'm Tom Mathews. I'm a registered representative with ABC Securities. The reason I'm calling is I'd like to offer the services of myself and my firm to you. We've been in business for 80 years helping investors build their assets to achieve their financial goals. Can you tell me what your investment objectives are?

Prospect: To tell you the truth, I dabble in a few local stocks for speculation and I have some money in long-term growth mutual funds.

Broker: What do you do with your serious money?

Prospect: I've got some tax-deferred annuities and a few municipal bonds.

Broker: What are you looking to do now? Do you have some investable funds you're looking to put to work at this time?

Prospect: I have some money to invest if the right thing comes along.

Broker: Are you looking at anything right now?

Prospect: I've been looking at some of these high-tech stocks.

Broker: Any in particular?

Prospect: I'm sort of interested in Apple. I think they may have turned things around there.

Broker: I'll tell you what, Mr. Smith, I think our firm has a research report on Apple. Why don't I send you that report, and I'll follow up with you in a week or so?

Prospect: Well, if you want to.

FIGURE 6–6   The Need Approach

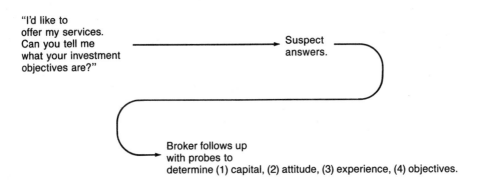

"I'd like to offer my services. Can you tell me what your investment objectives are?"

Suspect answers.

Broker follows up with probes to determine (1) capital, (2) attitude, (3) experience, (4) objectives.

And with that, the broker ends the call and enters the investor's name into his suspect file. The need approach is a little more difficult than the product approach because it's more direct. Prospects are often reluctant to openly discuss their investments with a broker making a cold call. The need approach works better face-to-face than it does over the phone. But some brokers have found it to work very effectively even by phone.

FOLLOW-UP: THE 90-SECOND SALE

The purpose of cold call technique is to build up a file of well-qualified prospects—to "fill the pipeline"—so that when the broker comes up with an investment idea that looks attractive, he has a list of qualified prospects to call.

Brokers generally keep a card file with information on each active prospect. The cards, which help the broker keep track of each prospect's status and investment objectives, typically look something like this:

Before making their follow-up calls, brokers refer to these cards to re-

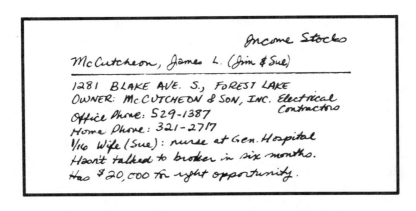

Income Stocks

McCutcheon, James L. (Jim & Sue)

1281 BLAKE AVE. S., FOREST LAKE
OWNER: McCUTCHEON & SON, INC. Electrical Contractors
Office Phone: 529-1387
Home Phone: 321-2717
1/16 Wife (Sue): nurse at Gen. Hospital
Hasn't talked to broker in six months.
Has $20,000 for right opportunity.

fresh their memory and to decide which investments to recommend. Then, in the course of the follow-up call, they may jot down other facts that come up during the call. "I have a personal computer at the side of my desk," says Thomson McKinnon's Horrall, "and I am constantly following up with a note after a phone conversation, and I keep notes on what we said in each conversation."

Brokers classify prospects according to investment interests—"income stocks" or "tax-free income" or "long-term growth" or "active trading"—and contact those prospects when they have an investment opportunity that seems suitable. For instance, if a broker's firm underwrites an income stock, the broker will go through his or her card file and compile a list of prospects who have shown a preference for income stocks. The. , before making calls, the broker will develop a "story" about the investment—an enticing verbal picture that makes the investment come alive.

The best stories have substance and sizzle. First comes substance:

"The last time we talked," the broker might say, "you said you were interested in income stocks. Traditionally, investors have found that high-quality utility stocks are excellent income-producing investments. The particular utility stock I have in mind is Western Public Service. As you may know, Western has been a strong company in this area for many years. Right now, it's selling at $25 a share and pays a $2 dividend—that's an 8 percent return. Furthermore, the stock has traded as high as $30. If it returns to that level, you could get not only a good current return but also substantial appreciation. Besides, the stock has a history of increasing its dividend almost every year. We've projected that within five years that dividend could increase by 50 percent. Those are the main reasons you should buy the stock. But there's one more reason . . ."

Here the broker shifts from substance to sizzle:

"Western Public Service gets 80 percent of its energy from hydroelectric power. That means it is not vulnerable to the ecological problems of burning coal or the difficulty of buying oil or all of the problems of nuclear power. It is beautifully positioned not only for this decade but well into the 21st century."

Then comes the sell:

"So with the stock trading at $25 a share, you could buy 400 shares for about $10,000, plus commissions, and that's what I would recommend that you do at this time."

Brokers try to keep their entire pitch—substance, sizzle and sell—to under two minutes. If it lasts much longer, prospects start to lose interest. The rule on Wall Street is that if you can't sell a stock in 90 seconds, you probably can't sell it at all.

Some brokers say that they'll make as many as 20 follow-up calls to try to earn a strong prospect's business. Others give up after three or four calls. "You're constantly assessing the situation and trying to determine if it's worth pursuing," says Horrall. "My average is about eight calls before we start doing business."

Adds Buehler: "If they kept putting me off, I would say, 'I've spoken to you four times now, and I've brought you some good ideas, but I'm kind of new in this business, and I wonder if you could tell me what I'm doing wrong. Help me be a better broker.' The guy may say, 'You just hit me at the wrong time' or 'You didn't qualify me right—I really want income and not growth.' Or the guy may not have a good reason. He may have just been stringing me along. If that's the case, I'll tear up his card and never call him again."

Brokers are encouraged by their firms to have a "hit list" or a "ten most wanted" list made up of prospects with high net worth. "We're supposed to call each week and do whatever it takes to earn their business— even if it means making 20 or 30 calls to that prospect," reports one broker. The pursuit of these wealthy clients is sometimes referred to as "elephant hunting." If the account is big enough, the broker may continue to call faithfully, week after week, for several years to crack it. Or the broker may try to set up a personal appointment, either for breakfast or in the afternoon after the market is closed. The personal appointment is often the best way to win the trust of older investors or substantial investors.

And that leads us to the 14/71 rule.

THE 14/71 RULE

In 1975, the marketing director of PaineWebber discovered that the top 14 percent of the firm's clients generated 71 percent of its commissions. Further investigation showed that the top 14 percent of the typical broker's accounts generated 71 percent of his or her income. These discoveries generated a chain reaction of inferences. For example, it was concluded that brokers could increase their income by 71 percent simply by replicating the top 14 percent of their clients and that the entire firm could increase its revenues by 71 percent by finding another group of clients just like its best 14 percent.

Later studies yielded additional information along the same lines. For example, PaineWebber found that a mere 7 percent of its clients accounted for more than 50 percent of its revenues. And when A. G. Edwards did a study of its top-producing brokers (those with annual gross commissions of at least $300,000), "What we learned," says D'Arcy Fox, the firm's director of training and development, "was that typically they had about 300 clients but that 17 of those clients accounted for 60 percent of their commissions."

What all of this means to brokers—and indirectly to their customers—is that the big clients are extremely valuable to them. Brokers need to identify those clients, cater to them, do everything possible to retain them, and find other investors just like them.

Many brokers use a systematic three-tier pecking order for keeping tabs on their clients. They use small three-ring binders to log their clients' names, phone numbers and addresses and other pertinent information on the clients. Their best clients—the 14 percent who keep their bread on the table and their yacht in the water—go into their "A book." When the market is moving, brokers turn first to their A book customers to keep them abreast of any developments.

The next group—the "B book" entries—are good, valued customers who make a handful of trades every year. A broker would have a hard time making a living off their trades, but they do help supplement the broker's income and they can sometimes be helpful in offering referrals. "C book" customers are the least active. They may not have made a trade in the past 12 months. Brokers don't expect much from them but keep their names on file just in case they call again to place another order.

One industry insider describes the commission breakdown this way:

A book: Customers doing at least $2,500 in annual commissions (the equivalent of $125,000 in stock buy or sell transactions or $250,000 in bond transactions)

B book: Customers doing between $1,000 and $2,500 in annual commissions

C book: customers doing less than $1,000 in annual commissions

These figures, however, are all relative to the individual broker. Some of an experienced broker's C accounts might be considered A accounts by a newer broker who is still building a clientele.

Al Heiam of Drexel Burnham takes a slightly different approach. "I don't categorize my clients by commissions generated. I classify them by the size of the account. The commissions are up to me." For Heiam, an A account is one that contains more than $100,000 in assets, a B account is one that contains $35,000 to $100,000 and a C account is one that contains less than $35,000.

Dain Bosworth's Buckley takes a less structured approach. "I have A book accounts with a half million dollars and others with $50,000 who I really like. I have one account that started out as an $80,000 IRA rollover that I've turned into $120,000; and I just sense something wonderful is going to happen there."

The vast majority of a broker's clients—roughly 86 percent—are categorized as B and C book customers, yet these clients generate only about 29 percent of the broker's gross commissions. Brokers carefully budget the amount of time they spend with such clients—preferring to devote most of their time to their A book customers. Just the same, B and C book customers are still held in high esteem by most good brokers.

"We tell our brokers that if you're dealing with a guy who has $1,000, don't be short with him," says Joe Baxter, vice president and training director of Smith Barney. "Give him the amount of time you think you can, and give him the right products, because you never know when his Uncle Harry is going to die and leave this guy a quarter of a million dollars. If you've treated him well, he'll come back to you to invest that money. That happens more often than you might think." Smaller investors can also be a good source of referrals if they're impressed by their broker.

In addition to names, phone numbers and addresses, brokers keep a history of their clients' investment purchases, preferences, assets and general financial status in their A, B and C books. Thus, a broker can see at a glance, for instance, that a client likes energy stocks, has a tax problem, expects to inherit some property soon, bought 600 shares of Texaco on August 9 for $35 per share and is occasionally interested in buying tax-exempt municipal bonds.

In short, the A, B and C books serve two key purposes: they give brokers instant access to all the information they might need on any client, and, more important, they help separate the big-ticket clients from the rest of the pack. And in the high-pressure, bottom-line-driven brokerage business, knowing who has the money is paramount to survival.

INCENTIVES

At times, securities firms offer brokers special incentives to sell a specific investment. For instance, a securities firm may have purchased a large block of an over-the-counter stock from an institutional investor at a favorable price—as much as a point below the market price. To unload the stock, the firm may offer shares to clients at a 1/8 (12^1/2 cents) to 1/4 (25 cents) discount to the market, with no commission charge. At the same time, the firm may give brokers 1/4 point per share as a special incentive to sell the stock. Even with the discount to clients and the incentive for brokers, the firm will still realize a small profit on the stock because it purchased shares in volume at a below-market price.

But beware of the overzealous broker—particularly if the broker is pushing a speculative stock you've never heard of. One small California brokerage house that was making a market in a speculative stock called RCM Corporation told its brokers to sell the stock—or else. According to an SEC report, the brokers were told to "get on the phone and pick up clients . . . any way we could." Recalled one broker: "We were told that if we didn't go ahead and produce, we would be kicked out of the office. We were taught to say certain things about RCM Corporation. We said it could be a $10 to $20 stock . . . [and] that it had moved up steadily the whole year without a drop. Then, in a frenzy, we would tell prospects to get some RCM before it went up some more."

And indeed, the stock was climbing steadily, going from 1^1/4 to 3^1/4 during a six-month span. But not because RCM's success warranted such growth. In fact, the brokerage firm's own research director said she thought the stock was overpriced. But the brokers at the firm just kept pushing the stock and driving up its price. "We were essentially told that this is the stock," said one broker. "It's an inventory. Work on it. And if we didn't, [the office manager] might get upset." The brokers apparently followed their orders well—the firm sold 543,000 shares of RCM stock to more than 1,000 investors before NASD investigators stepped in. It was later charged with several SEC violations, including manipulation, high-pressure sales tactics and unfair prices.

Many securities firms also offer special incentives to brokers to sell company-packaged investment products such as mutual funds and unit investment trusts. The incentives may come in the form of higher commissions or in the form of perks, such as free trips to Hawaii.

New stock offerings often involve special incentives. Clients are sometimes able to buy the new stock under the market price and with no commission, while brokers are compensated with a special fee that exceeds their usual commission rate. The extra cost is covered in the underwriting charges.

Another motivator is what brokers facetiously refer to as "scramble day." Scramble day falls five business days before the end of the month. Securities transactions take five business days to be officially "settled" or completed, so scramble day is considered the last production day of the month. Any sales made after scramble day are credited to the next month's production. When brokers have a slow month, they sometimes have to "scramble" to drum up sales on that final day in order to meet their personal quotas. In fact, some brokers have been known to do as much as half of their business on scramble day. "A guy can do a hell of a lot of business in a couple of days if he really burns the phone," says David Thompson of Prudential-Bache. "There are brokers who do that. They're blasé all through the month, not servicing their clients, and then a day or two before scramble day they start phoning clients to generate some business and salvage some commissions. They are acting out of desperation—serving their own interests rather than their clients'. If a client continually gets calls from his broker at the end of the month, he should take a closer look at his broker's recommendations."

RESPONDING TO THE COLD CALL

Next time a new broker calls you, how should you respond? As we mentioned in Chapter 5, "Making the Final Choice," there are better ways to choose a broker than through a cold call. We strongly recommend that, if possible, you meet the broker face-to-face before opening an account.

But if a broker does catch your attention with what you consider an outstanding investment opportunity, the best way to agree to make a purchase is by repeating what you are agreeing to. You might say, "OK, I'm going to buy 200 shares of Western Public Service at the market price. It is currently selling at $25, so I will be paying about $5,000 plus commissions." If you want to hold the stock certificate yourself, mention that, and make sure that the broker agrees to have it mailed to you promptly. If you want the brokerage firm to hold the certificate (which is normally the case), tell the broker to hold the stock "in street name."

What's the best way to turn brokers down? Don't lead them on. Level with them. It's in their and your best interest. They don't want to waste their time or yours. The biggest enemy of a broker is a prospect who keeps agreeing to have the broker call back but has no intention of ever investing. A polite rejection is much kinder. You might say, "I'm really not a good prospect for you." Or, "I have no available funds and don't anticipate having any for a couple of years." Or, "I've had the same broker for the past five years, and I'm very happy with that broker."

If you are genuinely interested in doing business with a broker but don't want the particular investment he or she is offering, explain your objections to the investment and tell the broker what specific type of investments you're interested in. And then, if possible, take one more step—meet the broker at his or her office to find out more about the broker's background and investment strengths. Remember, in choosing a broker, it's to your advantage to be in full control of the selection process.

It's also to your advantage, once you've chosen a broker, to manage that relationship effectively. You should expect certain courtesies from your broker, just as your broker expects certain courtesies from you. The following chapter focuses on how to establish and maintain a viable, mutually satisfying relationship with your broker.

CHAPTER SEVEN _____

Broker's Pet

It's not always easy to love your broker. After all, brokers are like any other professionals. They make mistakes. Attorneys lose cases, physicians lose patients and brokers lose money. Brokers' recommendations do not always work out. In short, brokers are human. They err. And for that, some clients never forgive them.

But if it's human to err, it's also human to play favorites—which is a very good reason to be kind to your broker and to forgive your broker's innocent mistakes. Brokers have pet clients—people they go to first with every new tip, every public offering, every good joke. If you want to get the most from your relationship with your broker, you should get to be one of his or her pets. Take your broker to lunch, offer referrals, say thanks when your broker makes you money, and, as one veteran broker puts it, "Don't bug me."

The surest way to become one of your broker's pets, of course, is by investing large sums of money with him or her on a regular basis. The more you invest, the more your broker is likely to do for you. Dale Grubb of Shearson Lehman says that he sometimes offers discounts for bigger accounts and that he also sends out regular detailed computerized account statements to his top 50 clients. Some get them monthly, others twice-monthly and the biggest accounts get them every week.

But unless you have a few hundred thousand dollars to toss your broker's way, you probably won't be able to invest your way into his or her heart. Instead, you've got to resort to Plan B: common decency.

That may sound simple enough (especially if your broker is consistently making you money), but strangely, a lot of investors never catch on. "I had one guy I did 18 trades with," recalls Don Tidlund of E. F. Hutton; "14 were winners, 4 were losers—and small ones at that. Yet the guy would always call me and cry about it. 'Gee,' he'd say, 'what did we buy that one for?' I finally told him that maybe he'd better just call his own shots. I made it very clear that I didn't want to deal with him anymore."

Bill Blount of PaineWebber talks about a local businessman he once had as a client. "He was a very vindictive, very obnoxious person. When he came into the office, he would often have my assistant in tears. My daughter, who works with me, always chose to avoid him. He was always making derogatory comments about rich brokers." Still, Blount continued to do business with this client until the client ordered $65,000 in Daimler-Benz stock (against Blount's strong recommendations to the contrary) and then refused to take delivery of the stock. That left Blount holding the stock and a $5,200 spread between the bid price and the ask price that he and the firm had to cover. "The real rub," says Blount, "was that just to put the order through, I had to make about five long-distance calls, and the firm charged him only $102 commission for the entire $65,000 transaction." Needless to say, that was the last transaction Blount ever executed for the client.

Outright banishment may be the gravest consequence of incurring your broker's wrath, but it's certainly not the only one. Brokers tend to try harder and perform better for clients they like. Brokers are also likely to offer their opinions more freely to clients who they feel trust them. When the market is down and everyone is selling rather than buying, a good broker might call his pet clients and say, "I think we're pretty close to the bottom, and while I can't tell you this is the bottom, I think we should start investing now." Brokers are far more likely to make such recommendations and to take calculated risks with clients whom they like and who trust them than with clients who are constantly berating and second-guessing them.

Betsy Buckley of Dain Bosworth talks about one relatively small investor whose personality alone has earned him A book status—with the weekly phone updates, the special mailings and the other privileges that A book clients are accorded. "I may never get another dime out of him," she says, "but he gives me good insights and I love to talk to him. He's a motivator. When I feel down, I call him up and he makes me laugh. If I have a new idea, I'll always run it by him. If it's a bad idea, I'll know it immediately, because if it doesn't sell to him, it isn't going to sell."

"What I like in a client," says Tidlund, "is someone who is totally realistic with you (not expecting the moon), someone who can accept risk, knowing he's not going to win every time but understandably expecting to win more times than he loses."

Brokers often withdraw from and stop calling clients who are distrustful or difficult. Even if they continue to make recommendations to such clients, they do so in a very careful, guarded way. They won't put themselves on the line and risk further criticism from these clients. "In that type of situation," explains Henry Basil of PaineWebber, "I will not turn down a guy's business, but if he calls me for something, I may put it on the back burner. I continue to be very polite, very formal and I just let it fade away."

Bill Koriath of Prudential-Bache talks about one investor, a noted heart surgeon, who he says is far and away the most perverse client he's ever dealt with. "There aren't many like this guy," says Koriath. "It's a dramatic character flaw in the individual, compounded by the incredible success he's had in life. Some people get to the point in life where they feel that everyone around them is there to serve them. When that happens, something has to jump up to bring them down to earth. Unfortunately, that has never happened to this individual. He saves a life here and a life there, and he's put on a pedestal. He's completely lost touch with what is socially acceptable. If he were ever to take a close look in the mirror and see what everyone else sees, he'd be horrified.

"The sad thing about him is, he goes from broker to broker and he's always unhappy. No trade is ever executed properly. If he buys the stock at $90 a share and later learns that the stock was trading that day for $89, he thinks he should have gotten it at $89—even if the following day it's trading at $94. If your recommendation went down, he thinks you should reimburse him for the loss. I ask him, 'Well, what about the recommendations that went up—are you going to share the profits with us?' He's made a lot of money with us. He's way up on his investments, but he's never satisfied.

"So you quit giving him recommendations. You don't do anything for him other than maybe send him an article or call him with some news, but as far as giving him advice on whether to buy or sell, you don't. You completely stay on the sidelines, because if you make recommendations, he's going to blame you no matter what happens. In fact, even though you don't make recommendations, he still finds ways to blame you. He sold out some stock and options in one company at $160 (totally his own decision), and within two weeks it was up to $198. He missed out on $60,000 in profits by selling out early. But, of course, he's above error; he's never made a mistake in his life. Somebody else has to take the blame. So what does he do? He comes up with another reason to be argumentative. He calls up and goes into this tirade about my secretary avoiding him. But, of course, the underlying reason he's complaining has nothing to do with my secretary. He's complaining because he missed out on $60,000 in share appreciation. He has to be mad at somebody, and he's not going to be mad at himself. He'll go into some remarks about brokerage companies and how they're always out to get him, and how he's never had a fair shake and how he never has any recourse.

"The question you might have next is, why would I ever tolerate something like this? The reason is, he does the business, and the business is all unsolicited. If he's going to generate $3,000 a month in stock commissions, why look a gift horse in the mouth? But I expect him to transfer the account soon. That's his pattern, to go from broker to broker to broker.

"He's a classic tragic figure. He has this great gift for saving lives, but what he doesn't realize is that the day he dies, the sun is going to come up in the east and set in the west and no one is going to give a damn."

RULES FOR BECOMING A BROKER'S PET

It doesn't take a lot of effort to develop a mutually beneficial relationship with your broker. It just takes common courtesy and adherence to the following informal rules of etiquette:

- Rule 1: Be honest. Tell the truth. Most stockbrokers regard their relationship with their better clients as almost a sacred trust. As their clients' personal financial advisors, they are privy to much of their clients' most confidential information. There's a chance that the clients will discuss anything that relates to money with them—and that could include anything from a pending vacation to a pending divorce. Brokers, aware of the sensitive nature of this relationship, try not to violate their clients' trust. For that reason, it is very disillusioning for brokers to learn that clients have lied to them.

    What do clients lie about? They lie about how much money they have to invest, or about their use of other brokers, or about their investments elsewhere. Such lies can be damaging for a couple of reasons. It can undermine the rapport a broker has with a client, and it can diminish the effectiveness of the broker as a financial advisor. It's a bit like not telling your doctor about the chest pains you've been experiencing. Doctors can't treat illnesses properly if they don't know the symptoms. Brokers make their investment recommendations based on the information clients provide. If clients give brokers incorrect information, the brokers are much more likely to give the clients unsuitable recommendations.

    This is not to say, however, that you must always tell your broker everything. If all you want are some good stock recommendations, your broker may not need to know your entire financial situation. But there's no point in being dishonest. If he or she asks you for information you feel uncomfortable providing, simply say, "That is something I would rather not discuss at this time." By doing that, you can be forthright with your broker and yet not reveal anything that you would rather keep to yourself.

- Rule 2: Return phone calls promptly. Brokers have a very clear sense of who returns their phone calls and who doesn't. When the market is moving and time is of the essence, brokers don't like to waste precious minutes calling clients who are hard to reach. A broker, for example, may have dozens of clients who are sitting on cash during a bear market, waiting for the market to turn before making further investments. When the broker sees that the market is up 20 points and that trading volume is snowballing, who is going to be called first? Will it be clients who are hard to reach and slow to return calls? Not on your life. The broker will call the clients who have consistently made themselves accessible.

Some clients go to almost ridiculous extremes to take their brokers' calls. Dentists have been known to step away from their patients in mid-root canal to answer such a call. Corporate presidents interrupt important meetings when their broker is on the line. "One time," recalls Al Heiam of Drexel Burnham, "I called one of my clients, an anesthesiologist, who actually had the nurse put the phone right in front of him while he was involved in an operation. He said he wasn't in a position to carry on a lengthy conversation, but if it was an emergency in his account, he was certainly willing to listen to a recommendation. I told him, 'For God's sake, get on with the operation and call me back when you're through!' He did."

The select group of clients who can be reached whenever brokers have something worth discussing will always be among the first to be called. If you want to be included in that select group, be prepared to respond quickly when your broker calls.

- Rule 3: Once you've found a broker you feel comfortable with, accept his or her recommendations. Once again, remember that successful brokers usually have several hundred clients with a wide variety of investment objectives. It takes considerable time and effort to come up with suitable investment recommendations for all of those clients. If you've told your broker what your investment objectives are and how much you have to invest, then follow your broker's advice when your broker calls you back with a recommendation he or she considers suitable. As one broker grumbled, "My most frustrating clients are the guys who yes me to death. 'Yes, that sounds good,' they'll say, 'but I just don't think I want to put any money into it at this time.'" We're not saying you should feel compelled to invest all of your money in the first investment your broker recommends. But you should be willing to invest some of it—unless this would mean compromising your moral principles. For instance, your broker may recommend a high-yielding stock of an electric utility that uses nuclear energy. If you're morally opposed to nuclear energy, simply explain your objections to your broker, and he or she should be able to come up with something else that's acceptable.

Brokers become very demoralized if clients repeatedly decline their recommendations. Eventually, they give up on such clients and either put them on their inactive list or refer them to another broker. "I had one client who came to me after she had inherited $120,000," says Lee Kopp of Dain Bosworth. "I put her in some smaller growth stocks that didn't do well right away, so I suggested we move the money into some other investments. She would never take my suggestions. All she would do was complain. 'Why did you do this? Why is this happening?' Despite my recommendations, no change ever resulted. Finally, I just gave up and asked her to transfer her account to another broker."

So if you want a good relationship with your broker, give your broker the benefit of the doubt. (Have a bias toward accepting his or her recommendations.) If you have questions about a recommendation, restate your investment objectives and then ask, "Do you really feel that this is the best thing you can come up with right now to meet those objectives?" If the broker says yes, then you've got a decision on your hands: either you accept the recommendation or you find another broker. But if you want your broker to keep bringing you new investment ideas, be prepared to accept his or her recommendations. In the long run, you both may benefit. As David Waterbury of Dean Witter explains, "When something good comes up, the first people I'll call are the ones I think will give me the order."

- Rule 4: Set realistic expectations. When you sit down with your broker, describe your goals and find out how much money you can realistically expect to make. In a survey of its top clients, PaineWebber learned that even the most aggressive were hoping for a 15 to 20 percent annual return. Many were happy with a 10 percent annual return. "If you want to start with $1,000 and become wealthy," says Bob Dunwoody, president of Van Dusen & Co. in Denver, "then you will have to approach investing either assuming enormous risk or having enormous patience."

Remember, risk rules the potential of almost every investment you'll make. If you want absolute safety, be ready to settle for the low-interest income of government bonds or insured bank accounts. If you insist on stocks with the potential to double the first year, be prepared to take the failures with the successes. "Everyone is willing to accept risk for a greater reward," says Waterbury. "The problem is too often they're assuming the greater reward without the real presence of risk."

"A perfect client for me," adds Dain Bosworth's Kopp, "is a person who understands the risk of business, who understands that not all businesses are successful, who understands that brokers can make mistakes, that we cannot always predict tomorrow. They also have to be able to look out over a two- or three-year time horizon rather than to pick up the paper tomorrow or next week and wonder why their broker's idea hasn't worked out yet. My clients have to have a certain amount of patience."

Dunwoody offers this perspective: "If you double a thousand dollars ten times, you are a millionaire. And if stockbrokers were really able to do that, they would not be stockbrokers, they would all be multimillionaires. So the first issue is, let's get everybody's expectations on a reasonable plane—both the broker's and the client's."

- Rule 5: Share any relevant news about your company or your industry with your broker. Think of your broker not only as a source of information for you but also as a grateful recipient of information from you. We're not talking here about insider information—in fact, there's a good chance your broker would rather not hear it. Says PaineWebber's Basil: "If a client calls me with what he thinks is inside information, I tell him I don't even want to know about it. He can give me a buy or sell order, and I'll mark it 'Unsolicited.' I tell him, 'You can do what you want, but *you* have to answer the questions—not me.'"

While brokers should not welcome insider information, the chances are that they'll greet other types of information with open arms. For instance, if your company has just introduced a product that's blowing off the shelves faster than you can produce it, your broker would probably like to hear about it. If you're in the printing business and you're doing an increasing volume of business for a small over-the-counter company, mention that to your broker. If you're a car dealer and you find yourself with a disturbing backlog of inventory, your broker would probably appreciate knowing about that. Many brokers say that they get some of their best ideas from clients. The information you provide—coupled with similar bits of information that your broker collects from other clients—will help your broker stay a step ahead of the market. And it could also make you a treasured client.

- Rule 6: Say thank-you. This should be obvious, and to many investors it is. Brokers who have been in the business awhile universally acknowledge that they get a lot of postcards, Christmas cards and thank-you notes from appreciative clients. But some clients never utter a word of thanks—even after watching their portfolio double in a matter of years. So show some gratitude. Brokers, like everyone else, love the sound of praise.
- Rule 7: Provide referrals for your broker. It's no secret that brokers hate cold calling. From almost their first day in the business, new brokers look forward to the time when they can put their power dialing behind them and acquire new clients exclusively through referrals. By their third or fourth year in the business, brokers are usually able to get most of their new clients through referrals. "That's probably the best way to say thank-you—through referrals and through more money coming into the account," says David Thompson of Prudential-Bache. "Rather than hearing a client say, 'Gee, David, you did a hell of a job,' it gratifies me much more to see another $50,000 check coming in. I have one client who has referred his mother, brother, stepfather, previous boss, current boss and two current coworkers to me. That's the type of compliment I like best."

If you think your broker would do a good job for a friend who's shopping for a broker, try to get the two together. You could either have your broker call the friend (with the friend's prior consent), or you could make the grand gesture and invite them both to lunch or an early breakfast in order to introduce them. "Referrals are my lifeblood," says Jim Vieburg of Piper Jaffray. "I had one client, an accountant, who referred me to a businessman who bought $5 million of a mutual fund from me. Now the businessman has referred me to his

---

**Seven Rules for Becoming
One of Your Broker's Favorite Clients**

1. Be honest.
2. Return calls promptly.
3. Follow your broker's advice.
4. Set realistic expectations.
5. Share relevant news.
6. Say thank-you.
7. Provide referrals.

---

son, who inherited a large portfolio of stocks from his grandfather." If you like your broker, spread the word.

THINGS TO AVOID

Just as there are ways to earn your broker's respect, there are also ways to lose it. Brokers all have pet peeves. If you want to be one of your broker's favorite clients, you need to be aware of the things that brokers hate most.

• The squeaky wheel does *not* necessarily get the grease. Brokers are nearly unanimous in their disdain for what they customarily refer to as "the whiners."

"One woman who came in to open an account with me started complaining about her former broker," recalls PaineWebber's Blount. "She said, 'I threatened to shoot that guy.' I told her in a very tactful way that I was not interested in doing business with her."

Adds Grubb of Shearson Lehman: "I don't like people who call me every time the market goes down. I tell them from square one, 'I cannot control the volatility of the market. It's going to go up, and it's going to go down, and if I'm doing my job right, the stocks we have positions in will go up more than they go down.'"

Tom Hudson, branch manager of PaineWebber's Jacksonville, Florida, office, says that clients who continually overreact to issues outside their broker's control risk being fired by their broker. "If you give me grief and mess up my mind to the point that I cannot deal effectively with the next person I talk with, I can't really afford that. Furthermore, it's not fair to me. I can only control certain things. I cannot control what the chairman of the Federal Reserve says in a speech, and I cannot control whether the Iraq air force attacks the USS *Stark* in the Persian Gulf."

If you want your broker to do a good job for you, give him or her the benefit of the doubt and don't call every time the market weakens.

This is not to say that you should never call your broker out of concern for your position; just don't make a habit of it.

- Don't hook your broker into taking responsibility for your ideas. Typical example: A client calls his broker and says he's thinking of investing in XYZ Corporation and wonders what the broker thinks. What the client, in essence, is trying to do is to get the broker to ratify his idea and thus take some of the responsibility for it. This is a no-win situation for the broker. In such a situation, brokers will often say that they have no information upon which to base a recommendation, and will offer to take the order as unsolicited—a condition some clients are reluctant to accept. So the clients may pass up investing in the stock, perhaps to watch it rise steadily in value. If that happens, clients may later say something to this effect to their brokers: "XYZ Corporation has really been climbing. It's too bad we didn't get into it"—implying that the brokers are at least partly to blame for the decision not to buy the stock. On the other hand, if brokers offer even the softest endorsement (they might say, "From what little I know about XYZ Corporation, I think it may have some potential"), clients may go ahead and buy the stock, then blame the brokers if it doesn't perform. That's not fair to the brokers, and they will resent any implications to that effect. Don't hold your broker responsible for your ideas.

- Don't make a habit of second-guessing your broker. Expecting your broker to be on the money with every recommendation is expecting the impossible. Your broker is absolutely committed to making money for you. Brokers make their living helping clients make money. The more they make, the more the clients have to invest with them and the more likely clients will refer friends to them.

In fact, the urge to do well for clients goes well beyond mere economics for most brokers. Helping clients succeed in the markets is what gives brokers their greatest sense of professional satisfaction. It's like a surgeon saving lives, a lawyer getting a client out of a tough jam, a reporter breaking a big story. "I have a lot of millionaires among my clients," says PaineWebber's Blount, "and the beautiful thing about it is that I made them millionaires."

When brokers put clients into investments that don't work out, they often take it harder than the clients. "I'm my own worst critic," says Dain Bosworth's Kopp. "I try to be right all the time, and obviously nobody can be right all the time. I get so down on myself, I feel worse than anyone. So when someone says, 'Hey, so it didn't work out,' that makes me feel terrific. That's a person who understands the risks in this business and understands the fact that we can't be right all the time."

Kathy Soule of Merrill Lynch says that she always took her clients' losses so hard that her manager finally had to remind her, "You don't take their profits home with you, so don't take their losses home either."

Don't belabor the failures. The best policy—if you want to be one of your broker's favorite clients—is simply to offer the broker a word of encouragement and move on to the next investment. "What I appreciate," says Prudential's Koriath, "is a client who's maybe had a couple of croppers and still thanks me for calling, and then he gives me another order. He understands that no one is perfect, and he knows you're doing the best job you can."

- Never, never use a discount broker to buy or sell stocks recommended by your broker. That is the cardinal sin of the investment business—the lowest, most vulgar professional discourtesy you can ever direct at your broker. "I'll never forget the guy who bought a utility stock from me, made money on it, then sold it through a discounter," says Paine-Webber's Basil. Most brokers will automatically dump you as a client—no questions asked and no apologies accepted—if they find out that you've been using their recommendations to buy stocks from a discounter.

One broker talks about the time he recommended that a client buy stock in Sanders Associates. "He bought a couple of hundred shares through me, and then the next day I see a check cut out of his account for a substantial sum. The man was indiscreet enough to have the check made out to another brokerage house—a discount firm. So I called him and said, 'Hey, I'd like to apologize for not serving you better.' He said, 'What do you mean?' 'Well,' I told him, 'anytime a check goes out of the account, it has to meet my approval.' There was dead silence on the phone. I continued, 'I just wondered what I did to make you take your money out.' He said, 'Oh, no reason. I just liked your idea and couldn't reach you, so I bought it through this other broker.' Well, when we later sold his stock, I sent all the money out, enclosing a note telling him, 'I work for a living, and I am hereby closing the account. I am not here to do my job for free.' "

It's OK to use a discounter to buy (and sell) securities that you've selected independently of your broker's advice. But your broker's company goes to considerable expense to research the market and come up with investment recommendations. If you're using that service, then you have a moral obligation to pay for it. You expect your broker to deal with you in an ethical manner. Return the courtesy.

"Sometimes if a broker has a guy who wants to deal with a discounter," says Joe Baxter, Smith Barney training director, "he'll offer the client a discount on all the trade ideas the client comes up with on his own, but the broker will charge full price on all the stock ideas he recommends to the client."

- Don't ask your broker to do research on your ideas. Several thousand publicly traded stocks are sold on the various exchanges, plus thousands of bonds, mutual funds and other investment products. Most brokers—in fact, most firms—limit their realm of expertise to a relatively small number of those investments. Although it is true that most brokers have access to a wide array of research information, considerable effort is often needed to track down information on investments that their firms do not actively follow.

In certain instances, however, you can expect research assistance from your broker. If one company in particular catches your eye—maybe you saw an article about it, maybe you have friends who work there, maybe it's your own company, or maybe it's a company you've heard some rumors about—it would be appropriate to ask your broker: "Does your firm follow this stock?" If the answer is yes, ask your broker what his or her firm thinks of it. The broker may either give you an immediate answer or offer to send you a research report on the company. You might also ask whether the stock is on the firm's buy or sell list. But you should keep such requests to a minimum, especially if you're not an active trader. "I would have people who did almost no business with me," recalls one former broker, "and they were always asking me 'look up this' and 'look up that.' If you try hard enough, you can find something out about anything, but sometimes it takes an awful lot of digging and an awful lot of time."

You can also expect research assistance from your broker if you already have some investments when you first begin doing business with the broker. If you've just moved in from another city, for instance, and you open an account with a new broker, he or she should be willing to look over your portfolio and offer recommendations on which investments to keep and which to sell. Your broker will probably have no recommendation on some investments in your portfolio because his or her research department doesn't follow them. The broker might tell you, "If you want to hold onto this stock, you're certainly welcome to. But if you want to own investments I can give you advice on, I recommend that you sell it. I'm not saying it's a bad stock. I'm just saying I can't be of service to you on this stock."

It's important to understand that brokers do not see their role as that of answering an infinite number of questions that clients have about the market. As brokers see it, the clients' role is to tell the broker how they want to make their money—growth stocks, blue chips, speculative investments, income-oriented investments—and the broker's role is to find the investments that will work best. "Once I understand your tolerance for risk and your expectation for reward, it's my job to figure out what investment is going to do that for you," says Dain Bosworth's Buckley. Generally, the more experienced the broker, the more adamant the broker will be about his or her role in the relationship. As Dean Witter's Waterbury puts it, "My clients will adopt my way of investing, or else they'll find someone else who can do what they want to do." Adds Blount: "If you come to me, I'll tell you I don't have time to do much hand-holding. I'll tell you the philosophies I work by, and if you agree with that, then maybe we'll do business."

• Don't pester your broker for quotes every day. This is a very

---

Things to Avoid

1. Don't whine.
2. Don't hook your broker into taking responsibility for your ideas.
3. Don't second-guess your broker.
4. Don't execute your broker's recommendations through a discount broker.
5. Don't continually expect research on your ideas.
6. Don't continually call your broker for quotes.

---

common—and universally disliked—annoyance for brokers. "One of the biggest hassles in this business is giving quotes," says Hutton's Tidlund. "It just galls me." Why such a strong reaction to such a seemingly innocuous request? Again, the answer is time—and in this case a very senseless waste of time.

If you're a long-term investor (you buy stocks and expect to hold them for one or two years), what your stocks are trading at in the middle of the day is absolutely irrelevant. You can follow your stocks in the paper every morning or every weekend and rest assured that their prices will not vary much during the day. "You don't call your real estate agent each day to see how the price of your house is doing," says Tom Asher of Robinson-Humphrey. "Why call your broker to find out how your stocks are doing?"

If you're an active trader and you're interested in getting quotes, ask your broker what quote requests would be reasonable. But remember that your broker is presumably following your stocks for you. If the broker is recommending that you hold a stock to $39^1/_2$, he or she will call you when the stock gets up there and let you know it's time to sell. On the other hand, if you want to make the timing decision yourself, you can put in a buy or sell limit order at a specified price and the broker will execute it for you. If you feel that you absolutely must call to get midday quotes, ask your broker's sales assistant to get them for you. But don't tie up your broker's time with quote requests.

Your success in the stock market will be governed to a great extent by your ability to establish a successful working relationship with your broker, and you are every bit as important to the success of that relationship as your broker. Your attitudes, your behavior and your willingness to take the losses with the gains will play a key role in your broker's ability to make you money.

However, we don't mean to imply that you should give your broker license to ignore you, to consistently put you into bad investments, to pressure you into buying investments you don't want. After all, it's your money. There's a time for leniency and a time for assertiveness, as the next two chapters explain.

CHAPTER EIGHT _____

The Unscrupulous Broker

In the summer of 1985, a distraught 41-year-old plumbing services worker stepped into his garage, started his car and dozed off to a peaceful death. The authorities said that carbon monoxide poisoning did him in, but in his suicide note the victim claimed that his stockbroker drove him to it.

Those familiar with the case say the man had remortgaged his house, pulled together his life savings and gambled it all on the stock of a small specialty company. His broker, a friend of the company president, had apparently assured him that a pending buy-out offer by a large conglomerate would cause the price of the stock to soar. Alas, the buy-out never materialized and the stock plunged to about a third of its original price. The man's loss came to about $55,000—roughly twice his annual salary. The prospect of rebuilding his life savings from scratch was apparently too much for him to bear.

In Florida, a 61-year-old multimillionaire turned over his investments to his 21-year-old grandnephew, who had just taken a job with one of the nation's largest brokerage firms. According to investigators, in the next two years the grandnephew made thousands of trades in his granduncle's account, collecting nearly $5 million in commissions. In the early stages of the relationship, the grandnephew managed to win his granduncle's trust by turning some profitable trades. But before long, the young broker's inexperience began to catch up with him and the trades started going the other way. When he tried to recoup the losses, matters only seemed to get worse. To hide his failings, he intercepted the regular account statements intended for his granduncle and mailed out falsified statements in their place. When investigators broke the case open, the granduncle was mystified to learn that he had "only" $8 million left in his account. The final statement he had received—presumably falsified by the broker—showed an account balance of $55 million less a $19 million margin debt.

A Midwestern couple sold an interest in a real estate investment to raise $45,000 that they would need the following year to pay off a bank note secured by a second mortgage on their home. But before the note came due, they wanted to put their $45,000 to work in an investment that would provide short-term earnings. Their broker recommended that they open a margin account and put all of their money into a small speculative stock called AML. (A margin account enables the investor to, in essence, buy stock and then use that stock as collateral to buy more stock.) By buying on margin, the couple acquired $89,000 in AML stock with their $45,000 investment. Unfortunately, AML began dropping shortly after they bought it and the margin maintenance calls began to mount. Over the next few months, the couple had to kick in another $9,111 to cover the losses from the falling stock. Finally, with their reserves depleted from margin calls, the couple ordered the broker to sell out their position. By then, the value of their stock had fallen by $40,000 and they received a mere $4,953 from its sale. In all, during a seven-month span the couple lost more than $9,000 from margin calls and $40,000 from direct losses on their stock, which comes to a grand total of $49,000 in losses on a $45,000 investment.

Woody Allen defines a stockbroker as someone who invests other people's money until it's all gone. The consumer affairs office of the Securities and Exchange Commission reports that each year it receives more that 15,000 complaints from consumers who feel that they've been victimized by their brokers. The fact is that no matter where you live, no matter what securities firm you do business with, there's always the risk that you will lose your money due to the incompetent or unscrupulous practices of your broker.

Fortunately, that risk is far smaller than you might expect. The vast majority of brokers are honest, reputable and competent professionals who go through their entire careers without a serious investor complaint. The chances that your broker will ever maliciously defraud you—skim money from your account, sell you counterfeit bonds or put you into bogus partnerships—are very, very slim. Most brokerage firms go to great pains to encourage their brokers to deal with clients honestly. "We spend a substantial block of time training new brokers in compliance matters," says John Sundeen, compliance director with Robert W. Baird & Co. "We give them a series of situations in which we show them why they should do things right instead of just sliding through. Then we give them a test at the end as a form of review to reinforce their understanding." Breaking the rules is a prescription for disaster for brokers—and for brokerage firms. Those who cross the line rarely last long in the business. The brokers who ultimately succeed are those who play by the rules and handle every account in an honest, straightforward manner.

THE MIND-SET OF A STOCKBROKER

Securities firms have developed some very sophisticated tests to screen applicants and to single out the best possible broker candidates. Through psychological tests, assessment exercises, interviews and reference checks, they attempt to identify candidates who score high on the scale for initiative and aggressiveness. Securities firms have learned that the type of individual who sits quietly by and waits for instructions rarely succeeds in the high-pressure, highly competitive securities environment.

But as Dr. Robert Lefton of Psychological Associates in St. Louis points out, "Whenever you hire highly ambitious, highly energetic people, a certain percentage of them are also going to be people who like to take unusual risks. That's why it's important to make sure they have a sound basic character underneath." Most brokers are able to toe the line of legality, but a small percentage let their aggressiveness get the better of them. Although their intentions may be honorable, they feel that they know what's best for their clients, and if that means bending the rules a bit, so be it. Perrin Long, an analyst with Lipper Analytical Services, who has been observing the securities industry for almost 30 years, estimates that 99 percent of all brokers are honest. "But bear in mind," cautions Long, "that all of us are dishonest to a degree."

While you're not likely to ever be maliciously defrauded by a broker, you could fall prey to a broker's overzealousness on a given investment. With the very best of intentions, a broker might offer you unsuitable recommendations, make exaggerated claims on a certain stock or even make trades in your account without your prior authorization—all of which are violations of U.S. securities regulations.

In most cases, it's possible to get some financial relief from your brokerage firm if you've been ripped off, if you act promptly and if the brokerage firm is still around to collect from. The plumbing services worker who committed suicide, for example, may have died needlessly. If he had pressed his case, he would probably have been able to collect most of the $55,000 he lost—minus some high legal fees. On the other hand, if you're dealing with a small securities firm that goes out of business after losing all your money, there's a good chance that you'll never see the money again. Even under the best of circumstances, reaching a settlement with a securities firm often requires a lengthy and expensive court battle. That's why it's in your best interest to keep a sharp eye on your account and to insist that your broker chart a prudent, diversified and scrupulous investment course—which, obviously, is far easier said than done.

CROSSING THE LINE

Scrupulous: having moral integrity: acting in strict regard for what is considered right or proper (*Webster's Ninth New Collegiate Dictionary*)

If you want to be assured of long-term success in the investment market, then you want a broker who is scrupulous. "If I felt I couldn't trust the person," says Donnis Casey, assistant training director for A. G. Edwards, "I wouldn't do business with him. I wouldn't do business with a broker I was intimidated by, and I wouldn't do business with a broker who was vulgar. I would only do business with a broker I felt very comfortable with, who could be a friend."

The problem is that our impressions can sometimes be fatally inaccurate. There was a broker in Iowa—a young, attractive son of a banker— who exuded sincerity. "If you saw him, if you talked to him, you'd swear he had a Bible in his hand," says a former acquaintance. "He looked like a preacher. He sounded like a preacher. This guy was incredible." Yet before this broker's spree of securities violations was finally brought to a halt, he had defrauded hundreds of investors and had helped put his own father's bank out of business.

It all started when, through an inept options trade in the margin account of one of his clients, the broker lost several thousand dollars of the client's money. To cover the loss, the broker sold some of the client's bonds, a move that the client objected to strongly. So the broker promised that he would buy back the bonds. Instead, he simply printed up false confirmations of the sale and sent those to the client. To cover up his scam, he intercepted the client's monthly statements and wrote out checks from his own account to cover the client's quarterly interest payment.

At the same time, the broker was handling the account of an orphanage in North Carolina. In six months, he lost a quarter of a million dollars for that orphanage due to unsuitable speculative positions. After those improprieties were discovered, he lost his job at the brokerage firm—but he held onto his securities license. A few months later he opened his own brokerage firm, and there he began a new chapter in compliance violations. As he began to build his business and bring in new clients, he decided to use their assets to corner the market in the stock of a small Pennsylvania auto parts company. He reasoned that by controlling the market for the stock, he could slowly drive up its price, earning large profits for himself and his clients.

Unbeknownst to his clients, he opened margin accounts in their names at two or more brokerage firms and pushed their accounts to the limit. He also invested much of the assets of his father's bank in the stock—a strategy that later would put the bank out of business. At one point, he controlled several hundred thousand shares of the stock, but even that was not enough. What he didn't realize was that about half of the stock of the auto parts company was held by key persons in the company. Every time he drove the price of the stock up a dollar, those key shareholders would sell off more of their shares and send the price back down. Finally, SEC investigators discovered his ploy and stepped in to shut him down. He then stole what was left of his firm's money and disappeared. A couple of weeks later, he turned himself in to the authorities. He was convicted and served a few months in prison. The final tally on his career: falsification of securities documents, unsuitable recommendations, exaggerated and fraudulent claims, market manipulation, unauthorized trades, misappropriation of funds and theft of client funds.

Of the 15,706 investor complaints filed by brokerage firm clients with the SEC in 1986, the greatest number fell into these six categories: failure to deliver stocks or funds (1,492 complaints); delays in transferring accounts (1,409 complaints); problems in execution of investment orders (1,370 complaints); high-pressure sales tactics, churning and fraudulent statements made by the account representative (1,319); mishandling of accounts—books and records problems (1,025 complaints), and problems in delivery of funds—getting the money for investments that an investor has sold through the broker (1,016 complaints).

The category of greatest concern for investors is "high-pressure sales tactics." You should be aware there are several common securities violations that are classified within that category: making misleading, exaggerated or fraudulent statements to induce a client to buy a certain investment; making unsuitable recommendations; churning (excessive trading in a client's account) and making unauthorized trades. Two other problem areas—unsuitable options and commodities trades and misappropriation of funds—are also worth noting.

Misrepresentation

In one respect, stockbrokers play the same role as car dealers, vacuum cleaner salespeople and aluminum siding vendors. They earn their living by inducing you to buy (or sell) something. In most cases, they sincerely believe that you should buy what they're recommending. But in their enthusiasm, they can be tempted to exaggerate. For instance, when your broker should be saying something to this effect: "Based on this company's earnings growth, our research department believes that the selling price of its stock could double in the next year," the overzealous broker might say, "I guarantee that you'll double you money on this stock in the next year." If your broker ever "guarantees" the future performance of a given stock (or stock mutual fund), he is in violation of securities laws. The fact is that a company's earnings may double or even triple in a given year, but if the overall stock market takes a nosedive, the selling price of that company's stock could actually decline.

Another common method that brokers use to induce clients to buy a stock is by saying something to this effect: "I have it on good authority that when this company's next earnings report is released, the price of its stock is going to double." The fact is that brokers in most cases really don't have this on good authority, and even if they did, they'd probably be violating insider information laws by telling you so. Would you have a strong case against your broker if you invested in the stock and it went down? Probably not, unless the broker's claims were blatantly fraudulent. This is a very gray area of the law, and it would be difficult to prove that the broker was in violation.

"A successful broker is often going to appeal to an investor's greed," says Jack McTaggart, a former broker and compliance officer who is now with Longman Financial Services Institute. 'I'm going to show you how to get rich,' they'll say. 'If you don't do this, you ain't going to get rich.' I've heard brokers say this right over the phone."

The best way to react when a broker seems to be overselling a stock by making exaggerated claims is to say, "Look, I appreciate your enthusiasm for this stock, but you and I both know you're in no position to personally guarantee its success. So what I would like you to do in the future is to give me solid recommendations based on your research department's information, based on facts and based on reasonable projections."

Unsuitable Recommendations

A 75-year-old upstate New York widow opened an account with a new broker and allocated most of her life savings—$115,000 in all—to that account. Since most of her income was derived from her investments, a logical course would have been to buy conservative, income-oriented investments. Instead, her broker recommended options and speculative stocks purchased on margin and worked her account like an active trader. In a single year, he effected more than 130 transactions, generating more than $25,000 in commissions. The woman finally turned to the authorities when she got a margin call for $80,000—which represented more than 75 percent of her life savings at the time—for a speculative gold mining stock that the broker had recommended. The broker was charged with unsuitable recommendations and excessive trading. He was fined $10,000 and suspended from serving as an NASD representative for six months.

Securities law stresses that recommendations must be suitable for investors in light of their investment objectives, their capital, their age, their income and their experience. Brokers sometimes tend to be more aggressive in investing than their clients. They see their job as helping their clients get rich, which—strange as it may sound—is not always in the clients' best interest. The clients may already be rich, and their objective may be to stay rich and not become poor. They may be perfectly at ease investing in low-yielding U.S. Treasury bonds, and their brokers should respect that.

But the responsibility of brokers goes beyond merely following the wishes of their conservative clients. They must also temper the aggressive tendencies of those clients who want to buy speculative stocks when their circumstances call for a more prudent portfolio. If a 75-year-old widow instructed her broker to put her life savings in a speculative stock, the broker could be held at fault for following her orders. Placing a small portion of her money in speculative stocks might be OK, but most of her money should be placed in safe, long-term investments.

While the brokers may be legally responsible for their clients' investments, the clients must also bear some of the responsibility. "Most of the problems in a broker-client relationship occur because the client is intimidated, or doesn't demand to understand what's being presented to him, or doesn't want to take the time to review the information that's being presented by the broker," says Advest's Judy Johnson. "You've got to remember, it's your money. Nobody is going to care about it and watch it as much as you do."

"During one particularly bad time in the market," relates a broker, "I had investors calling me saying, 'How could you do this to me? You just lost all the money for my daughters' education.' The fact is, they should never have given me that money. You should never invest any more money in a speculative stock than you can afford to lose."

As a client, if you suspect that your broker has put you in an unsuitable investment, you should act quickly to resolve the problem. "Timeliness is very important," says Johnson. "If a client comes to me six or eight months later, after his $2 stock has dropped to a dollar (the client had received confirmation of the trade and statements of the trade showing this position in his account), and now he says he doesn't want the stock, I'm not so inclined to believe the person. Maybe if the stock had gone to $6, he wouldn't be here."

What's the best way to handle a broker who offers you unsuitable recommendations? Simply remind the broker of your investment objectives and ask the broker not to recommend any more investments that don't conform to those objectives. If that doesn't work, then you should find a new broker. After all, no matter how much you earn, if it's safety you want with your investments, you shouldn't have to keep fending off the speculative recommendations of an overly aggressive broker.

Churning

"Churning," as the colorful term would imply, refers to rotating the securities in an account at a high velocity. The greater the velocity (the faster securities are bought and sold), the greater the commissions that the account generates.

What, specifically, constitutes churning? How much velocity is too much? That depends on the investment objectives of the client. Some investors buy securities and never sell them, or at least hold them for a number of years. Other investors, commonly referred to as traders, may buy and sell a stock within a period of days or even hours.

As a general rule, however, brokers are expected to abide by a 300 percent guideline. If you start out a year with $100,000 and you end the year with $100,000 and if your investment trades totaled 300 percent of

---

The Most Common Broker Violations

- Misrepresentation (making misleading or fraudulent statements)
- Unsuitability (putting clients in unsuitable investments)
- Churning (excessive buying and selling of the securities in a customer account)
- Unauthorized trades
- Unsuitable options and commodities trading
- Misappropriation of funds

---

that, or $300,000, no charges of churning could be made. You would fall within the 300 percent guideline if in the same year you invested $100,000 in IBM stock and sold that, bought $100,000 in General Motors stock and sold that and bought $100,000 in Pillsbury stock. Any more than that could make your broker vulnerable to charges of churning. Most investors turn over their portfolios far less than 300% per year.

But like misrepresentations and unsuitable recommendations, churning is ensconced in a gray area of the law. Churning, after all, is not something that is done overnight. Clients whose accounts are being churned may be perfectly happy with their brokers as long as they're making money. After allowing their brokers to make excessive trades for a period of months or years, such clients would have a tough time holding their brokers accountable if they started losing money on those trades. Once again, the best response to churning is to nip it in the bud. Tell your broker, "Look, I'm a long-term investor. I don't have the resources, the time or the inclination to be an active trader. So please don't call me and encourage me to buy and sell these securities. I want to buy good long-term stocks, and unless we decide otherwise, I want to hold onto them for the long term."

Unauthorized Trades

One broker talks about a telephone conversation he overheard between another broker and one of that broker's clients. "He had been trying to convince one of his customers to buy a certain stock, and the customer just couldn't seem to make up his mind. All of a sudden, I hear this broker say, 'What? I can't hear you. I don't know if you can hear me, but I'll put your order in for that 10,000 shares. Sorry, I can't make out what you're saying. I'm going to put that order in for 10,000 shares.' Then he hung up the phone and looked at me with a sly grin and said, 'Sometimes these people need a little motivation.' "

Although the client probably never complained, the broker had just violated a key securities law—which prohibits unauthorized trades. An unauthorized trade occurs anytime a broker buys or sells a security in a client's account without the client's prior approval.

Unauthorized trades can take place in several ways. Before leaving on an extended vacation, for example, a client might tell her broker to buy something for her if it looks attractive. In most cases, such transactions will proceed without a hitch. But if the investor comes home to find that the new stock has dropped ten points, she could complain, with some basis in fact, that the broker bought it without her prior approval. What experienced brokers do to avoid such problems is to discuss specific stocks with clients beforehand. The broker might say, for instance, "XYZ Corporation could be in the buying range if it drops one more point. If it drops to $19^1/_2$, I'll buy 300 shares for you." The client's agreement to that constitutes prior authorization.

What you as a client should be most concerned about is a broker who buys or sells stock first and tells you about it afterward. "Nothing should happen in your account that you haven't approved," says Lee Kopp of Dain Bosworth. Even if your broker has a very plausible reason for making the transaction (the stock was dropping, the broker tried to reach you but couldn't, and the broker wanted to sell out your position before the stock dropped any further), you should still not tolerate unauthorized trading. Complain to your broker immediately. You might say, "I just want to remind you that it's my money, that you are my agent and that you carry out my instructions. I make the decisions. If you're concerned about the stock dropping in value in the future, I would be more than happy to give you a limit order instructing you to sell it if it drops to a certain level, but I don't want to lose control of my account."

If you wish, you can grant your broker the authority to make your investment buying and selling decisions for you by signing a discretionary power authorization. But that sharply changes the broker's role. Rather than serving as an agent who carries out your decisions, the broker becomes a money manager with full control over your account. Even in a discretionary account, however, the broker must still buy investments that are consistent with your stated objectives and is still liable for churning violations and unsuitable trades. Because of these liabilities, most brokerage firms and most brokers avoid discretionary accounts. And you should too. If you want someone else to manage your investments, buy a mutual fund or hire a money manager. It's the rare broker who can serve simultaneously as both your commissioned sales agent and your discretionary money manager.

Options and Commodities Violations

A growing number of investor complaints have involved options and commodities. Both options and commodities are complex and difficult to understand, and both can make the investor liable for losses in excess of his or her original investment. "Probably one of the largest compliance problems—which you don't hear about at all—involves the sale of options," says Long of Lipper Analytical.

Options are securities that give the buyer the right to buy or sell a quantity of stock at a specified price within a specific period of time (see "Options Trading" section in Chapter 13). For most investors in options, options activity starts in a conservative fashion, with the broker writing "covered call options" (option contracts backed by the shares underlying the options). Covered options involve relatively little risk and can often provide additional income for the investor.

Problems arise, however, because some brokers move on to riskier strategies with inexperienced investors. Some options can result in a loss of 100 percent of the investment. Others, "naked calls" (which are not backed by securities), can result in losses in excess of the original investment.

In one case, a broker began writing covered calls for a client against stocks that she held in her portfolio. The early trades worked out well, so the broker gradually moved to a more aggressive options strategy. At one point, he wrote 60 put options on a stock. When that stock dropped in value, the client was obliged under the terms of her option contracts to buy 6,000 shares of the stock—which put her deeply in debt. To make matters worse, the stock quickly declined by $6 a share, strapping her with an immediate $36,000 loss.

Brokerage firms take extra precautions to minimize the risks of investing in options. They require that each investor receive a document disclosing those risks and that he or she sign a specific options agreement. They also try to ascertain what kinds of options strategies are suitable for the investor, given that investor's financial resources, investment objectives and financial sophistication.

Despite these precautions, many problems continue to exist. Most investors do not read or do not understand the risk disclosure booklet. "The main problem," says Long "is that brokers can convince customers— let's say widows and orphans—that they should protect their investments by buying a put on an underlying equity. It's not that the broker is doing it without the approval of the customer. It's just that the customer doesn't understand the puts and calls and the straddles and other aspects relative to options."

Most brokerage firms find that although options trades account for only a small part of their business, those trades account for a relatively high percentage of their complaints and legal problems. "If individuals complain about options transactions, the firm will often settle immediately with no litigation," says Long. According to the SEC, relatively few options complaints go beyond the brokerage firm. In 1986, the SEC received fewer than 300 complaints from investors regarding options trad-

---

Protecting Yourself in Options Trading

1. Read the options disclosure statement carefully, and ask your broker to clarify points you don't understand.

2. Discuss in advance exactly what kinds of options strategies you will engage in. Have your broker describe the maximum gain and maximum loss of these strategies.

3. Write a letter to your broker summarizing your verbal agreement, and save a copy of the letter. Stipulate, for example, "As we agreed in our meeting on July 6, consistent with my investment objectives of safety and income, the only options strategy that we will employ in my account is covered call writing."

4. When you begin making options transactions, ask your broker to outline the maximum profit and maximum loss potential in each trade. Write down exactly what the broker says.

---

ing. "In many cases," says Long, "the brokerage firm will cancel the contracts and refund the money, and the company or the salesman will take the loss—if there is a loss." Just the same, there's no guarantee that settlements will come that easily, so investors should be particularly cautious when engaging in options trading.

Misappropriation

According to Long, misappropriation—which occurs when a broker juggles funds in your account or takes money out of your account—is one of the most serious legal problems involving securities transactions. "There are several types of misappropriation—a broker may move funds backwards and forwards in a customer's account, for example," says Long. "Or a broker goes to the cashier and says, 'Let me check on so-and-so's account. Let me have the statement (or the check), and I'll mail it out.' Well, that doesn't always happen."

It's often difficult to detect when a broker is tampering with your account even when you know what to look for. The NASD reported one case where a broker interposed his wife's account between his clients and the market. When a client placed an order, the broker would fill it by selling shares short in his wife's account and then buying those shares for the client. After completing the transaction, he would routinely purchase more shares for his wife's account to cover her short position—always at a price lower than the price he had charged the client. As SEC investigators pointed out, the broker was making a double profit on each transaction—a profit on the stock for his wife and a commission from the client for himself.

Increasing Abuse

Whether the violation is churning, misrepresentation, unauthorized trades or unsuitable recommendations, serious problems generally emerge, not as the result of a single, spontaneous act, but rather as the result of a process, a series of ongoing actions. And usually there is a pattern of increasing abuse. A typical broker who engages in unauthorized trading, for instance, will probably do so on a small scale at first to see what happens. The solution, as we've stressed, is to respond clearly and firmly the first time this is done. In almost every instance, your broker will comply with your wishes, because good brokers recognize the importance of avoiding sticky legal issues. As Tom Asher of Robinson-Humphrey puts it, "This is such an exciting, lucrative business, why would anybody want to jeopardize their career?"

What should you do if your broker ignores your warnings? If the problem is unsuitable recommendations (that is, your broker continues to recommend investments that don't meet your objectives even after you've complained), you should find another broker. But if the problem is unauthorized trades and it occurs a second time, you should not only fire your broker; you should also go to the company's compliance officer and cite the facts: "This is the second time this has happened. The stock was bought in my account on this date, and I want to rescind that trade." By acting quickly, you should be able to avoid any further problems.

The Other Side

Two can play the game of deceit. Although the abuses of brokers seem to get most of the ink in the media, clients can also be unscrupulous. Despite the enormous amount of money that changes hands, investing is a business that's conducted primarily on an oral basis. "In real estate," says Advest's Johnson, "if it isn't written down, it never happened. But brokers conduct their business by word of mouth. Every day brokers conduct billions of dollars of business on mutual trust sealed with nothing more than a verbal agreement."

Sometimes that can cause major problems for brokers who are preyed upon by dishonest investors. An investor, for instance, might place an order for a large block of a volatile stock and then wait to see whether the stock moves up or down. When payment for the stock is due (a week after the order has been placed), if the stock has dropped in value, the investor might deny having ordered it.

Jim Vieburg of Piper Jaffray relates an incident from his early days in the business. "I was the broker of the day, and this well-dressed lady came into the office. She probably sensed that I was a rookie. She started talking to me about Control Data, which was then a real mover. She said she was thinking of buying some and wondered if I thought it would keep going up. I told her I thought it would. She said, 'Why don't you buy me a thousand shares?'

"I told her that our firm had a policy that I had to have a $2,000 deposit before I could accept such as order. She said she had never heard of such a thing. I insisted it was firm policy. (Actually it wasn't, but I wanted to protect myself. She seemed too smooth.)

"The next day she returned and peeled off twenty $100 bills and said, 'There. Buy it.' So I opened an account for her, deposited the $2,000 and entered the order to buy 1,000 shares of Control Data at the market.

"The next week when her payment was due, the stock was down a point. When I called her about the payment, she said, 'Oh, Mr. Vieburg, that stock is too risky for me. I don't think I should be in that stock.'

"I told her, 'You gave me an order to buy 1,000 shares of Control Data stock at the market, and that is exactly what I did. If you no longer want to own it, I will enter a sell order, and whatever is left from the $2,000 deposit, we will mail to you.'

"I later found out that she was investigated by the IRS for income tax fraud. I wonder if she pulled this trick on a lot of young brokers in those days."

Vieburg continues, "It's a two-way street. Not only do customers have to worry about brokers, but brokers have to worry about customers. It's like playing poker. I play a lot of poker, and I have learned to pick out a thief or a cheat pretty quickly. Trust is the key—mutual trust. The client must trust you, and you must be able to trust the client."

D'Arcy Fox of A. G. Edwards shakes his head at the creative devices some investors employ to defraud their brokers. "One client made a photocopy of a $2,500 check we sent him, cut it out and somehow managed to cash both the original and the copy. I don't know how it ever got through the bank, but we had to sue him to get our money back."

In some cases, clients will encourage their brokers to trade in speculative stocks and then try to sue if the stocks don't work out. Or clients will tell their brokers that they want to be active traders and later sue the brokers for churning if the trades don't work out. "There are a lot of greedy people out there," says Bill Blount of PaineWebber. "That's why brokers need to very carefully scrutinize the people they do business with. Those opportunists who are out there looking for a fast buck—I don't want them as clients. It's those types of people who are the source of 90 percent of the problems in the brokerage business. You've got to weed those people out."

So if your broker seems hesitant to make sweeping recommendations on a stock, or cautions you against making too many trades, or refuses to buy stocks for you while you're on a fishing trip in Canada, the broker is probably looking out not only for your best interest but for his or her own best interest as well.

GETTING RELIEF

If you feel that you've been victimized by your broker, there's a process we recommend to help you get relief.

Step 1.   Talk to your broker. Tell your broker the problem. Perhaps your complaint is that you wanted safety and he or she put you in a margin account in a volatile stock. The result was that you lost most of your investment when the stock dropped. If you think a proper remedy would be a full refund of the money you lost, tell your broker that. In many cases (particularly where you have a strong argument and act quickly), your broker will find a way to offer you a satisfactory settlement. If that doesn't work, move on to Step 2.

Step 2.   Contact the branch manager. Write a letter stating your complaint and outlining exactly what happened. If you have any corroborative items (your statement, a listing of your investment objectives, etc.), enclose a photocopy of each item and put the original in a safe place. Then state the remedy you expect. If the stakes are high, you should consider having an attorney draft the letter for you. By using an attorney, you might avoid saying things in your letter that could later weaken your case and you might stand a better chance of catching the manager's attention. After mailing your letter, follow up with a phone call to the manager. "We would like to be advised of any problems a client might have," says Kopp, a branch manager at Dain Bosworth's Edina, Minnesota, office, "because the last thing we want is to have our reputation damaged by a broker in our office." Kopp says that, depending on the seriousness of the complaint, the broker could be put on notice or even dismissed. "I will not have that type of person working for me." He adds, "Your best line of defense is to contact the branch manager right away. Don't let it drag out if you as an investor have any doubts about the integrity of your broker. It's too easy to let it drag out and then have to go through the courts to get it settled." If the branch manager does not resolve your problem, move on to Step 3.

Step 3.   Phone the branch manager and ask for the name and address of the firm's chief compliance officer. Then send a similar letter to that person. Again, stipulate the remedy. If your relations with the branch manager have chilled, you might want to take another approach. Check your monthly statement to find the location and phone number of the firm's headquarters. Then call headquarters and ask for the name of the chief compliance officer. You may wish to send your letter to the chief compliance officer by certified mail in order to verify that he or she receives it.

Step 4.   If Step 3 doesn't work, you might consider filing a formal complaint with the SEC or either the New York Stock Exchange or the National Association of Securities Dealers—whichever self-regulating organization has jurisdiction over the dispute. Bonnie Westbrook, director of the SEC Office of Consumer and Information Services, asks that to avoid duplication of effort you write only to one of these organizations rather than to all three.

Sometimes a letter to one of these organizations will bring prompt results. An investor who held a Dreyfus bond mutual fund said that he wanted to redeem his shares in the fund when interest rates were rising in the summer of 1987 but that because of the rush by other investors to sell out their shares, it took him several days to get through on Dreyfus's 24-hour toll-free line. "I finally got through at four o'clock in the morning one day," said the investor, "but by then, the value of my shares in the fund had declined by $400." However, within a few weeks after he wrote to the SEC and explained his problem, he received a check in the mail for $400 from Dreyfus.

Westbrook recommends that investors who want to file a complaint write to one of the 15 regional SEC offices (see Table 8.1 for addresses). Include an explanation of your problem and photocopies of any related documentation. "But please," Westbrook stresses, "send us copies only! Keep the originals yourself."

The SEC will follow up your complaint within two to three weeks by contacting your brokerage firm to request an explanation. "We generally also forward a copy of the investor's letter, and we sometimes ask the brokerage firm for additional documentation to accompany that response," says Westbrook. "Many times, when we bring the matter to the attention of the brokerage firm compliance department, they will look into it, and if they find they've made a mistake, they will offer corrective action and solve the matter right there. Obviously, though, that is not always the case," she adds. "If that does not solve the complaint, our office is not authorized to act as an arbitrator or judge to decide who is right or wrong. But we will furnish the investor with information on arbitration, or other courses of action if arbitration is not appropriate."

Westbrook asks that investors try to resolve their problem through the brokerage firm before turning to the SEC for help. "We also recommend that at the first sign of a problem, the person start documenting it with a written record. That helps us in looking into it, and it would also help the investor if the case goes to arbitration. That way, they have a written record as opposed to just relying on their memory."

While your complaint to the SEC or one of the exchanges could help solve your problem, there is certainly no guarantee. If your claim is for a substantial amount, brokerage companies would be very unlikely to settle up based strictly on such a complaint. One investor who claimed losses of $25,000 due to churning and unsuitable recommendations says that, in effect, she received this response from the New York Stock Exchange: "Thank you for bringing this matter to our attention. If we can be of further assistance, please let us know." At most, you might be

TABLE 8–1   U.S. Securities and Exchange Commission Regional and Branch Offices

Region 1
New York Regional Office
26 Federal Plaza
New York, NY 10278
(212) 264-1636
Region: New York and New Jersey

Region 2
Boston Regional Office
150 Causeway Street
Boston, MA 02114
(617) 223-2721
Region: Maine, New Hampshire, Vermont, Massachusetts, Rhode Island and Connecticut

Region 3
Atlanta Regional Office
1375 Peachtree Street, NE
Suite 788
Atlanta, GA 30367
(404) 881-4768
Region: Tennessee, Virgin Islands, Puerto Rico, North Carolina, South Carolina, Georgia, Alabama, Mississippi, Florida and Louisiana east of the Atchafalaya River

Miama Branch Office
Dupont Plaza Center
300 Biscayne Boulevard Way,
Suite 500
Miami, FLA 33131
(305) 350-5765

Region 4
Chicago Regional Office
Everett McKinley Dirksen Building
219 South Dearborn Street, Room 1204
Chicago, IL 60604
(312) 353-7390
Region: Michigan, Ohio, Kentucky, Wisconsin, Indiana, Iowa, Minnesota, Missouri and Illinois

Detroit Branch Office
1044 Federal Building
Detroit, MI 48226
(313) 226-6070

Region 5
Fort Worth Regional Office
411 West Seventh Street
Fort Worth, TX 76102
(817) 334-3821
Region: Oklahoma, Arkansas, Texas, Louisiana west of the Atchafalaya River and Kansas

Houston Branch Office
7500 San Felipe, Suite 550
Houston, TX 77063
(713) 226-2775

Region 6
Denver Regional Office
410 17th Street, Suite 700
Denver, CO 80202
(303) 844-2071
Region: North Dakota, South Dakota, Wyoming, Nebraska, Colorado, New Mexico and Utah

Salt Lake Branch Office
Boston Building, Suite 810
9 Exchange Place
Salt Lake City, UT 84111
(801) 524-5796

Region 7
Los Angeles Regional Office
5757 Wilshire Boulevard, Suite 500 East
Los Angeles, CA 90036-3648
(213) 468-3098
Region: Nevada, Arizona, California, Hawaii and Guam

San Francisco Branch Office
450 Golden Gate Avenue, Box 36042
San Francisco, CA 94102
(415) 556-5264

TABLE 8-1 *(concluded)*

Region 8	Region 9
Seattle Regional Office	Washington Regional Office
3040 Federal Building	Ballston Center Tower 3
915 Second Avenue	4015 Wilson Boulevard
Seattle, WA 98174	Arlington, VA 22203
(206) 442-7990	(703) 235-3701
Region: Montana, Idaho, Washington, Oregon and Alaska	Region: Pennsylvania, Delaware, Maryland, Virginia, West Virginia and District of Columbia
	Philadelphia Branch Office
	William J. Green, Jr. Federal Building
	600 Arch Street, Room 2204
	Philadelphia, PA 19106
	(215) 597-3100

referred to another agency. But such organizations as the NYSE and the NASD will not take the place of your own legal counsel. They will not go to bat for you and serve as adversaries against their own members. Move ahead to Step 5.

Step 5.   You might consider pursuing your case in court—if your case involves a substantial amount of money. You will need a lawyer who has experience in securities cases involving brokers and who works for a firm that takes plaintiff cases. The easiest way to find a qualified securities attorney is through a referral from either your regular attorney or the local bar association.

Once you find a qualified attorney, briefly explain your case to the attorney and ask whether it warrants legal help. What you're really asking is, "Are the dollar stakes big enough here?" An investor who had a $25,000 dispute with a brokerage firm decided to forgo the legal process after talking to his attorney. "The attorney said that because of the backlog of cases we'd have to wait at least five years to get to court, and he estimated his legal fees would exceed $30,000. That would have meant spending $30,000 to collect $25,000. As the attorney put it, 'If you win, you'll still be out $5,000; if you lose, you pay me $30,000 and you've still lost the $25,000, so then you're out $55,000. Not a very good bet.' "

Even the smallest cases could easily consume 100 hours at $100 an hour, according to Paul Neimann, an experienced securities attorney. So the minimum cost would be about $10,000, and in most cases it would go much higher. Neimann recommends that an investor should have a claim of at least $25,000, and preferably $50,000, before seriously considering going to court. "Even if your case is successful," says Neimann, "the final result would be very rough justice. Most clients will look back and not consider the whole process to be very satisfactory. They will have borne the grief and emotional stress of a long, one- to five-year dispute; they will have spent their personal time in conferences with their attorney; they will have gone through the rough business of adversary proceedings, and their best hope will be to recover some of what they lost."

There are, however, a couple of other options that you might consider. If you know of other investors who were also victimized, you might want to file a class action suit and split up the legal fees. Or you might consider Step 6—arbitration.

Step 6.   Arbitration is a mechanism that has been set up by the securities industry to resolve securities disputes quickly and inexpensively. In most cases, to apply for arbitration you would need to contact the NASD Office of Arbitration in New York.

To proceed with arbitration, you will be asked to fill out five copies of the official complaint form, stating the facts of your case, and to include any corroborative material. You will be assessed a $500 hearing fee, which may be refunded at the discretion of the arbitrators. On disputes involving more than $5,000, a three-person arbitration panel will hear your case. The panel will include two representatives of the securities industry and one member from outside the industry. After you have filed your complaint, the defendant (your broker) is given 20 business days to reply. After all papers have been filed, your hearing is convened and the arbitration panel considers your situation. You would be well served to have your attorney present, because the brokerage firm will certainly be represented by its counsel. The final decision in arbitration is considered final, and it is almost impossible to appeal that decision in court.

One June 8, 1987, the U.S. Supreme Court ruled that a brokerage firm may enforce a standard written agreement in which the investor agrees to binding arbitration. The case, *Shearson/American Express* v. *McMahon* (No. 86-44), may prevent investors from filing lawsuits against their brokers and may relegate to arbitration nearly all complaints of investors against brokers. Because of this decision, most brokerage firms are expected to require all customers to sign a form agreeing to submit all disputes to arbitration.

To proceed with an arbitration claim, contact:

Arbitration
National Association of
    Securities Dealers, Inc.
Two World Trade Center, 98th Floor
New York, NY 10048
(212) 839-6251

**Arbitration versus a Court Proceeding:
Advantages to the Investor**

Arbitration

1. Faster
2. Less costly

Court proceeding

1. No possible bias in favor of the brokerage firm
2. Possible award of monetary damages in excess of actual dollar losses

---

What are the pluses and minuses of arbitration? The pluses are that arbitration is cheaper and faster than going to court. The minuses are that arbitration is not that cheap and it's not that swift. It's not cheap because in order to have a decent chance in arbitration, you need to hire a lawyer to research your case, compile evidence, interview witnesses, prepare the complaint and represent you in the hearing. Your legal costs would run into the thousands of dollars. It's not swift because the broker can request numerous extensions and your hearing might be set months after all the papers have finally been filed. Critics of arbitration also say that it may be stacked against investors because the panels are dominated by securities industry representatives, who tend to be more lenient on their industry associates. In a court proceeding, moreover, the investor can be awarded damages far exceeding the actual monetary loss in his or her account, whereas in arbitration the settlement will never be more that the investor's actual out-of-pocket loss.

There has been a tremendous increase in customer complaints in the past several years (see Figure 8.1).

FIGURE 8–1   Number of Customer Complaints to the Securities and Exchange Commission

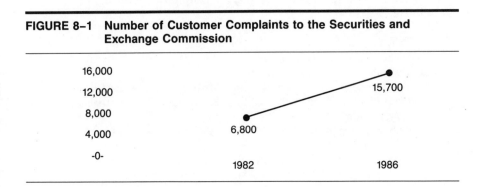

Figure 8.2   Number of Arbitration Cases with the New York Stock Exchange

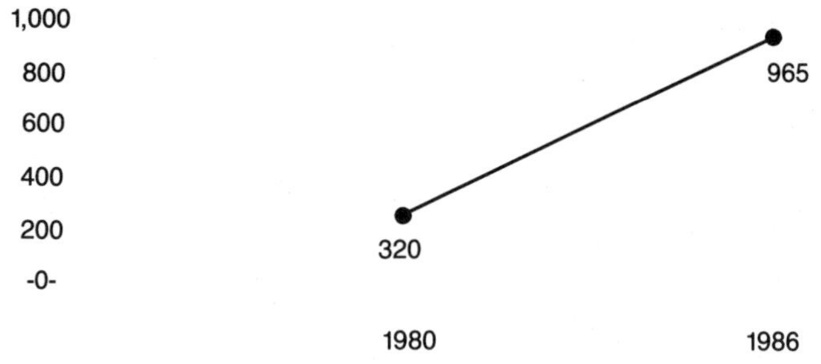

And the number of arbitration cases has also multiplied (see Figure 8.2).

Of all the arbitration cases settled by the NASD in recent years, approximately 50 percent have been settled in favor of the investor and 50 percent have been settled in favor of the brokerage firm.

If you want to preserve your right to sue in court, strike out the clause in which you are asked to agree to submit any dispute to arbitration, initial that section and then sign the agreement. If the brokerage firm accepts your customer agreement in its amended form, you have preserved your right to sue.

If your options for dealing with securities violations sound limited, it's not by mistake. The sad truth is that there are no good, simple remedies for investors. One investor talks about a $6,000 loss he took because his broker failed to execute a trade he ordered. "I called and complained to the compliance officer. You know what he said? 'Sue me.' What could I do? For $6,000, it just wasn't worth it."

The Investor's Steps for Resolving a Compliance Complaint against a Broker

1. Talk to your broker.
2. Write to the branch manager.
3. Write to the chief compliance officer.
4. File a formal written complaint with the Securities and Exchange Commission, the New York Stock Exchange or some other regulatory authority.
5. If the claim is for at least $30,000 to $50,000, hire an attorney to file a lawsuit.
6. Or submit your dispute to arbitration at the New York Stock Exchange or the National Association of Securities Dealers

The Securities and Exchange Commission offers this advice for investors:

1. Before buying...think!
2. Don't deal with strange securities firms. (Consult your broker, your banker or some other experienced person you know and trust.)
3. Beware of securities offered over the telephone by strangers.
4. Don't listen to high-pressure sales talk.
5. Beware of promises of spectacular profits.
6. Be sure you understand the risks of loss.
7. Don't buy on tips and rumors. Get all the facts!
8. If you don't understand all the written information,...consult a person who does.
9. Give at least as much consideration to buying securities as you would to buying other valuable property.
10. Don't speculate. Speculating may serve a useful market purpose when carried out by those who understand and can manage the risks involved. For the average investor, speculation is not investing—it's gambling.
11. Beware of "confidence" schemes. If you're promised "quick profits," "a sure thing," "double your money," be skeptical—and get in touch with either the SEC's closest field office, or with your State Securities Administrator, to help the SEC track down operators in the business who deserve to be put out of the business.
12. Ask for information. Reputable securities salespeople will be happy to mail you a "prospectus" or "offering circular" on any security that you're interested in. Ask for these documents—and save the information.
13. Be prudent. Don't invest until your financial situation permits. Have you made provisions for a home? life and health insurance? savings? Only then, consider investing in stocks, bonds or other instruments.
14. Follow your investments. After you've invested, keep on top of your investments. Read information sent to you by the company or companies in which you've invested. Look at statements from your broker. Overall, after buying securities, think!

The best answer to securities disputes is to do everything in your power to avoid them. That's why it's important to have a good broker at a good firm. "Get to know your broker," Neimann urges. "Ask yourself if you are comfortable with his advice. There really aren't that many bad eggs, but there is an inherent conflict in the role of the broker who makes his living on commissions. So you have to know who you're dealing with—the broker as well as the firm. Deal with a good firm—a firm that's solvent, a firm that won't disappear, that has a reputation to protect."

Remember also that you are a partner in the relationship and that you have a lot more at stake than your broker. Keep a close watch on your investments, and make sure your broker abides by your investment objectives. If problems do arise, be sure to act quickly. "If there is ever a problem with your account," advises Casey of A. G. Edwards, "if the money is not there, or if there is a purchase or sale that you had nothing to do with, I would go directly to the broker to try to get it resolved. But if the broker can't resolve it within a few days, I would go to the manager. Often customers realize there's something wrong with their account, but they trust the broker, who may give them the runaround for six months or so. By then, the problem will often have become even bigger."

"This is serious money," adds Longman's McTaggart. "This is money we're going to retire with. If you lose it all when you're 50 years old, it's pretty hard to make it all back again."

That's why it's important to choose your broker carefully. With a little care in your selection process, you should be able to find a broker who will deal with you honestly. D'Arcy Fox of A. G. Edwards points out that the well-known "80/20 rule" applies to both brokers and investors. "Less than 20 percent of our clients cause us more than 80 percent of our problems. And far less than 20 percent of our brokers are involved in far more than 80 percent of our complaints. The typical client and the typical broker are honest and straightforward, and are never involved in a legal dispute throughout a career of investing."

But while honesty may be the most important virtue to seek in a stockbroker, it is certainly not the only one. A broker should also bring a number of other key qualities to the relationship, as the following chapter details.

CHAPTER NINE

When Things Go Awry

An aging Midwestern woman, her eyesight failing, found that she could no longer keep up with the paperwork associated with her investments. She had inherited a securities portfolio worth about half a million dollars from her husband, and she personally held the certificates for every stock and bond in the lot. The blizzard of account statements, earnings reports, dividend checks, prospectuses and miscellaneous legal notices that came in the mail each week just gathered dust on the dining room table. For help, she turned to her daughter.

The daughter, a bright middle-aged professional woman, thumbed incredulously through the stack of stock and bond certificates. Fifteen shares of a manufacturing company, 1,500 shares of a high-tech firm, 12 shares of a communications firm, 500 shares of a utility—there were 15 or 20 different stocks and bonds in all. Which stocks were worth keeping, which bonds should be sold? The daughter had no idea, and like her mother, she was overwhelmed by the mountain of paperwork that accompanied the securities. She suggested the only solution that made sense to her: Find a good stockbroker.

Logical as this sounded, the mother was not easily swayed. These stocks and bonds were her life savings, everything she would ever have. How could she entrust them with a stranger? The daughter reassured her and offered to seek out a broker they could trust. Reluctantly, the mother agreed.

After consulting some friends at her church, the daughter was referred to a veteran broker at Merrill Lynch who was well known for his investment expertise. Mother and daughter talked with the broker, set up an account and signed over their securities to be held at the firm. The process went smoothly enough—there were a few forms to fill out, some dotted lines to sign, but both mother and daughter felt that this effort was well worthwhile if it would put an end to their problems. The truth, however, was that their problems were just beginning. Although their broker was well versed in investment matters, his attention to other important details of the brokerage business left much to be desired.

Shortly after opening the account, the daughter received a check in the mail from Merrill Lynch. When she asked the broker why the check was sent to her, he said, "I'm not sure. It must be a mistake. Send it back." The daughter, understandably, wondered why a major securities firm would send her a check out of the blue and then, with no explanation, ask her to return it.

To make matters worse, instead of being sent to the daughter, as the women had instructed, the account statements were being sent to the mother, who couldn't read them because of her poor vision.

The mother had also requested that $10,000 in stocks be transferred from her account to her daughter's each year, but the broker forgot to do that too. After he finally got that straightened out, the daughter asked him to give $2,000 of her appreciated stock to her church. By donating the stock directly, the daughter would be spared any capital gains tax on the sale of the stock. But what happened instead? You guessed it. The broker sold the stock instead of turning it over to the church, and the daughter was assessed several hundred dollars in taxes on the appreciation.

In spite of their troubles, mother and daughter might have been content to keep the broker except that he never showed any real concern or remorse over their problems. His response was always condescending. "Oh, don't worry about it," he'd say. "It'll be taken care of." Mother and daughter decided that they had had enough. It was time to fire their broker.

In one of the hardest calls she would ever have to make, the daughter phoned the broker to break the news. She was cordial but direct. "Look," she said, "this just isn't working out. I don't think we're the right type of clients for you. I really think we need another broker. I'm going to call the [branch] manager and ask him to recommend someone else." Despite the awkward nature of the conversation, it went reasonably well. The broker didn't protest and didn't seem to have any hard feelings. In fact, he may have been relieved. He was a big producer with a lot of other clients, and he may not have had the time to tend to the unique problems of the two women.

The daughter's next step was to meet with the branch manager at the Merrill Lynch office. Without getting into a lot of detail about her first broker, she explained her situation: "My mother is almost blind, and I have some responsibility for working with her investments. Basically, I need an arrangement in which I serve as the intermediary between my mother and the broker. Sometimes I have to ask a lot of questions in my mother's behalf, and I need a broker who has a little more time to spend talking with me and explaining things to me."

The manager said he understood. "I think I have just the broker for you," he said. The broker he introduced her to was a 50-year-old woman with a gift for explaining complex investment matters in simple terms. For the next half hour, this broker listened to the daughter's story, asked some pertinent questions and made some helpful suggestions. The relationship between the broker and the daughter has been flourishing ever since. The broker unwound the operational problems of the mother and daughter and began keeping a close eye on the mother's account. She also started to help the daughter with her stock picks, and later she handled the investments of some other members of the family.

WHEN TO FIRE YOUR BROKER

Operational problems—incorrect financial statements, late dividend payments, errant mailings, missing verifications and the like—are just part of life in the securities business. No matter whom you work with, you're going to experience some operational problems. The key in a broker-client relationship is how the broker handles those problems. If the broker resolves them quickly and efficiently without further inconvenience to the client, the chances are that the relationship will continue smoothly. But operational problems left hanging can turn into a chasm of frustration and distrust. No matter how minor the problems, most serious investors will soon lose their patience—as well they should—with a broker who fails to solve them quickly. Operational problems are the responsibility of the broker, and the broker who doesn't resolve them is not doing his or her job.

On average, brokers lose 20 to 25 percent of their accounts a year for a variety of reasons. Clients may move away, die, leave the market or simply switch to another broker. "Brokers are like baseball managers," says Tom Hudson of PaineWebber; "they are hired to be fired. An investor hires a broker by deciding to do business with him. And he can fire him just as easily. He simply stops doing business with him." While losing clients is just part of the business, that doesn't mean the parting is always easy. "It's not like changing gas stations," contends Tom Asher of Robinson-Humphrey. "When one of my clients left, it hurt. It meant I had done something wrong." Some investors will switch brokers at the drop of a hat; others stick with a broker far too long, even though that broker is doing a poor job of serving their needs. "Part of the problem is inertia," says D'Arcy Fox of A. G. Edwards. "They've finally learned how to read their account statement, so they don't want to change."

In most cases, rifts that develop between client and broker occur, not because of illegal acts or bad investment advice but simply because "things aren't working out." Lingering operational problems are just one of many reasons that broker-client relationships break down. Here are some other common reasons:

1. *Broker doesn't call when your investments are down.* This is far and away the most frequent cause of a deteriorating relationship between

FIGURE 9.1   Brokers Lose 20 Percent of Their Clients Each Year

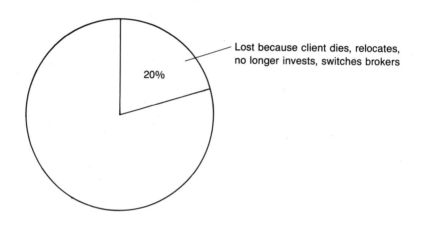

20%

Lost because client dies, relocates,
no longer invests, switches brokers

client and broker. "Brokers get enough rejection trying to get new clients," says David Thompson of Prudential-Bache. "They don't want to look to their current clients as a second source of rejection. That's the main reason for a breakdown in a broker-client relationship. The broker is unwilling to call a client who has a loss." If you own stocks that your broker recommended and those stocks are down, your broker has an obligation to get in touch with you to offer an explanation. After Black Monday, October 19, 1987, the best brokers called all of their clients—sometimes working well into the evening—to reassure their clients and discuss strategies. But it shouldn't take a market disaster to merit a call from your broker. If you have a stock that you bought at $20 and it's fallen to $12.25, your broker should be in touch with you to ease your concerns and offer a recommendation on whether to sell, hold or add to your position. "Brokers are often long on buy ideas and short on sell ideas," says Donnis Casey of A. G. Edwards. "It seems like they're calling clients to get them to buy something when often they should be taking a look at what the person is holding to see if it is still appropriate."

In some cases—particularly during bear markets—an investor may be sitting on half a dozen stocks that are all down. Yet the broker still doesn't call. The reality is that the broker is probably very discouraged. The phone becomes "heavy," as brokers say. The broker has sold a product that is disappointing almost everyone who bought it. The broker may have several hundred clients, all of whom are losing money in the market. It's very difficult for the broker to pick up the phone and make one call after another to those clients, to try to explain why his or her recommendations aren't working. But that is what brokers are paid to do, and you should expect your broker to call you when your investments are down. "That's got to be the worst part of a broker's job," says Dale Grubb of Shearson Lehman, "to call clients to advise them to get out of a position either because the market has changed, the fundamentals have changed or the stock has suddenly become less attractive. When you have a large position in a stock with a lot of clients in that stock (as I did a couple of years ago with an airline stock that took a dive), you just know you're going to have some angry clients and you're going to lose some of those clients."

Jim Vieburg, managing director at Piper Jaffray says that he thinks one of his most important jobs is to give people good, professional advice when their stocks are down. "They're tough phone calls to make, but here's what I do: I call them, identify myself, and I say, 'Remember what they do to the messenger who comes with bad news?' The clients usually laugh—a little—and say something like 'Yeah, they chop off his head.' Then I say, 'Well, I hope you're not going to do that to me.' That tends to disarm them a little, and if it doesn't disarm them, it helps me to say what I need to say. Then I explain the situation and give them the best advice I can as to what they should do."

2. *Broker doesn't solve operational problems* (as discussed earlier in the chapter).

3. *Broker pressures you to make investments you are not interested in.* This is a major complaint of investors—and a legitimate cause for concern. Sometimes brokers can be very intimidating. "Come on," the broker might say, "this is a bull market. Everybody's making money except you. This is the chance of a lifetime, and you're going to miss it." You shouldn't be subjected to that type of pressure. You don't want a broker who is constantly urging you to invest against your will—whether it's in stocks, bonds or prepackaged investment products. "I would wonder if my broker had my best interest at heart if he was constantly trying to push his company's own proprietary products on me—their mutual funds, their tax shelters or their unit trusts," says Casey.

"The acid test," says Phil Clark of Roney & Co., "is, does this person really care about my needs? If the broker wants to sell you something without knowing what you have or need, that gives you a pretty good idea that he is more interested in selling rather than filling your needs. Try to analyze whether the broker is trying to fulfill his need to sell or your need to buy."

If you've explained your objectives to your broker, your broker should respect your wishes. A broker who is constantly pressuring you to make other investments needs to be set straight. "Maybe I didn't express myself clearly," you might say. "I'm an occasional investor whose chief interest is in buying stock in the company I work for. I'm a busy person, and I would prefer not to be bothered with recommendations that don't comply with my objectives." If the broker continues to call, we recommend that you find another broker.

4. *Poor communications.* "Does your broker listen?" asks Bob Cohn, training director of Drexel Burnham. "Does he hear? Can you understand what he says and why he thinks that way?"

The symptoms of poor communications are numerous—the broker fails to follow your instructions, seems too busy to answer reasonable questions, can't speak in terms you understand, or simply never calls. All are reasons to find another broker.

If you're not an active investor, you shouldn't expect to hear from your broker every week or even every month. "It may be," says Robinson-Humphrey's Asher, "that your broker only needs to get in touch with you every two or three years, if that's what your financial situation dictates." But you still should hear from your broker from time to time if for no other reason than to review your portfolio to see whether your investments are still appropriate. According to Roney's Clark, "Your broker should call you whenever you need him. If I buy General Motors stock and I'm not going to sell it for ten years come hell or high water, then there's no reason for my broker to call me every 30 days. But if I bought General Motors as an investment and would relinquish it for another investment of superior quality whenever the time is right, I would expect my broker to tell me when the time is right. If I bought CDs that were going to mature in 12 months and I wasn't going to buy anything for the next 12 months, I wouldn't want a broker calling me every week trying to sell me something else. But I would expect him to call me before my CD expires and tell me what to do with the money."

"With that type of client," says Bill Koriath of Prudential-Bache, "I'll call him up maybe a month ahead of time to let him know I'm alive and I'm thinking of him. That gives him a chance to start thinking about how he's going to reinvest that money."

Adds A. G. Edwards's Casey: "If you have money to invest a couple of times a year, your broker should be in touch with you. If you have a stock and you're looking for it to make a move, your broker should be in touch with you to tell you when to get out. If you haven't heard from your broker for a year or two, or you're missing the market, or you're in a stock that went up and came back down without your taking a profit, then your broker was not paying much attention to your account."

Another problem clients face is the unwillingness of their brokers to answer reasonable questions. While brokers earn their commissions effecting transactions, the presumption is that they should also render additional service for their clients roughly proportionate to the amount of business the clients do with them. Part of that service involves answering reasonable questions. You buy a stock that splits, for instance, and you don't understand the new price of the stock. You have every right to call your broker and say, "I've never had a stock that split before. Can you take a moment and explain this to me?" Or you have a question about something on your account statement. You should feel free to ask your broker for an explanation. If your broker is always too busy to answer your questions, that's a good indication that the broker may not be a good fit for you.

Another test of your broker's communications skills is his or her ability to follow your instructions. Clients are often frustrated by the mistakes that brokers make in their accounts. You order $5,000 worth of General Motors bonds, and instead your broker buys you 5,000 shares of General Motors stock. You ask your broker to reinvest your dividends, and instead the checks keep coming to you in the mail. You instruct your broker to buy some stock in a custodial account for one of your children, and instead the broker buys the stock for another child. If you invest in the stock market for long, you're going to experience some problems with your account. But a good broker will keep the mistakes to a minimum and will resolve any problems that do crop up as soon as you bring them to his or her attention.

5. *Lack of rapport.* You talk stocks; your broker talks bonds. You talk preservation of capital; your broker talks speculation. You talk dividends; your broker talks capital growth. One investor recalls a problem he had with his former broker. "I was interested in tax-sheltered investments, and my broker didn't deal in them, didn't know much about them, and he really wasn't all that interested in them. I called him and asked if he would check into a limited partnership for me. While he didn't absolutely refuse, I could sense a lot of reluctance from him." Rather than pursue the subject any further with the broker, the investor simply called the branch manager, explained his problem and asked to be assigned to a different broker. The branch manager referred the investor to a broker in the same office who specialized in tax-sheltered investments, and the relationship between the investor and his new broker has worked out exceptionally well ever since.

Rapport problems can come in many forms. Maybe your broker talks too fast or uses investment jargon that you don't understand. Maybe he or she is arrogant and condescending or chauvinistic and patronizing. "I have one client," says Betsy Buckley of Dain Bosworth, "who was very dissatisfied with her former broker. She's not a good communicator, and he wouldn't probe. He was very macho, and she was offended by how macho he was, so she was going to outmacho him. The relationship just didn't work out."

There may be other reasons for a breakdown in rapport. Perhaps your broker's political views are different from yours—your broker is a right-wing reactionary, and you're tired of listening to his or her complaints about these crazy liberal schemes, some of which you believe in. Or perhaps you just don't trust your broker. "You need to be able to feel that this is a person I can trust," says Buckley, "just like I trust my dentist and I trust my doctor. I instinctively have not only professional confidence in them, but I have a feeling of personal rapport as well. They are sort of 'my kind of person.' "

Adds Koriath: "I don't think you necessarily have to have things in common with your broker, but you should be able to converse with that broker as neighbors would across a back fence."

If you don't have rapport with your broker, you'll probably know it instinctively. You may not be able to put your finger on exactly why. But whatever the reason, the bottom line is that you feel uneasy with the relationship. "Sometimes the chemistry is not quite right," says Gary Cohen of E. F. Hutton. If you're not comfortable with the relationship, that's all the justification you need to look for another broker. Remember, it's your money. You should invest it with someone with whom you feel most comfortable.

6. *Poor performance.* Are your investment objectives being met? Are you earning the kind of return on your investments that you think you should earn? This may be the most difficult reason to assess accurately. Often, if your investments are not performing up to your expectations that may be no fault of your broker's.

For instance, if you told your broker to put your money into conservative investments and you now find that you're earning 8 percent a year while the market is moving up 28 percent, don't blame your broker. You wanted conservative investments, so you should be satisfied with conservative returns.

On the other hand, if you told your broker to invest in highly speculative stocks and now the market has dropped and your stocks have dropped even further, don't blame your broker. You knew the risks when you ordered the stocks.

Then there's the matter of investor impatience. Some brokers offer their clients long-range recommendations—stocks that are trading at low levels but have the potential to climb dramatically over time. If your broker put you into such stocks, don't lose patience after six or eight months. It could take two or three years before those stocks begin to reach their potential.

Bull markets often give investors a distorted view of how well their investments should be doing. In the bull market of 1985-87, the Dow Jones Industrial Average doubled, but very few investors did that well. A more accurate measure of overall market performance is the Standard & Poor's 500 index, which gauges a much broader cross section of stocks than the Dow. The S&P 500 didn't experience nearly the growth that the Dow did. And smaller over-the-counter stocks underperformed the S&P 500. As Adrian Banky, executive vice president of the Securities Industry Association, points out, "The Dow is a highly visible benchmark, but it may not be a fair benchmark for a particular investor. If you allocate 20 percent of your assets to money market funds, 30 percent to bonds, 25 percent to blue-chip stocks (which tend to reflect the Dow) and 25 percent to aggressive stocks, then it is not appropriate to use the Dow as a benchmark, because only 25 percent of your portfolio is invested in stocks that mirror the Dow."

Bull markets also tend to bring out a lot of one-sided claims among investors. Investors like to boast about how well their best stocks are doing, but they typically neglect to mention their losers. If you accept what other people say at face value, you're bound to feel that everyone is doing better than you.

The best policy is to determine your objectives and judge your broker on whether or not he or she is meeting those objectives. If you wanted absolute safety, then be happy with the 7^1/$_2$ percent your broker got you with government securities. If you find you're not happy with that kind of return, then change your objectives, not your broker.

Of course, there are times when it may be appropriate to change brokers because of poor performance. If the stock market is moving up and your stocks are moving down, that is reason for concern. Don't be too quick to judge, but if the poor performance continues, then you should consider changing brokers. "If the broker loses the client a lot of money on a consistent basis, then the broker's obviously doing something that's not in the client's best interest," says David Waterbury of Dean Witter. "Long term, if the broker's not making money for the client, then the client should be asking why."

7. *Broker switches firms frequently.* There may be some very sound reasons for your broker to move from one firm to another. If your broker has been with the same firm for the past five years and has just announced a move to a new firm, you have no real reason for concern. But if he or she has worked for four firms in the past four years, you should strongly consider finding another broker.

For one thing, moving your account from one firm to another can be a major inconvenience. More than likely, your old firm is holding your securities in street name, so you would need to fill out authorization forms to have the securities moved to the new firm. In this process, errors are sometimes made—the wrong securities may be transferred; records may get lost or fouled up. And your broker, who is probably contacting other clients and helping them transfer their securities, may be too busy to offer much help. If you're an active investor, the transfer of your account could take two to three months to complete, and during that period your account could well be in a state of limbo.

More important, it's very likely that your old firm keeps a closer watch on the securities in your portfolio than does your broker's new firm. The fact is that you may have chosen this broker because of his or her firm. You were interested in regional stocks, so you went to a regional firm and found a broker there. Now that your broker is leaving the regional firm to move to a national firm, he or she would no longer be able to serve your interests as well. If you own any of the old firm's prepackaged investment products, you could face additional complications. An investor who had an account with a broker at Dean Witter talks about her situation: "I bought a Dean Witter unit investment trust and some other Dean Witter products which worked well while my broker was there, but when he switched to Drexel Burnham, he no longer had access to investment information on those products. So I was basically left on my own. I had no way of knowing how my investments were doing or what I should do with them."

Brokers generally switch firms for one of two reasons:

1. They have been offered an attractive financial incentive to switch to another firm. "Often what happens," says Koriath, "is that a broker will have incredible success one year and is offered an opportunity to

pick up a large financial bonus by moving to another firm. The broker rationalizes that he's done as well as he's ever going to do—that he's achieved more than he could ever possibly achieve, so why not grab that extra cash and move on."

2. They are not getting along with their branch manager.

Neither reason is necessarily a good reason for you to follow your broker to the new firm.

When To Fire Your Broker

1. Doesn't call when your investments are down
2. Doesn't solve operational problems
3. Pressures you to make investments you are not interested in
4. Poor communications
5. Lack of rapport
6. Poor performance
7. Switches firms frequently

MAKING THE SWITCH

Any of the preceeding problems is a valid reason to fire your broker. You may also wish to fire your broker for committing any of the unscrupulous or illegal offenses mentioned in the preceding chapter. If your broker commits certain offenses, such as unauthorized trading, you should fire him or her immediately. Otherwise, if the problem seems correctable and manageable, you may wish to give your broker a warning and a second chance. But if the offense is repeated, find another broker.

What's the best way to do that? It takes a little effort on your part. "There's no easy way to change brokers," says Asher. "That's why it's important to make the right decision the first time." However, you may be able to save some steps by switching brokers within the same firm. In that way, you can avoid the paperwork and inconvenience of transferring your investments. "Many investors think that once they have a broker, they're stuck with that broker as long as they want to do business in that office," says Judy Johnson of Advest. "To change brokers, they think they have to go through the pain and anguish of transferring their account out to a broker at another firm. That's not true. Changing brokers can be as simple as going to the branch manager and requesting another broker at the same firm."

What follows is a step-by-step approach for switching brokers.

1. As a courtesy to your broker, you should contact the broker first to say that you are switching. You can do that through either a letter or a call. There is no need to apologize or to defend your decision. If you have a specific reason for making the switch (for example, that your broker is not well versed in the investments you're interested in, or calls you too often, or doesn't call often enough), you may wish to mention it. But there's no real point in belaboring the issue. This is simply a courtesy call. You're not asking for excuses; you're not asking for permission. You're simply informing your broker of your decision to get another broker. The best approach is to say something like this: "I don't feel comfortable with our relationship. I don't think things are working out the way I'd like them to, and I think I need another broker." If the broker presses you for reasons, you can briefly state your reasons or you can simply say, "I'm not even sure I can explain it, but my conclusion is that I need another broker." Then add something to this effect: "No hard feelings. I like your firm, and I intend to keep my account here. I'm going to ask the branch manager to assign me to another broker. I appreciate the work you've done for me. Good luck."

2. Set up an appointment with the branch manager to explain your situation, and ask the branch manager to assign you to another broker.

Tell the manager what your investment needs are. Be very open about your circumstances. You might say, for instance, "In dealing with my present broker, here is what I've learned about my investment needs . . ."

Then talk briefly about your needs. You might say, "I need a broker who has strong expertise in direct participation investments," or "I need a broker who is willing to answer some basic questions about my account," or "I need a broker who is conscientious about solving operational problems," or "I need a broker who has the intestinal fortitude to call me when my stocks are down," or "I need a broker who is tuned in to preservation of capital," or "I'm a new investor, and I need a broker who is willing to spend a little more time with me to keep me informed."

You can expect your discussion with the manager to go very well. Managers see themselves as problem solvers and matchmakers. In most cases, a manager would welcome the opportunity to set you up with another broker and would do his or her best to find one who would be a good fit for you. After all, the manager realizes that the firm is being given one last chance to keep you as a customer and that if a good match isn't found for you this time, you're almost certain to take your business elsewhere.

3. When the branch manager assigns you to a new broker, sit down with the broker and explain your needs, your objectives, and your expectations (as discussed in Chapter 5, "Making Your Final Choice"). The broker will probably ask you a few questions, go over your portfolio and try to learn what went wrong in your relationship with your first broker. In the vast majority of cases, your new broker will work out extremely well for you because the broker was handpicked by the branch manager.

If after making the switch, you're still not satisfied (for instance, you want to trade in small speculative growth stocks, and the best your new broker can do is suggest midsized stocks from the company's recom-

---

How To Switch Brokers

1. Inform your current broker.
2. Meet with the branch manager to request a different broker.
3. Explain your needs, objectives and expectations to your new broker.

---

mended list), then we recommend that you shop around for a brokerage firm that specializes in your type of investments (see Chapter 4, "What's out There: From Different Firms Come Different Services").

Thousands of outstanding brokers are ready and willing to offer you their services. If you're dissatisfied with your present broker, let your broker know what's troubling you. If he or she can't solve your problems, rest assured that plenty of other brokers can and that you owe it to yourself to find one.

PART 4

Getting the Most for Your Money

CHAPTER TEN _____

_____

Buying at a Discount

Service has its price. Bag your own groceries, bus your own dishes, pump your own gas and you'll get a break on the price. The same can be said for buying securities. If you want personal service and attention, you'll pay a premium. But if all you want is a simple buy or sell transaction, you can fill your order for less through a discount broker.

"Discounters are in a different business than we are," says an executive of a large full-service firm. "What they're delivering is execution of orders. What we deliver is information. Yes, we will buy and sell the securities for you, but essentially that extra commission dollar you pay for a full-service broker is for the information. If you don't need or use the information, then you're overpaying."

How big are the savings at a discounter? The answer depends on whom you ask:

Says Charles Schwab, chairman, CEO and founder of discount giant Charles Schwab & Co.: "By now, it's certainly no secret that investors can save a lot of money using a discount broker."

Counters Tom Asher, executive vice president of the full-service firm Robinson-Humphrey: "The difference in commission costs is minuscule compared to the total investment purchase."

Discounters will tell you that the savings can be as great as 75 percent of the commission per trade—which happens to be true. Full-service brokers, on the other hand, would argue that the difference is a paltry 1 percent or so of the total trade—which also happens to be true.

As Asher points out, "If you invest $20,000 for a thousand shares of a $20 stock, it may cost you $400 in commissions at a full-service brokerage and $200 at a discounter. The difference in commissions may be 50 to 60 percent, but on a $20,000 purchase that extra $200 represents a very, very small part—just 1 percent—of the total transaction."

More to the point is PaineWebber's Bill Blount: "Our commissions amount to peanuts," he says. "Since 1970, my customer accounts, on average, have grown 20 percent per year. What difference is a measly quarter of a point on a purchase or sale of a stock if your turnover is minimal and your success has been what ours has?"

But Schwab sees it another way: "If an investor buys and sells 500 shares of a $15 stock three times a year (six transactions), the annual savings would be close to $600. Commission costs can add up quickly."

GROWTH OF DISCOUNTING

Discounters were once looked upon as the poor stepsisters of the full-service houses. Cut-rate firms first began to emerge in 1975, when the SEC scrapped the long-standing compulsory commission rate schedule. Despite the savings, investors were slow to embrace the discount concept. But over time, investment bargain hunters and do-it-yourselfers began to turn increasingly to discounters. Perhaps the final stride in the discounters' climb to respectability came in the early 1980s, when banks and savings and loan associations began to add discount brokering to their list of services (cash a check; get a loan; buy a stock).

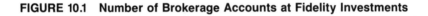

FIGURE 10.1   Number of Brokerage Accounts at Fidelity Investments

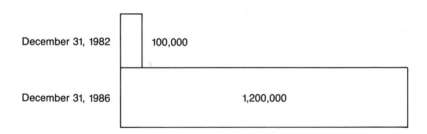

Fidelity Investments, which claims to be the second largest discount firm portrays its growth as shown above.

At present, about 25 percent of all retail investors have an account with a discount broker. Many investors use both a full-service broker and a discounter.

Discount houses, for the most part, offer fast, efficient transactions for all stock exchange and over-the-counter securities and options. While they give no investment advice, discounters do provide some of the other

FIGURE 10.2   Retail Market Share of Discount firms

According to sources within the discount securities business, in mid-1987 discount firms were transacting approximately 15 percent of all retail trades and generating about 7½ percent of all retail stock commissions in the securities industry. The full-service firms have maintained a dominant 85 percent market share for the past several years.

amenities offered by full-service houses. Most discount houses will hold your securities in street name, mail out regular account statements and insure the cash and assets in your account. They also offer money market accounts, margin accounts, self-directed IRAs, Keogh accounts and, in some cases, asset management accounts, such as the Fidelity USA Account. And as Schwab points out, a few discounters offer some services that you still can't get from most full-service brokers—"24-hour-a-day, seven-day order entry; instant trade confirmations, and the ability to buy a wide range of no-load mutual funds." The 24-hour service has proven particularly popular at Fidelity Investments. The firm receives about 200,000 calls during a typical 24-hour period, including as many as 10,000 calls between midnight and 4:00 A.M.

As you see in the following cost comparison chart, prices vary widely not only between discounters and full-service brokers but also between one discounter and another and between one full-service broker and another:

	100 Shares @ $40	300 Shares @ $30	1,000 Shares @ $20
Discounters	$35-50	$58-90	$100-165
Full-service firms	$70-90	$160-195	$335-400

PROS AND CONS

Discount brokers are best suited for investors who make all their own buying and selling decisions. "Many investors don't want a broker's investment research and advice," says Schwab. "They either don't need it or they prefer independent, objective sources of information. We've found that some don't want the attention of a commissioned broker because of potential conflicts of interest. What these investors want, either for all their transactions or a part of them, is executions at the best possible prices, along with commissions which reflect only the cost of the service."

But with the cheaper prices come some predictable problems. If you have an error in your account at a discount house, you don't have a personal broker who can go to bat for you. More important, if you need advice on a particular investment, a discount broker cannot help you. "It does get a little frustrating at times," says a longtime discount user. "The firm I use is always sending me brochures on different types of investments, but when I call up to ask about them, no one there can answer my questions. In fact, it's as though they go out of their way not to answer any questions."

That inability to respond to investment questions manifests itself in other ways as well. For most investors, finding promising investments to buy is not a problem (the financial press is loaded with information on investments that prominent brokers are recommending), but knowing when to hold and when to sell represents a difficult dilemma. Rarely are the financial publications of any help after you've bought an investment.

"I've always used a discounter because I like the idea of making my own decision and tracking my own stocks," says one 36-year-old investor. "I don't really want the pressure of a full-service broker. But there have been times when I wished I had someone to go to for advice. I once read about a company called Pharma Control. A top broker was recommending the stock as 'a flier with the most potential of anything I've ever seen.' That sounded good to me, so I bought several hundred shares at $13. It eased up to $14 and moved around a little—an eighth here, a quarter there. Then suddenly in one day it dropped two points. Then two more points over the next two days, and before I knew it, it was trading at $7^1/_2$. I had no idea why it dropped and no way to find out. Every time it dropped a point, I was out a few hundred dollars more—which for me was serious money. I was thinking, 'Should I sell it, should I hold, should I go for dollar-cost averaging and buy more, or is this going to just keep dropping?' That's when you need a broker. I mean, I've watched a $19 stock drop to $11 the week I bought it, I've had a $2 stock slide to zero (that was another one of those highly recommended ones in the newspaper), I've watched a $15 stock drop to $6 inside of a month. Sometimes it works out OK; the stock bounces back. But when they're dropping a point or two a day and you don't have a clue as to why, it really is a helpless feeling. It makes for some restless nights. And there's no one to call for advice." Pharma Control, by the way, did move back up briefly, he says. "When it finally got back up to $13, I sold out of it that day—which was lucky because then it started dropping again. I just wish I was so lucky with all my picks."

Providing advice on specific stocks and bonds is just one aspect of the full-service broker's job. Equally important is the ability of the full-service broker to motivate clients to continue investing through good times and bad. "There are some investors who absolutely must have a shoulder to lean on when making investment decisions," concedes Schwab. Without the prodding of a broker, many clients would lack the discipline necessary to maintain a consistent investment program.

One 34-year-old businessman talked about his experience with discounting. "I had never invested myself," he explains, "but I worked with a lot of people who played the market." From one source, he heard that the stock of a computer network company was expected to jump in price in the near future. "So I bought the stock, and sure enough, within a few weeks the price doubled."

Buttressed by that bit of success, he became more serious than ever. In talking with other investors, he heard several favorable comments about Jaguar, the British motor company. He bought Jaguar stock at $5 and sold it at $7.

Slowly, he began to develop his own system. He searched *The Wall Street Journal* for "bouncers," stocks that tended to drop a few points and then bounce back to new heights. His strategy was to buy when they hit the bottom and sell when they bounced back to the top—a strategy that worked fairly well the first time or two he tried it.

Then one day he discovered Bird Finder, a cable television company that seemed to be a classic bouncer. He bought 400 shares at $3^5/8$. "From the split second I bought it," he reports, "it began to drop." It quickly fell to $5/8$ per share and never recovered. Discouraged by that one failure, he stopped investing in stocks—missing out entirely on the big bull market of the mid-1980s.

How could this investor have benefited from a good full-service broker? Certainly, using a broker is no guarantee against making a bad stock purchase. But the chances are that a good broker would have persuaded him to sell out sooner than he did—before his small loss became a big one. And just as important, a broker would probably have encouraged him to reinvest in other stocks so that he could keep his investment program up to speed.

WHEN TO USE A DISCOUNTER

"Generally," says Schwab, "discount brokerage is for self-directed investors who wish to conduct their own research and make their own investment decisions. Obviously, many investors maintain accounts at full-commission firms and use a discounter for those transactions where they are the ones making the investment decisions." Most discount investors fall into one of three categories:

- *Long-term investors who study the market.* Some investors enjoy studying the market, following industry trends and spotting stocks of high potential. It's an avocation for them, and if their own efforts work reasonably well, they may be better off using a discounter. The satisfaction of controlling their own investment program is the main attraction, and the discounted commissions are just an added bonus. Many of these investors have both a full-service broker and a discount broker.
- *Short-term technical traders.* Technical traders who chart stocks themselves and trade on a short-term basis commonly use discounters. It's a simple matter of economics. Active traders may turn over their entire portfolio once a month. With full-service commissions averaging 2 percent per trade, those costs can become enormous over 12 months. Every time you turn over a security, you pay 2 percent to sell and 2 percent to buy—that's 4 percent per month, or 48 percent per year. By using a discounter, you could cut those commissions by as much as 75 percent per year. And in this case, a 75 percent reduction in commissions translates into 36 percent of the entire portfolio value (48% x 75% = 36%). This means that active traders could save the equivalent of the entire value of their portfolio within three years (36% x 3 = 108%) simply by using a discounter instead of a full-service broker.
- *Investors with onetime transactions.* If you want to sell shares of stock that you've acquired as a gift, as a part of your company's benefits plan, or through inheritance, you should consider using a discounter to execute your trade. If you have a full-service broker, you might ask whether he or she would be willing to give you a onetime discount to sell the stock for you—since the transaction would require no special service or advice from the broker. A fair number of brokers will agree to handle such a transaction for you at a discount. If your broker refuses, then go to a discounter.

However, there is one exception—small lots of stock. It may be cheaper to sell small lots of stock through a full-service broker than through a discounter. You might begin by trying the shareholder departments of the companies whose shares you own. Some companies are now willing to buy back small lots of stock from shareholders at either no cost or a nominal fee.

If that doesn't work, some full-service firms offer special low-rate programs for small lots of stock. Under Merrill Lynch's Sharebuilder program, for instance, you would be charged 10 percent of the sales price for trades of up to $200, 5 percent of the sales price plus a $10 fee for trades of $200 to $500, 1.5 percent of the sales price plus a $27.50 fee for trades of $500 to $1,000, and 1.2 percent of the sales price plus $30.50 for trades of $1,000 to $5,000.

Profile of a Discount Firm Investor

1. Wants to make his or her own buy and sell investment decisions
2. Willing to assume above-average risks
3. College graduate
4. Above-average income and net worth
5. Urban
6. Manager or professional

For odd lots of under 100 shares, PaineWebber offers these rates:

- 17 percent of the sales price for trades of under $152
- 1.8 percent plus $23 for trades of $152 to $3,000
- 1.4 percent plus $35 for trades of $3,000 to $4,786

On the sale of ten shares of a $5 stock, for instance, your total commission at PaineWebber would be 17 percent of $50—which is $8.50. By comparison, most discounters charge a much higher flat minimum of roughly $25 to $40 per transaction, regardless of the value of the trade.

WHO SHOULD NOT USE A DISCOUNTER

Despite the growing popularity of discount brokers, the vast majority of investors still use full-service brokers for most of their trades. "There will always be room for the full-service broker," says Lee Kopp of Dain Bosworth, "for the person who is a true pro, who takes time to understand the business, does his homework and enjoys what he does."

The investors who are most likely to stick with a full-service broker are the ones who appreciate the convenience of having a professional advisor guiding their buying and selling decisions. These people see their broker in the same light as they see their attorney, their accountant or their real estate agent. They recognize their limitations in the complex investment market, and they see their broker as the industry specialist who can push the right buttons to keep their investments growing.

They also appreciate the personal attention of a full-service broker. They like having a broker who will keep an eye on their account, who will call when the need arises and who will answer their questions and tend to their problems.

In addition to advice, however, full-service brokers offer some other services that you aren't likely to find at a discounter. They have access to new stock offerings and to a wide variety of packaged investment products, such as unit investment trusts, municipal bonds, limited partnerships, life insurance and annuities.

"Discounters aren't going to talk to you about other investments you should have to balance out your investment portfolio," says Robinson-

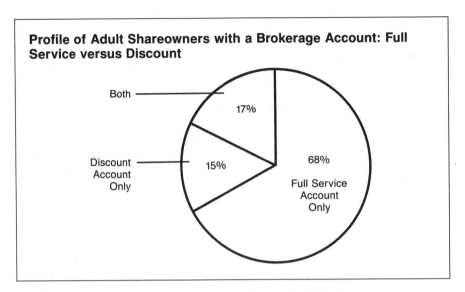

Profile of Adult Shareowners with a Brokerage Account: Full Service versus Discount

Both — 17%

Discount Account Only — 15%

68% Full Service Account Only

Source: New York Stock Exchange, Inc. "Shareownership 1985"

Humphrey's Asher. "What you get with a full-service broker is an advisor—an investment counselor with many good ideas and good products to help solve your financial problems—for a minuscule increase in costs over a discounter."

CHOOSING A DISCOUNT BROKER

Choosing a discount broker can be almost as difficult as choosing a full-service broker. "There is a large difference in discounters," says Schwab. "There are differences in size, financial strength, range and quality of services provided, number and location of branch offices and fees and commission charges. I believe investors should look first toward the well-established firms," adds Schwab, "and make the selection based on their individual investment needs."

While Schwab & Co. is by far the largest of the discounters, several other national firms have also made their presence felt. Fidelity, Quick & Reilly, Haas and Rose & Co. all advertise their rates in business and investment publications, often running charts that compare their rates not only with the full-service houses but with other discounters as well. Schwab, whose commissions are considered pricey by discount standards, cautions that rates should not be the only criterion in selecting a discounter. "There are a number of intangibles that can be equally, if not more, important," he says, "including safety, security, ease of access, convenience, quality and range of services. Most investors want more than just no-frills trading. They want the 'intangibles' that go with a wider range of services."

In addition to the national discount firms, a number of regional discount firms offer competitive rates. These regional firms are ideal for investors who want to keep their investments at a company close to home. Check the yellow pages under "stock & bond brokers" for the discount firms in your area, and then call around to see which firm offers the best prices and services for you. Many banks and thrifts also offer cut-rate brokerage services. Their commissions are likely to be somewhat higher than those of the discount houses, but the added convenience may be worth the price.

If you study the choices long enough, what you will probably find is that there is no clear-cut favorite—either for convenience or for price (see accompanying box).

Haas Securities ran a price chart in the June 2, 1987, *Wall Street Journal* comparing its rates for selected transactions with the rates charged by Schwab, Rose and Fidelity. We've added to that chart the rates of the other major national discounter, Quick & Reilly, and of a Wisconsin-based regional discounter, Ziegler Thrift Trading. This information shows that there are wide variations in rates among discounters. It also shows that a discounter who is the cheapest at one volume can be the most expensive at another.

	100 Shares @ $26	300 Shares @ $20	500 Shares @ $18	1,000 Shares @ $42	2,000 Shares @ $28
Schwab	$45	$72	$84	$183	$225
Rose & Co.	35	71	89	169	197
Fidelity	40	72	86	151	165
Haas	30	58	65	140	150
Quick & Reilly*	35	59	83	138	174
Ziegler*	27	58	83	229	289

* As of July 1, 1987.

If after comparing prices and services, you still can't decide on a discounter, it might pay you to visit the discounter's local office—if there is one. Set up an appointment with the local branch manager or with a registered representative in the local office, and ask that person to describe the firm and its services. If there is no local office, most of the national discounters list an 800 number in their advertisements that you can call to ask questions and request more information.

Selecting a Discount Broker by Phone

Rab Bertelsen, a vice president with Fidelity Investments, suggests this approach for investors who want to choose a discounter by telephone:
1. Refer to ads in *The Wall Street Journal, Money* and other investment publications to get the names and 800 phone numbers of several discount firms.
2. Phone those firms using the toll-free 800 number, and ask for materials describing the firm, a new account form and a commission schedule.
3. Notice how long it takes for the phone to be answered.
4. Evaluate the professionalism of the person answering the phone.
5. Notice how long it takes for the requested information to arrive.
6. Evaluate the products and services available.
7. Evaluate the competitiveness of the commission schedule.

Choosing a Discount Broker Face-to-Face

For face-to-face dealings, Fidelity Investments' Rab Bertelsen offers this advice:
1. Identify discount firms with offices near your home by consulting the yellow pages or local newspaper ads.
2. Visit several offices.
3. At each stop, ask to speak with a registered representative. Inquire about products, services and how to open an account.
4. If you anticipate making a specific transaction, describe the transaction and ask for a commission quote on it.

Once you've weighed the choices and made your decision, opening an account with a discounter is generally as easy as dialing the phone, providing some basic information and placing an order.

COMMISSION-FREE STOCKS

A few publicly traded corporations offer stockholders the opportunity to buy additional shares of their stock directly from the company with no commission or administrative fees. Some corporations also offer free dividend reinvestment plans and small contribution plans for individual investors.

Aetna Life and Casualty, for instance, offers a monthly stock purchase plan with as little as $50 or as much as $5,000 per payment. In addition, it agrees to reinvest cash dividends at a 5 percent discount from the average price of its stock.

McDonald's and Walt Disney have monthly no-commission plans that start for as little as $20. Quaker Oats, Ashland and the St. Paul Companies accept payments of as little as $10.

One problem with buying stocks through the company, however, is that investors have no control over the price they pay for the stock. Generally, the company will set aside one day a month to purchase all the stocks for participating shareholders, and those shareholders will pay the going price for that day. "I had one gentleman call recently who wanted to know why he had to pay so much for his stock," says Ed Gerber of the St. Paul Companies. "The stock was trading at $47 a share the day he sent his money in, but by the 17th of the month—when we bought the stock—it was up to $50. So that cost him a lot of money."

By the same token, Gerber points out, the stock sometimes drops in price and investors end up paying less per share than they would have paid if they had bought it the day they sent in their money.

If you're interested in making a long-range buying commitment to a specific company (perhaps the one you work for or one in which you have a strong interest), you might consider opening an account directly with the company. To qualify for dividend reinvestment plans, you need to hold your stock in your own name and to fill out an authorization form requesting the company to reinvest your dividends. Contact the company's shareholder relations department to see whether the company offers such a plan, and if so, ask for additional details on how to open an account. It's an excellent way to build a stake in a company with a nominal periodic payment—and absolutely no commissions.

TAKING CHARGE

If you choose to use a discounter, you will need an outside source of investment information to help you stay attuned to the market. Where can you turn for help?

* *The financial press.* Investment ideas are everywhere. The business section of your newspaper will normally carry articles on local companies as well as nationally syndicated investment columns that offer investment advice. *The Wall Street Journal, Money, Investor's Daily, Forbes, Fortune, Barron's* and a number of other investment publications provide a wealth of promising investment recommendations. The PBS program "Wall Street Week" features investment recommendations from some of the nation's top financial experts.

How accurate are these published recommendations? Probably about as accurate as the typical brokerage house recommendations—primarily because most of the published recommendations are drawn from brokers and analysts. Obviously, when you rely exclusively on the press for your investment ideas, the biggest problem you'll face is getting up-to-the-minute information on the status of the company, and you'll have no source of guidance on when to sell, hold or buy more of your stocks. You may also face some other problems as well. Some financial experts contend that by the time a stock makes it into the press, there's a good chance that its price has already been run up. "When a stock makes it on the cover of *Forbes* or *Fortune*," says one broker, "I want to be out of that stock."

Moreover, investors tend to suffer from the candy store syndrome. Instead of building a position in a handful of stocks, they tend to sample a few shares of two or three dozen stocks. It's difficult to effectively follow and trade that many stocks—especially when your chief source of information is the press. But some investors have managed to invest very successfully using only the financial press and their own market instincts.

- *Investment clubs.* Investors in communities across America have been forming investment clubs to join forces in uncovering hidden values in the stock market. Typically, the members of such clubs research the companies themselves and vote on what to buy at club meetings. While results vary from club to club, some of the clubs do very well. The Lorain County Investment Club, an all-black investment group in Lorain, Ohio, has been among the top performers. In 1985 alone, its portfolio rose 39 percent.

Two large national associations—the National Association of Investors Corporation (NAIC) and the American Association of Individual Investors (AAII)—cater specifically to investment clubs and independent investors.

The NAIC boasts more than 100,000 members and 7,000 investment clubs. You can join it for $30 a year. Membership entitles you to the association's investor's manual, a no-commission stock purchase plan with more than 25 stocks; a subscription to *Better Investing*, the monthly association magazine; and discounts on some other helpful services. Association figures show that stocks featured on the cover of *Better Investing* have outperformed the Dow Jones Industrial Average 23 of the past 31 overlapping five-year periods. From 1982 to 1986, the Dow climbed 146 percent while the association's picks jumped 322 percent.

To join the NAIC, send a check for $30 to: NAIC, 1515 East Eleven Mile Road, Royal Oak, MI 48067.

For $48 a year, you can join the American Association of Individual Investors. The AAII claims about 100,000 members and 40 local chapters. Membership entitles you to an annual guide to no-load mutual funds, a year-end tax strategy guide, and discounts on software and subscriptions to such publications as *Money, Investor's Daily, Business Week* and *Fortune.* Members also receive a free subscription to the *AAII Journal,* an investment magazine that is published ten times a year.

For another $24, you can join the AAII computer users group and get access to an electronic investment bulletin board and a subscription to a bimonthly newsletter called "Computerized Investing."

To join the AAII, send $48 to: AAII, 612 North Michigan Avenue, Chicago, IL 60611.

* *Market newsletters.* Many investors use market newsletters to make their investment selections. Hundreds of such newsletters provide detailed investment evaluations and recommendations. The subscription prices of market newsletters vary, but you can usually expect to pay at least $100 a year. While some investors adhere closely to the recommendations of a single newsletter, others subscribe to a number of services and selectively glean investment ideas from each of them.

One of the most successful newsletters has been *Value Line Investment Survey*, which costs $425 a year. *Value Line* is popular with serious investors because it offers not only investment recommendations, but also in-depth financial reports on all of the major publicly traded companies. Some of the other leading newsletters are the *Standard & Poor's Outlook, Growth Stock Outlook, United Business Service, Market Logic, Dow Theory Forecasts* and the *Zweig Forecast.*

Perhaps the biggest problem that investors face with newsletters is deciding among the hundreds of choices available. One enterprising publisher, Mark Hulbert, has even started a newsletter that evaluates the performance of other newsletters. His *Hulbert Financial Digest* (643 South Carolina Avenue, SE, Washington, DC 20003; $37.50 for a five-month trial subscription) provides performance ratings for most newsletters based on the recommendations they offer. It also gives risk-adjusted performance ratings.

Hulbert suggests that anyone shopping for newsletters look at the performance of newsletters for as long a period as possible, then take out trial subscriptions to the newsletters with the best long-term record (a trial subscription generally costs about $20). When you read through a newsletter, Hulbert suggests that you pay particularly close attention to several factors:

* *Risk level.* How risky are its recommendations? "You may find," says Hulbert, "that the letter has done very well over the past several years but its portfolio has been fully margined. You may decide that that's just not for you.
* *Tone.* "If the newsletter does a lot of apologizing, that's a giveaway that they're more interested in protecting their ego than in making you money," says Hulbert.
* *Follow-up.* Does the newsletter tell you not only what to buy but when to sell?
* *Approach.* "In reading the letter," says Hulbert, "see whether you're comfortable with its philosophy and its writing style or if you find its approach irritating, egotistical or obnoxious."

The important thing about a newsletter, says Hulbert, is not how it arrives at its recommendations but how accurate those recommendations turn out to be. "I don't care if they use astrology to chart the stocks; if it's performing well, I'll sit up and take notice. The proof of the pudding is in the eating. It would be nice to say that PhDs in finance end up doing better than people who have high school educations, but that's just not the case."

A word of caution about going strictly by track record: As with stocks and mutual funds, the performance of investment newsletters can vary greatly from one year to the next. Joe Granville was once hailed as one of the top gurus in the investment industry. But from 1982 to 1986 (during one of the greatest sustained bull markets in history), according to Hulbert's rating system, following the advice of the *Granville Market Letter* would have yielded disastrous results—a loss of 63.9 percent. By contrast, following *Value Line*'s advice would have resulted in a net gain of 169.3 percent.

In the end, choosing a newsletter involves some of the same problems as choosing stocks. Even when you take the time to choose carefully, there is no guarantee that the newsletter you choose will continue to perform as it has in the past. And there is certainly no guarantee that it will outperform your full-service broker. As Hulbert puts it, "There will be plenty of people who will do better with a broker than with a newsletter and a lot who will do better with a newsletter than with a broker."

For many investors, however, there is only one way to go—the full-service route. And as the next chapter explains, alert investors have been able to get added value for their commission dollars by cashing in on some of the lesser-known advantages of the full-service firms.

CHAPTER ELEVEN —————————————————

The Extras

You pay more for a full-service broker. Logically, you should get more.

And you can, if you know what to ask for. The range of services that brokers provide goes well beyond buy and sell recommendations: brokers sometimes offer house research reports, newsletters, discretionary services, discounts on trades, checking accounts, flexible lines of credit, comprehensive financial planning and other customer services. But brokers are not always quick to volunteer these extras. More often than not, only if you ask shall you receive.

DISCOUNTS

Forgive your broker for wincing at the word *discount*. Brokers, understandably, don't like that word—or the concept it represents. Some brokers refuse to offer discounts under any circumstances. But others have grudgingly come to accept discounting as part of the business and are willing to cut costs on certain trades.

"I discount," says Jim Vieburg of Piper Jaffray. "It's stupid not to. If a client calls in and says, 'Buy me 1,000 shares of XYZ,' I will tell him, 'Thanks for the order. I am giving you a 25 percent discount on this order.' On the other hand," Vieburg continues, "if the trade is my idea, I expect to get paid full commission for it. I realize that some brokers don't bring up discounting and will not grant a discount unless the client insists on it. That's dumb."

Generally speaking, discounts are reserved for larger accounts—either frequent traders or large block buyers. You should feel comfortable about asking for a discount if:

- your order is for 500 shares or more of a stock;
- you do $5,000 or more a year in gross commissions with your broker; or
- your order is unsolicited.

It's probably best to negotiate discounts when you first set up an account with a broker. Many brokers say that upon request they would offer discounts of roughly 25 percent on ideas that the investor comes up with and no discount on ideas that they provide. In your initial interview with your broker, you should ask the broker what type of discount arrangements he or she offers. Or you might say, "I plan to do this volume of business. What type of discount can I expect?"

"When I decided to do a lot of trading," says one investor, "I got the name of a broker who was supposed to be a good trader and gave him a call. We set up the ground rules for my discounts before I made my first trade. Here's the way we set it up: If it was my pick, I'd get a discount to buy and sell. If it was his pick, I'd pay full price to buy and sell unless the stock didn't do well, and then I'd get a discount on the sale."

Negotiating the discount, says the investor, was no problem. "From the second I suggested it, he said, 'Fine.' The biggest key, I felt, was to find a young, hungry, aggressive broker—this guy had three years' experience—who wanted the business. Buying stocks is just like anything else in sales—you're not going to get a discount if you don't ask for it."

When you're selling a stock, your ability to negotiate a discount varies with the circumstances. When you're calling your broker to unload a stock, don't expect a discount. "But when it's your broker calling you to urge you to trade out of one stock and into another," says one investor, "that's when you have some bargaining power. One time, on a stock that hadn't done well, my broker handled the sale for me for free—contingent, in this case, on the condition that I pay full commission to buy into the stock he was recommending."

Another investor who trades in large volumes says that his broker offers discounts on rare occasions. "I once bought about 70,000 shares of a $3 stock my broker's firm was making a market in, and he sold it to me for one-eighth over the bid price. There have also been times when a stock he recommended didn't work out too well, so he offered to sell out my position at no commission."

Although no-commission trades are a rarity, a number of brokers offer discounts on the sale of stocks they recommend if the stocks perform poorly. Even with a discount, however, you generally pay more with a full-service broker than you would at a discount house. "I usually give 25 to 35 percent discounts on unsolicited trades," says Vieburg. By contrast, discounters offer savings of 50 to 75 percent. So if price is your overriding concern, you would be better off dealing with a discounter than constantly badgering your full-service broker to shave a few dollars off your commissions.

MARGIN ACCOUNTS

If you know much about the Crash of 1929, then you know the grim side of margin accounts. A margin account is a credit arrangement that enables investors to use their securities as collateral to buy more securities. In a bear market, margin accounts tend to create a snowballing effect. When stocks drop in value, margin investors are forced either to put up more collateral or to liquidate some of their securities. If they choose to sell out their stocks, that tends to drive prices down still further. And that, in turn, forces other margin investors into a similar selling position—which drives prices even lower. Under the worst circumstances, that downward cycle can build a momentum that is virtually irreversible (e.g., the Crash of 1929, and, to some extent, the Crash of 1987).

In 1929, the downward cycle began suddenly and moved swiftly. When it was over, many investors on margin had lost both their money and their stocks. Even those who weathered the crash with their holdings intact found that their securities were either of no value or a fraction of their former value.

Margin requirements have been tightened considerably since then. At that time, for every dollar you paid in cash, you could buy $10 worth of equities on margin. An investor with $10,000 in cash could buy $100,000 in stocks. In a bull market, the earnings could be phenomenal. A 20 percent rise in the price of your stocks would mean a tripling of your equity. (Example: If the price of your stocks rose from $100,000 to $120,000, your equity would rise from $10,000 to $30,000. With $30,000 in collateral, you could now buy up to $300,000 in equities.) The downside, however, could be equally breathtaking. A mere 10 percent drop would wipe out your entire $10,000 in equity—and force the brokerage company to sell out your remaining $90,000 in stock unless you came up with more cash. Imagine, if you will, a market that drops 10 to 20 percent under such conditions. Frantic to meet their margin calls, investors flood the market with stocks. With more sellers than buyers, prices fall rapidly. Of such conditions are Great Depressions born.

Nowadays, one dollar's worth of stock (or other investments) owned outright will get you an additional dollar's worth on margin—a 50 percent margin requirement. The investor with $10,000 who could have leveraged his or her way to $100,000 in stock in the 1920s, can now get only $20,000 worth. As a result, the gains in a bull market aren't nearly as big (a 20 percent rise in the price of your stock means a 40 percent rise in your equity)—but neither are the losses. If your stock drops 10 percent, your equity drops 20 percent—a far cry from the 100 percent drop of the 1920s.

Margin accounts are generally associated with aggressive traders, but they offer advantages that even the most prudent investor would find tempting:

Margin Account Growth

Total market value	$20,000
Debit balance	− 10,000
Your equity	$10,000

A 20 percent increase would mean:

Total market value	$24,000
Debit balance	− 10,000
Your equity	$14,000 (40 percent increase)

- You have $10,000 in stock (fully paid for), and you have a $10,000 CD expiring soon, the funds from which you hope to reinvest in a young growth stock. Your broker calls to tell you about a high tech medical stock that's expected to do well. With a margin account, you can use your stock as collateral to buy up to $10,000 worth of the new stock without having to cash in your CD and incurring the penalty that comes with early withdrawal.
- Emergency expenses come up unexpectedly. You need cash in a hurry, but you don't want to sell your stocks to get it. By drawing on your margin account, you can have a check sent to you immediately—no muss, no fuss.
- You want to buy a car, and you don't want to hassle with the bank over a loan. You can use your stock holdings as collateral to pay for the car. And by borrowing from your margin account instead of the bank, you can pay back the loan when you want to—if you want to. Otherwise, as long as your stock stays at a healthy level, all you're ever required to pay is the interest on the margin loan—which is generally a very favorable rate.

The interest rate you're charged is usually tied to the "call loan rate," which is a fluctuating rate closely aligned to the prime rate but usually slightly lower. Large clients can get margin loans at a rate just over the call loan rate, and smaller clients generally pay a point or two higher than that. Either way, your margin rate would often be lower than the bank interest rate.

Competitive as it is, however, your margin rate can still be a major drag on the overall profitability of your investments. If you're paying ten percent interest and your stocks are going up 8 percent a year, you're cutting into your profits by using margin. Even if the stocks you buy on margin go up a very respectable 15 percent, after you've paid the ten percent margin fee, that would leave you with only a five percent gain on your margined stocks. That isn't much of a payback considering the flipside risk which is this: If the stock you own goes down 15 percent, your total loss would be significantly greater because of the extra ten percent interest charge.

- Another effective way in which investors have used margin accounts is by buying stocks or bonds that offer a high yield. If you're paying a ten percent margin rate and the utility stock you've bought is paying a 12 percent dividend, you enjoy a positive two percent spread even if your portfolio doesn't move.

Margin Calls

Should the price of your stocks decline significantly, you may be subject to a "margin call"—that is, a notice from your broker instructing you either to add cash to your account or to liquidate some of your securities. Margin calls come when your equity drops to 25 percent of your total position (though many securities firms have established a slightly higher 30 percent maintenance requirement). For example, if you use $10,000 equity to buy $20,000 in stock and the total value of the stock drops to $13,333, you would have to either deposit additional cash to meet the minimum 25 percent level, or have your broker liquidate some stock. If you are ever subject to margin call, it is our recommendation that under most circumstances you meet the call by selling part of your position instead of pouring more cash into your floundering investment.

Calculating Your Margin Call

Total market value	$20,000
Your debit balance	− 10,000
Your equity	$10,000

To determine the level at which you will receive a margin maintenance call, you can multiply your debit balance by $4/3$:

$$4/3 \times \$10,000 \text{ debit balance} = \$13,333$$

The $13,333 represents the level to which the market value can fall before you are required to ante up more money or liquidate part of your position. The final figures would look like this:

Total market value drops to:	$13,333
Your debit balance stays at:	− 10,000
Your total equity falls to:	$3,333 (25% of market value)

Perhaps the biggest hazard with margin accounts is that investors tend to use them at the wrong time. Margin accounts are most appropriate when stocks are at bargain levels. However, when the market has rallied and stocks are high, some investors are swayed by the spirit of the moment and double up their investments with a margin account. If the market has a sudden reversal, those investors stand to lose a lot in a short amount of time.

Many investors who owned stocks on margin were devastated on Black Monday when the market crashed. In retrospect, October 1987 was a perfect example of when NOT to be heavily margined. The stock market was near its all-time high, five years into a bull market. Price earnings ratios of many stocks were at or near their all-time highs. By historic standards, there were very few real values in the market. Yet many investors, buoyed by their success over the previous five years, continued to buy stocks on margin. In fact the amount of margin buying had increased significantly from $22 billion in 1985 to $44 billion by October 1987.

The Dow had reached a peak of nearly 2750 in late August 1987, and had gradually declined to about 2200 by Oct. 19, so investors who owned stocks on margin had already seen an erosion of equity in their accounts. In many cases their equity had dropped from 50 percent to about 30 percent. For every $1 of stock they owned outright, they held $2 of stock on borrowed money. That put them right on the knife's edge. Any further erosion would force them either to put up more capital or sell some of their stocks to maintain their account.

Then came Black Monday, the disastrous 508 point drop. Many stocks dropped 20 to 40 percent on that day. Margin investors who were fully-invested lost all of their equity, and in some cases had to drain their savings to pay off their margin account debt. Millionaires became paupers overnight. It was an agonizing time for many investors. The most dramatic example of the emotional fall-out occurred in South Miami where Arthur Kane, a wealthy investor who lost everything in the crash (including $11 million in equities he had bought through heavy leveraging), walked into a Merrill Lynch branch office and fatally shot the branch manager, seriously wounded his broker and then killed himself.

The lesson? Investors should buy on margin only when they believe securities are undervalued—not when stock prices and price-earnings ratios are at all-time highs.

RESEARCH

Full-service houses spend millions of dollars tracking the market and monitoring the performance of the companies they follow. This research is generally manifested in buy and sell recommendations from your broker. But if you're interested in playing a more active role in your investment decisions, you can usually get research reports, newsletters and other investment-related literature from your broker to help you in doing so.

For instance, Merrill Lynch sends all of its clients a brief report on economic and investment issues along with the monthly account statements. The firm also offers a free weekly *Research Highlights* report for any client who wants it, a free weekly market analysis report called the *Farrell Report,* a free monthly publication called *Current Investment Strategy,* monthly or quarterly reviews on the various industry sectors and research reports on virtually any company that Merrill Lynch tracks. "My clients receive so much mail from us," says Merrill's Kathy Soule, "that they say they'll never be lonely as long as they have an account with us."

Brokers may also send their clients additional information about their specific investments. "If my clients own stock in ADC Telecommunications, for instance," says Lee Kopp of Dain Bosworth, "every time we see an article on that company, I'll send out a copy of it to those clients to keep them up-to-date on how the company is doing."

Brokers sometimes offer special gifts to new clients. For instance, if you're active in stocks, your broker may give you a complimentary *Standard & Poor's Stock Guide.* If you buy municipal bonds, your broker may send you a monthly listing of the firm's municipal bond inventory. Some firms have special publications that they send only to their wealthiest investors and other publications that they send to everyone who opens an account.

Ask your broker about available research services. Ask for samples of a typical stock research report. Ask about industry surveys, and perhaps about research reports on bonds. And get samples. Then ask your broker what material he or she thinks would be helpful to you, based on your own investment activity.

FINANCIAL PLANNING SERVICES

If you're interested in getting a comprehensive financial plan, you might ask your broker whether that's a service he or she can provide. A few brokers specialize in financial planning. Others avoid it at all costs. Brokerage firms offer a variety of financial plans:

- *Yellow pad plan.* With no charge, your broker jots down some basic financial information about you on a yellow pad and after some consideration recommends investments that he or she feels would be suitable for you.

- *Computer printout.* For roughly $250 to $500, you can get a computer-generated financial plan of about 20 pages that addresses your general needs but lacks specifics. Such a plan is geared toward individuals or couples with household incomes of $25,000 to $60,000.

- *Personalized computer printout.* For about $1,000, you can get a more detailed plan (50 to 100 pages). While such a plan is also largely computer-generated, it gives some extra attention to your special needs and circumstances. This type of plan is most appropriate for those with household incomes of $60,000 to $150,000.

- *Deluxe plan.* For about $8,000 to $10,000, you can get a comprehensive personalized plan that has been put together by a team of financial experts. The plan would run 100 to 200 pages. A plan of this kind is appropriate for millionaires and big-ticket executives.

See Chapter 4 for a more complete discussion of financial planning.

DISCRETIONARY ACCOUNTS

A discretionary account is one in which you let your broker make all of your buying and selling decisions for you. You give your broker written authorization to make purchases and sales in your account without consulting you. Generally speaking, discretionary accounts are more appropriate for blind trusts than for active investors. While it stands to reason that an experienced, highly competent money manager may very well do better managing your money than you would do on your own, you alone should have the final say in every investment decision that involves your money.

"I am paid on the basis of transactions," says Betsy Buckley of Dain Bosworth. "I do not want full discretionary authority where I take on the fiduciary responsibility and I'm compensated on a transaction basis. I don't feel that's ethical. Another broker might, and that's OK, but I don't. If a client needs a money manager to handle, say, a pension fund account, I'll help the client find a money manager, and then I'll monitor the money manager."

However, some investors have maintained discretionary accounts with their brokers for years with excellent results. PaineWebber's Bill Blount has discretionary authority over nearly a thousand accounts. He controls several hundred million dollars of his clients' assets, and his clients have fared extremely well over the past 15 years—about a 20 percent average annual rate of return (with compounding), says Blount. But Blount is an exception. Even within PaineWebber, discretionary accounts are generally discouraged.

BROKER PARTNERSHIPS

If you think two heads are better than one, you might benefit from a broker partnership. "A lot of brokers with different specialties are forming partnerships because they feel they can bring more to the table by joining together," says David Waterbury of Dean Witter. "Some have worked out very well; others haven't."

Dale Grubb, a young Shearson Lehman broker, joined forces with a more experienced broker at his office in order to appeal to a wider cross section of the public. "Between the two of us," says Grubb, "my partner and I cover the gamut. I'm 25, a native of this area and a Protestant. My partner is 60, from New York and Jewish. We found that some of his clients preferred to deal with me because I'm younger, more personable, and I put more stress on financial planning, whereas my partner is better at handling some of my older, more arrogant clients because he's been around so much longer. If one of us doesn't appeal to the client, the other one will."

In some partnerships, all accounts are handled jointly and commissions split evenly. In other partnerships, the partners merely serve as pinch hitters for each other. One partner can leave town—or merely step out for a round of golf—knowing that the other partner is fully prepared to handle his or her accounts. But taking on a partner carries added responsibility. Says Waterbury: "Both of us have to know all of the accounts—and not just what's in those accounts but why it's in there and what type of investment objectives each client has."

As an investor, you will find few disadvantages in using partners unless you're particularly discreet about your personal finances. Some investors are reluctant to share their personal financial information with more than one broker. But for the most part, investors can benefit from the added service and investment knowledge of a broker partnership. A husband and wife who have formed a partnership at Kidder, Peabody say that they brainstorm ideas for their clients to try to come up with better investing strategies for them.

However, partnerships, like marriages, are often fragile. "I think a relatively small number of partnerships have worked out well," says Waterbury. While partnerships may begin with the best of intentions, rifts eventually tend to develop between partners over two predictable issues: the division of labor and the division of commissions.

THE SALES ASSISTANT

To the good fortune of their clients, brokers don't have to wage the daily battle alone. For help, they have sales assistants. Get to know your broker's sales assistant. Learn the sales assistant's name. Treat the sales assistant with respect. And someday, your kindness may pay big dividends. "Establish a good relationship with your sales assistant," advises Merrilee Cole, a former sales assistant and broker, "and she'll knock herself out when you need help."

To a great degree, SAs are the foot soldiers of the securities business. They're the first line of defense between the public and the brokerage firm. "A good sales assistant can make or break a broker," says Cole. "I've heard customers say that the sales assistant is the main reason they keep their business at a firm."

Generally speaking, you should use a sales assistant when you have a question about an administrative or account matter, when you need information or a price quote, when you want a check sent out, when your address changes, or when you have any other questions or need any other paperwork regarding your account. On the other hand, unless other arrangements have been made, you should call your broker to obtain advice on investments and strategies and to place buy or sell orders.

When To Use a Sales Assistant

1. To answer any administrative questions
2. To answer any questions about your monthly statement
3. To obtain quotes on stocks, bonds, options, etc.
4. If you want a check sent out
5. If you want information sent out
6. If your address changes
7. To give instructions on how a security is to be registered
8. To have paperwork prepared for an estate
9. To transfer cash or securities
10. To determine the cost basis of a security
11. If you have questions about your IRA
12. If you have any other needs that involve paperwork

There are exceptions. Some houses use "registered" sales assistants who are allowed to handle many of the buy and sell transactions. "I only talk to my most active client a couple of times a year," says Don Tidlund of E. F. Hutton. "My assistant handles him. He usually calls her three times a day. Most brokers would kill for an account like that, but I just don't have the time to handle him myself. He makes most of his own decisions, and learns through my assistant what I'm recommending."

For the most part, however, sales assistants are not expected to give investment advice except in rare instances. "When my broker is out of the office or on vacation," says Lory Dubbels, a registered sales assistant with Piper Jaffray, "he will review with me his views on various investments. Based on that, I will pass along his opinions to clients who inquire about their investments."

Sales assistants are usually shared by three or four brokers, but the top producers generally have a full-time sales assistant. Some brokers, in fact, have two or three sales assistants who spend their time making cold calls to drum up new prospects for them.

The job of sales assistant seems to be one of the few areas that have been untouched by the feminist revolution. About 98 percent of all sales assistants are women. And most of them are poorly paid. "It's a wonderful position," says one former sales assistant, "but the money is terrible." "Parking lot attendants probably make more than sales assistants," says another former sales assistant. "I can't imagine a worse-paying job." In all fairness, however, it should be said that some sales assistants are paid considerably better than others. An executive placement counselor who deals with the securities industry says, "Sales assistants can make as little as $10,000 to $20,000 in some markets and as much as $40,000 in others. And in good years, they often receive bonuses from the broker they work for of $4,000 to $6,000—which often comes as cash, unreported and untaxed."

Sales assistants sometimes suffer from the Rodney Dangerfield complex—they "get no respect." Clients may be rude or abusive toward the sales assistant—a tendency that can ultimately hurt the client more than it does the sales assistant. "If a customer who has been inconsiderate or demanding needs a sales assistant's help to adjust his account," says one sales assistant, "and it's one of seven things on a 'to do' list, it will probably be the seventh thing that gets done."

In extreme cases, the consequences of mistreating a sales assistant can be far worse than mere inconvenience. "There is no point in being nasty to the sales assistant and sweet to the broker," says one sales assistant. "Eventually it all gets back to the broker." One broker talks about one client who was angry and downright abusive with his sales assistant. The sales assistant hung up the phone in tears. The branch manager stopped by to see what was wrong. When he heard what the client had said, he immediately phoned the client, verified the conversation, and then told the client that, effective immediately, he was closing the client's account with the firm.

When you open a new account, ask your broker how the sales assistant should be used. Then get to know the sales assistant. "One of the first things you should do is learn the assistant's name and direct dial number," says Piper's Vieburg. Then treat the sales assistant kindly. Because the next time your dividend is late or your statement is in error, you may need the sales assistant's help to put things straight.

ACCOUNT AND MONTHLY STATEMENT

When you open a new account, you should look over your account statement closely and ask your broker to explain anything you don't understand.

"I tell all my new clients, 'As soon as you receive your first monthly statement, give me a call and let me walk you through it, because there will probably be some things on there that you don't understand,'" says David Thompson of Prudential-Bache. Some firms hand out booklets on how to read the monthly statement.

"I always go over my statements with a fine-tooth comb," says one investor. "If I ordered 200 shares of XYZ at $10^1/8$, I want to make sure I got it at that price. I've fired two brokers since I've been investing, and both have been over problems I discovered on my statement. Once, I thought I was selling my stock at $12^1/2$. When I got my statement, it said I had sold it at $11^7/8$. I called my broker immediately and complained. Not long after that, I had another stock he sold for $1/4$ under what he had quoted. That time I called and closed my account. The same type of thing happened a couple of times with another broker. I thought I was buying one stock at $3^1/2$, but when I got my statement, to my surprise it said I had paid 4¹/₄. My present broker always calls me to let me know if there's been a change in price from the time I placed my order. I would much rather hear about it that way than to find out about if for the first time on my account statement."

Ask your broker whether his or her firm has a brochure on how to read the monthly statement. Also ask your broker for any other literature on the firm's products, services and specialties.

SPECIAL SERVICES

Brokerage firms offer a number of additional services, such as checking accounts, credit cards and special lines of credit.

Merrill Lynch, for instance, offers the Cash Management Account (CMA), which was originally developed during the tenure of Donald Regan, former president and CEO of Merrill Lynch and later President Reagan's chief of staff. For a fee of $65 a year, the CMA provides you with free checking, a VISA card, margin account privileges and an automatic "sweep" of your idle assets into an interest-bearing money market account. The CMA has proven extremely popular; about 1.3 million investors have opened CMA accounts.

Most of the major brokerage companies have introduced their own versions of the CMA—generically referred to as an "asset management account." Prudential-Bache, for example, has the Command Account; A. G. Edwards offers the Total Assets Account; PaineWebber has the Reserve Management Account. The names of such accounts vary from one firm to the next, but the services are very similar.

Ask your broker about the central assets account at his or her firm. Ask how credit balances are handled. Ask about research reports, about discounts, about margin arrangements. Whatever is on your mind, ask by all means. Otherwise you may never know what extras you're missing.

In addition to all the extras, brokerage firms offer a wide variety of products that go well beyond individual securities. Mutual funds are the most popular of these products. Although convenient to own, mutual funds are not always easy to select, as the next chapter explains.

CHAPTER TWELVE _____

Mutual Funds: The Fast Food of Investing

Stocks and bonds have always been the bread and butter of the brokerage business. But over the past few years, investors' tastes have changed, and so has the menu of investment products that brokerage firms offer. Investors can now choose from a varied fare of other investment staples: unit trusts, annuities, limited partnerships, certificates of deposit and the Big Mac of packaged investments—mutual funds.

This shift to packaged investments, to a great extent, has changed the nature of the stockbroker's job. "People still call them stockbrokers, but the broker of today does only a fraction of his business in stocks," says Bill Wise, a branch manager with Dean Witter who has been in the securities business since 1952. "In our firm, we get only 25 to 30 percent of our commissions from common stocks. We do more than that in mutual funds."

Mutual funds are considered investing's answer to fast foods. They're selectively blended servings of stocks or bonds that offer investors instant diversification, liquidity and professional management. Experienced portfolio managers hand-pick each security, charting the market, sifting through the financial statements of promising companies and using their professional instincts to make all the crucial buying and selling decisions. By pooling the assets of many investors, mutual funds are able to acquire a portfolio of dozens of securities. Investors who buy shares in a fund own a fraction of the entire portfolio and thus reduce their risk of a major loss. "With mutual funds, an investor can make a single investment decision and achieve diversification and complete record keeping," says Rab Bertelsen, a vice president with Fidelity Investments. "And you can get started for as little as a $500 to $1,000 investment." Another advantage of

Mutual Fund Benefits

1. Professional management
2. Convenience
3. Diversification
4. Liquidity

most mutual funds is that investors can redeem (open-end) funds at net asset value and receive their money in a matter of days.

Over the past decade, mutual fund assets have grown almost 20-fold, surging from about $50 billion in 1978 to more than $800 billion in 1987, with more than 30 million mutual fund accounts.

Why the sudden appetite for professionally managed funds? "For one thing," says William Bergstrom, a financial planner with IDS Financial Services, "there's been an explosion of investment magazines that have been publishing the rates of return that mutual funds are paying. Investors see that they can do better in mutual funds than they can do in their bank CDs and savings accounts."

Indeed, the pages of the financial press each year offer evidence of fabulous returns—30, 40, even 50 percent for the top-rated funds. But what is not so evident is that despite their diversity and professional management, mutual funds can be as volatile as stocks and bonds. The 44 Wall Street Equity Fund, for instance, performed spectacularly in the 1986 bull market, climbing 47 percent. But during the Black Monday days of October 1987, (from Oct. 1 to Oct. 20), it dropped 48 percent. The Hartwell Leverage Fund had similar results: it was up 50 percent in 1986, but dropped approximately 40 percent during October 1987.

"Some investors think that if a fund had a 20 percent return last year, that's the rate they can expect this year," says Bergstrom. "That's just not the case."

The fact is that most mutual funds generally underperform the overall stock market by a small margin. In the past five years, only 28 percent of all mutual funds have outperformed the Standard & Poor's 500. Would investors do better in mutual funds than in individual stocks and bonds? "Sometimes," says Bergstrom, "sometimes not."

A number of mutual fund owners are converts from individual securities. And while many made the switch because they were tired of getting pounded in the market, others changed over for less obvious reasons. One woman with $12,000 in her IRA account initially declined to put her money into a mutual fund because she wanted to try her hand with individual stocks. She invested in four stocks, all of which became takeover targets. Within 18 months, her $12,000 IRA had soared to $90,000. Despite her initial success—or, more accurately, because of it— the woman realized that she was suddenly in over her head with her new-

FIGURE 12.1   Typical Growth Mutual Fund Does Not Always Beat the Market

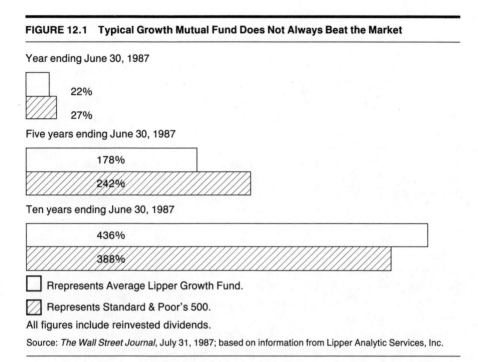

Year ending June 30, 1987

22%

27%

Five years ending June 30, 1987

178%

242%

Ten years ending June 30, 1987

436%

388%

☐ Rrepresents Average Lipper Growth Fund.

▨ Represents Standard & Poor's 500.

All figures include reinvested dividends.

Source: *The Wall Street Journal*, July 31, 1987; based on information from Lipper Analytic Services, Inc.

found wealth. "I'd never had that kind of money before," she explained. So she moved the entire $90,000 into mutual funds.

Convenience may be the most attractive feature of mutual funds. "I've had some older clients who had built up a large portfolio of stocks over the years but found that it was too much trouble to keep up with the paperwork," says Bergstrom. "So they cashed in their stocks and reinvested in mutual funds."

For all the advantages of mutual funds, buyers of such funds face a critical problem: choosing among the staggering number of funds. In 1986 alone, 500 new mutual funds were brought to market, raising the total to more than 2,000 funds. There are now more mutual funds than there are stocks on the New York Stock Exchange. So mutual funds are not quite the fast-food answer to investing that some would believe. The menu is overwhelming, the prices are confusing, and the quality is never guaranteed.

"WE DO IT ALL FOR YOU"

One of the obvious advantages of mutual funds is that you can buy many of the no-load funds directly from the investment company without paying a commission to a broker. Just the same, investors buy about

75 percent of their funds through their brokers—up from 55 percent just five years ago. Why? A broker may be able to help you in several ways.

A broker can do your research for you and give you recommendations on which funds to buy and on when to get in and when to get out. "First," says David Thompson of Prudential-Bache, "I ask clients what got them interested in a mutual fund. If they heard about a friend who made a 40 percent gain in a mutual fund last year and they are hoping to do the same, I want to know that so I can help them establish more realistic expectations. Then I want to find out what their risk threshold is and how much of a loss they feel they can take and still feel comfortable going to sleep at night. Once I've questioned them at length, I try to direct them to a mutual fund that is safe enough that both the investor and the spouse will be comfortable with it."

A broker can help you not only with your buying decisions but also with your decisions to sell. If you've made a lot of money in a high-tech fund, your broker may see the high-tech market beginning to flatten out and may recommend that you move into a fund in a different sector—a bond fund or maybe even a money market fund, where you can hold your money (with interest) until something more promising emerges. And if you stay within the same family of funds, you will have to pay a commission only once. After that, your broker's advice is free.

A broker can also troubleshoot for you. An investor who chose to buy mutual funds on his own, wanted to make regular contributions to four Fidelity funds. "I sent in my forms and told them to put $250 a month into each of the four funds, and I wanted the money automatically withdrawn from my checking account. I filled out each of the papers the same way; I sent in four checks and the authorizations from my bank, and I put them all in the same envelope and mailed them off. Nothing happened the first month, which was understandable. The second month, one fund was activated and three were not. I called an 800 number and talked to someone (I don't even know his name), and still nothing happened. A couple of months later, I called back and talked to someone else, and still got no results. Now it's been six months, and I don't really know what to do next. I could fill out new forms, but as soon as I do that, with my luck, they'll activate the first ones and I'll have $250 taken out for each fund twice."

The reality, then, is that if you don't buy mutual funds through a broker, there is no logical source to which you can turn to get your problems solved. But if you do buy through a broker, remember that brokers don't get paid to recommend no-load funds. You'll be expected to pay a commission in exchange for your broker's service and expertise.

"HAVE IT YOUR WAY"

You don't have to have a broker to buy a mutual fund. In fact, when you select a fund on your own, you can often save substantially on up-front fees. But choosing a fund takes a certain amount of effort and expertise. Where do you start?

"With more than 2,000 funds to choose from," says Bertelsen, "deciding on a fund sounds a lot more difficult than it really is." You can take several relatively simple steps to narrow down the field and select a mutual fund that's right for you:

- *Identify your investment objectives.* Do you want income, capital appreciation, safety or aggressive growth? "This will probably reduce the number of choices from 2,000 to perhaps 100 or fewer," says Bertelsen.
- *Identify your attitude toward risk.* "Are you a risk player, or are you concerned about volatility, or are you somewhere in between?" asks Bertelsen. "This may reduce your choices to a dozen or so funds."
- *Then begin your research.* There are a number of excellent reference sources. The *Forbes* August issue, the *Money* October issue, the *Business Week* special mutual funds issue in February, the *Barron's* quarterly review of mutual funds and several other investment publications offer rankings of mutual funds. In addition, several investment newsletters, such as the *Maximizer* and the *Mutual Fund Forecaster,* track the performance of mutual funds and offer advice on which mutual funds to buy.

The public library in most communities carries a wealth of reference material on mutual funds that would be well worth looking through. Lipper Analytical Services and the Wiesenberger Investment Companies Service publish in-depth evaluations of mutual funds. The Wiesenberger publication discusses not only the funds but the background of the fund managers as well.

Lipper Analytical Services periodically publishes the performance of different types of mutual funds.

This excerpt is from *The Wall Street Journal.*

LIPPER INDEXES

Tuesday, June 30, 1987

	Close	Percentage chg since Dec. 31	Percentage chg since Mar. 31
Growth Fund Index	393.84	+ 21.89	+ 2.34
Growth & Income Index	614.04	+ 22.31	+ 3.65
Balanced Fund Index	490.88	+ 14.17	+ 0.69
Gold Fund Index	172.49	+ 40.19	− 4.12
Science & Tech Fd Index	163.49	+ 28.44	+ 0.48
International Fd Index	273.73	+ 23.64	+ 8.11

Source: Lipper Analytical Services.

- *Weigh the choices.* According to Bertelsen, "There are three things to look for in assessing a mutual fund—performance, convenience and reputation."

Performance is the major consideration. We recommend that you look at the fund's track record over the past five to ten years. Good performance in a single year means very little. Very often, the best-performing funds one year become the worst-performing funds the next year. International funds, for instance, generally do very well while the dollar is declining, but what happens when it goes back up? Such funds are then more likely to show a loss. Gold funds do well when the price of gold is rising, but when it drops, those funds take a beating. According to Lipper Analytical Services, of the top 25 funds over the past five years, only three made it into the top 25 in the most recent one-year period. So with rare exceptions, you're probably better off avoiding the best-performing funds of the previous year.

Obviously, we suggest that you also avoid the worst-performing funds of the previous year. Often such poor performance is a more or less permanent condition. For instance, as of the end of March 1987, the Steadman American Industry Fund ranked in the bottom 25 percent for the past year, the past five years and the past ten years. During a five-year period in which the S&P 500 appreciated by more than 200 percent, the Steadman fund showed an average compounded gain of only 0.6 percent per year.

Our recommendation is that you look for funds that:

1. were in the top 10 to 40 percent in performance the previous year;
2. have had a strong track record over the past five to ten years;
3. have done well in good and bad markets (the last thing you want is a fund with an A in a bull market and a D in a bear market); and
4. have the same fund manager who was there during the fund's good years. (Such publications as *Money* list the number of years that fund managers have been with funds.)

"WHERE'S THE BEEF?"

There are mutual funds to meet the tastes and risk thresholds of nearly everyone who invests. The original mutual funds were designed to produce a combination of growth and income by investing in a diversified portfolio of dividend-paying blue-chip stocks. Many such funds—now referred to as "growth and income" funds—are still on the market.

- *Growth funds.* As mutual funds became more popular, new breeds were introduced. One of the earliest was the pure growth mutual funds, which concentrated on capital appreciation with little concern for (dividend) income. These funds characteristically invested in stocks of emerging industries or of classic growth industries such as drug companies, retailers and computer manufacturers.

- *Aggressive growth.* An outgrowth of the growth funds was the aggressive growth funds—called "go-go" funds when they were first introduced in the 1960s. The aggressive funds come in many forms. Some invest in depressed stocks that have turnaround potential—such as Chrysler, Manville, Union Carbide and Braniff. Others look for trendy stocks. For instance, in 1987, when condoms were a hot item (as a result of the AIDS epidemic), some funds began investing in such condom manufacturers as Mentor Corporation (which went from $12 a share to $47.50 in just over a month in early 1987). Other funds look for good start-up companies that could blossom into major corporations. And still others invest in potential takeover stocks that could experience a sharp run-up in prices. With aggressive funds, the portfolio managers play a numbers game. Some of their picks pan out; others fall flat. Their hope is to make enough money on the winners to more than compensate for the losers. In truth, the label "aggressive growth" applies more to the types of stocks that these funds invest in than it does to their overall performance. Although aggressive growth funds may outperform other stock funds at certain times, over the long run, many of them have proven to be no more profitable than other stock funds—just more volatile.
- *Bond funds.* Bond funds first became popular in the 1970s, when investors began opting for managed portfolios of corporate bonds rather than individual bonds. An offshoot of the traditional bond funds was the high-yield bond funds—portfolios of low-rated "junk bonds" that paid interest rates three or four points higher than those paid by many of the AAA-rated bonds. With individual junk bonds, safety is a major concern because of the risk of default. But with the diversity of a lot of different junk bonds, losses are minimal even if one or two of the bonds default. High-yield bond funds have enjoyed great popularity in recent years.

However, bond funds have one major flaw. Despite their diversity, they can be very volatile, depending on changes in interest rates. If you buy an individual bond that pays 10 percent and you want to hold it until 1999, you will get consistent interest payments and reimbursement of your invested assets in 1999. But that's not true for bond funds. Bonds rise and fall in value as interest rates fluctuate. When interest rates rise, bond values drop. When interest rates rise by two percentage points, your bond fund could decline in value by 10 percent or more. When interest rates were rising through the early 1980s, investors in bond funds were losing more in net asset value than they were receiving in interest payments. Conversely, as interest rates declined through the mid-80s, investors in bond funds enjoyed both excellent income and soaring net asset values. When inflation is on the rise and interest rates are following closely behind, you should not invest in long-term bond funds.

- *Tax-exempt bond funds.* These funds invest in municipal bonds and provide tax-exempt earnings for investors. Among such funds, you can find high-yield tax-exempt funds that invest in higher-risk municipal bonds paying higher interest rates.
- *Government securities funds.* These funds invest strictly in securities issued by the federal government. They are considered the safest of the bond funds, and therefore their yields are generally lower than those of other bond funds. But if it's absolute safety you want, you're better off investing in individual government securities, since government securities funds are just as vulnerable to swings in interest rates as any other bond funds. When interest rates are rising, these funds, like any other bond funds, will decline in value.
- *International funds.* This relatively new breed of stock fund had excellent success in the mid-1980s, when the U.S. dollar was declining relative to other currencies and foreign stocks were booming. International funds invest in the stocks of foreign countries (most commonly Japan, Germany and Great Britain). How does a declining dollar relate to the success of foreign stocks? Here's an example: If one British pound is worth $1, then a British company worth a million pounds is worth $1 million. If the pound rises in value to $1.50, then that company would be worth $1.5 million. The company's net asset value in U.S. currency has grown 50 percent, which means that the stock of U.S. investors in that company is worth 50 percent more. On the other hand, when the dollar is rising relative to other currencies, foreign stocks become less attractive to U.S. investors. Unless foreign stocks are doing particularly well in their home markets, currency translation losses can make investing abroad unprofitable.
- *Specialty funds* (also called "sector funds"). Funds are available in almost any market sector you could name—precious metals funds, utility funds, high-tech funds, medical technology funds, over-the-counter funds, regional funds. If you think gas and oil stocks are ready to take off, you might invest in an energy fund. If you want a hedge against inflation, you might invest in a gold fund that buys the stocks of gold mining companies. While specialty funds have broad stockholdings within a specific sector, they lack the diversity and safety of traditional stock funds. If the sector is faring poorly, so will the fund. For instance, while most stock funds did relatively well through the mid-1980s, energy stock funds were badly battered because of depressed conditions in the oil industry.
- *Ethical funds.* A number of mutual funds have been designed with the ethical investor in mind. These funds characteristically avoid investing in companies involved in weapons manufacturing, liquor and alcohol production, nuclear energy and anything that has to do with South Africa. Among the most successful of this group are Pax World Fund

(Portsmouth, New Hampshire), Calvert Social Investment Fund (Bethesda, Maryland) and Working Assets Money Fund (San Francisco, California).

- *Money market funds.* Although money market funds are a form of mutual fund, they are considered to be in a class by themselves. Of the $800 billion invested in mutual funds, more than $240 billion is invested in the more than 400 money market funds. Brokerage firms use money market fund accounts for clients who want to continue drawing interest on the money in their account when it is not invested in securities or other investments. There are three types of money market funds:

    1. regular money market funds, which invest in short-term government and corporate securities with maturities of less than a year (typically 60 to 90 days);
    2. government securities money market funds, which invest only in U.S. Treasury bills and other short-term securities issued by the federal government; and
    3. tax-free money market funds, which invest in short-term municipal notes providing federally tax-exempt income.

- *Mutual funds of mutual funds.* Since some funds are hot one year and others are hot the next year, why not buy a group of mutual funds or even a mutual fund of mutual funds? Such funds are available. But by using them, you diversify yourself so broadly that you consign yourself to mediocrity. In essence, you pay management fees for Portfolio managers to cancel one another out. Our recommendation is that you avoid such funds.

- *Index funds.* Index funds invest in a broad cross section of stocks that mirrors a popular stock index such as the Standard & Poor's 500 or the Dow Jones Industrial Average. Because index funds have no costs for research analysts and highly paid portfolio managers, their fees and expenses tend to be lower than those of other funds. And they're virtually guaranteed to match the performance of the market. The granddaddy of all index funds, the Vanguard Index Trust, has consistently shadowed the ups and downs of the S&P 500 throughout its 11-year history. The fund has an expense ratio of only 0.28 percent per year and no sales charge. By contrast, other index funds charge sales fees of up to $4^3/_4$ percent. Although the Vanguard fund has shunned advertising to help keep costs down, it has grown steadily through word of mouth and now has nearly $1 billion in assets.

    Index funds have become increasingly popular with institutional investors. Such investors recognize the difficulty of beating the market and are more than happy to just match it. (See Chapter 13 for further elaboration of index funds.)

- *Closed-end funds.* A closed-end fund is a professionally managed diversified portfolio that is closed to new investors. Much as with stock offerings, investment companies underwrite such funds to raise a limited amount of money. Once the cutoff point (say $100 million) has been reached, no new investments are accepted and the fund begins trading on the open market like a stock. Some of the best-known

You can find out how the prices of various closed-end funds compare to the net asset value of those funds by referring to the listing of "Publicly Traded Funds" in *The Wall Street Journal*. It is found on the mutual fund page in the second section of the *Journal*.

Notice that in this illustration the Korea Fund was selling at a premium of 114 percent over its net asset value, whereas the Gemini Capital Fund was selling at a discount of 15 percent.

Publicly Traded Funds

Friday, July 3, 1987

Following is a weekly listing of unaudited net asset values of publicly traded investment fund shares, reported by the companies as of Friday's close. Also shown is the closing listed market price or a dealer-to-dealer asked price of each fund's shares, with the percentage of difference.

	N.A. Value	Stk Price	% Diff		N.A. Value	Stk Price	% Diff
Diversified Common Stock Funds				CentSec	15.26	13½ −	11.5
				Claremont	57.38	57⅜	.....
AdmExp	22.85	22 −	3.7	CounsTndC	8.69	7⅛ −	18.0
BakerFen	59.54	49¾ −	16.4	DufPhUtils	8.39	9⅛ +	8.8
BlueChipVal	9.37	9⅝ +	2.7	EllsworthCv	9.86	8⅜ −	15.1
ClemnteGlbl	9.23	8⅞ −	3.8	EmgMdTh b16.47		14 −	15.0
DecisionCap18.00		16¾ −	6.9	Engex	17.60	15 −	14.7
EqGuard	b10.29	8⅝ −	16.2	1stAustralia14.21		11¼ −	20.8
GemIICap	19.38	16½ −	14.9	FstFnFd	9.04	7¾ −	18.4
GemII Inc	9.53	13⅛ +	37.7	FranceFd b14.73		11⅞ −	19.4
GenAmInv	24.02	20⅞ −	13.1	GabelliE	11.70	10 −	14.5
GlobGrCap	10.57	9¾ −	7.8	GermanyFd10.74		10⅞ +	1.3
GlobGrInc	9.37	11 +	17.4	H&Q Health	9.39	8⅜ −	1.0
GSO Trust	9.88	8¾ −	11.4	Italy Fd	b12.48	11⅞ −	4.8
Lehman	18.34	16⅝ −	9.4	Japan Fd b22.89		21½ −	6.1
LbtyAll-Star11.30		8⅞ −	21.5	Korea fd	32.90	70⅜ + 113.9
NiagaraSh	20.20	17½ −	13.4	MG SMLCap9.56		9½	.....
NchApGrEq	9.79	8¼ −	15.7	MalaysiaFd 11.09		13⅛ +	18.3
QuestFVICp11.71		9¾ −	16.7	Mexico Fdb10.83		7⅛ −	34.2
QuestFVIInc11.85		10⅝ −	10.3	NewAsiaFd 11.07		11⅜ +	2.8
RoyceValue	10.28	9¾ −	8.8	Pete&Res	33.31	32¾ −	1.7
SchaferValu10.24		8⅜ −	17.4	Pil Reg	9.85	8 −	18.8
Source	41.61	41¼ −	0.9	RegFinI/Shs 8.85		7¼ −	18.1
Tri-Contl b 33.76		33¼ −	1.5	Scandinav b11.16		9¾ −	15.9
WorldwdVal21.88		17⅞ −	18.3	TCW CvtFdb9.32		8⅞ −	4.8
Specialized Equity and Convertible Funds				TplEmgMk b9.68		9½ −	1.9
AmCapCv	29.89	32⅝ +	9.2	Z-Seven	d19.74	23 +	16.5
ASA	bc88.63	57¾ −	3.8				
AsiaPacific	9.92	10⅜ +	4.6	a-Ex-dividend. b-As of Wednesday's close. c-Translated at Commercial Rand exchange rate. d-NAV reflects $.85 per share for taxes. z-Not available.
BancrftCv	26.78	24⅜ −	9.0	
CNV	11.99	7⅛ −	40.6	
CNV Pr	9.64	12 +	24.5	
Castle	27.96	26⅞ −	3.9	

closed-end funds are Tri-Continental, Niagara Shares, Lehman, Gemini and Japan Fund. These are all traded on the New York Stock Exchange.

Unlike the conventional mutual funds, which are open-ended, a closed-end fund will not redeem your shares. The only way to get out of a closed-end fund is to sell it on the market. Although some closed-end funds trade at a premium (that is, sell for more than their net asset value), most of them trade at a discount. You may be able to buy a closed-end fund, for instance, at 95 cents on the dollar (which means that you're getting $100 worth of stock value for only $95).

Closed-end funds have become a specialty market. Some investors make their living buying and selling such funds, buying them when the discount widens and selling them when it narrows. The obvious disadvantage of closed-end funds is that you can't automatically redeem them at net asset value. Like stocks, closed-end funds are subject to the laws of supply and demand. This means that even if your closed-end fund is performing well, if the demand isn't there, the discount might widen and you could end up losing money on it.

- *Unit investment trusts (UITs).* UITs are very similar to mutual funds in the sense that they are professionally selected portfolios of stocks or bonds. But unlike mutual funds, UITs are not professionally managed. The portfolio selected for a UIT does not change until the UIT is liquidated. UIT portfolios often consist of bonds. A UIT portfolio might, for instance, consist of 30-year municipal bonds that pay a combined interest rate of 8 percent. That rate is locked in for the life of the trust. So trust holders receive monthly interest payments for the next 30 years. When the bonds come due, the assets are returned to the investors. UITs have no management fees, and they can be redeemed at their net asset value, but investors are charged a commission of about 4 percent to buy them. That commission rate is considerably higher than the approximately 1 percent commission charged to buy individual bonds. However, unit investment trusts offer three key advantages over individual bonds:

  1. A diverse portfolio spreads your risk.
  2. The bonds are professionally selected.
  3. You can receive income monthly instead of twice a year as with an individual corporate or municipal bond.

"THE WORKS"

Mutual funds are popular because they offer some unique benefits:

- *Periodic investment privileges.* You can set up an automatic investment plan in which a set amount is withdrawn from your checking account each month to be invested in mutual funds. Such a plan gives investors the benefit of forced savings and dollar-cost averaging (see "Dollar-

Cost Averaging" section in Chapter 13). And you don't have to invest a lot of money. You can put in $100 at a time (or less), an amount that would be impractical with individual securities because much of the money would go to commissions.

- *Reinvestment.* Most mutual funds allow you to reinvest dividends and capital gains at no charge. This is a great convenience for investors who would rather not have to deal with small dividend checks that come in the mail each month. It also contributes to the power of compounding. By reinvesting your dividends, you should be able to double or triple your investment in a relatively short time. Many of the top funds have increased 5- to 10-fold in compounded assets during the past ten years.

- *Withdrawal plans.* With sufficient assets (usually a $10,000 minimum), you can stipulate that you want a certain amount paid every month to whomever you designate.

  Example: You are retired, you have $100,000 in a mutual fund, and you specify that you want $500 paid out each month. Meanwhile, the fund is reinvesting all of your dividends and capital gains, and the amount of your assets can be growing faster than the amount of your withdrawals. If you have a 6 percent withdrawal rate and the fund is growing at a 9 percent rate, your nest egg will continue to grow and your capital will never be exhausted.

- *Families of funds.* If mutual funds are the fast food of investing, then Fidelity Investments is surely the Burger King—"Home of the Whopper." The company offers approximately 100 different funds for retail investors, including the largest of all equity funds, Fidelity Magellan which has more than $10 billion in assets. Magellan has had a legendary run of success. As the company points out, assuming that all dividends were reinvested in the fund, a $10,000 investment in Magellan in May 1977 would have grown to an astonishing $185,700 exactly one decade later. However, what the Fidelity marketing people tend to downplay is that you couldn't have bought the fund in 1977. As *The Wall Street Journal* reported in July 1984, Magellan "wasn't sold publicly until 1981, and it achieved most of those high returns at less than 1.25 percent of its [1984] current size."

Like Fidelity, many other funds are grouped into "families." Templeton has a family of funds, as do IDS, Vanguard, Kemper and many other investment companies. Some of the major full-service brokerage companies, such as Merrill Lynch, Prudential-Bache, Dean Witter and Shearson Lehman, have their own families of funds. By investing in a fund that is part of a family of funds, you qualify for certain special benefits.

The major benefit is an exchange privilege. If your needs change or if market conditions change, you can switch your assets from one fund to another with no additional sales charge. For instance, you might do well

in the Kemper Bond Fund while interest rates are dropping, but when interest rates start to move back up, you might choose to pull out of the
bond fund and put your money into the money market fund. You can do
that at no charge.

There is, however, one drawback to switching funds that some investors are not aware of. Every switch is considered a sale and therefore
qualifies as a taxable transaction. So if you've realized capital gains in a
fund through switching, those gains must be figured into your total income for the given year. "But that can work to an investor's advantage,"
says IDS's Bergstrom. "Let's say you're an aggressive investor in an aggressive growth fund. Well, most families have several aggressive-type funds,
and they all move together. When the market is up, they're all up; when
the market is down, they're all down. When your fund is down, you can
sell out at a depressed level, take a tax loss and switch your money into a
different aggressive fund which is also at a depressed level. So your position in the market is the same, you've incurred no new sales fees, but
you're getting the benefit of a tax deduction." Bergstrom points out that if
you expect to switch funds periodically, it's important to choose a fund
that is part of a family of funds that performs well. "Look at the overall
management of all the mutual funds in the group," he suggests.

"CHANGE BACK FOR YOUR DOLLAR"

The sales fees of mutual funds vary greatly. By shopping selectively,
you can save substantially on the up-front and annual fees you pay to
own mutual fund shares. Mutual funds fall into three general classifica-
tions: "load" funds, which usually charge a front-end sales fee of 3 to 8½
percent; "low-load" funds, which charge 1 to 3 percent; and "no-loads,"
which charge no initial sales fee.

All of this seems simple enough—until you read the fine print. Then
it gets confusing, because the fact is that in the long run it may cost you
more to own a no-load fund than it does to own a load fund.

Some no-load and low-load funds charge what is known as a "back-
end sales charge," which the investor pays when he or she sells the fund.
This charge can come in several forms. With some funds, you pay a "redemption fee" based on the price you sell the fund for; with others, you
pay a "deferred sales charge" based on the price you paid for your shares.
The deferred charge is definitely preferable.

Example: You put $10,000 into each of two funds, one with a redemp-
tion fee of 4 percent and one with a deferred charge of 4 percent. Your
holdings in each fund grow to $25,000 before you decide to sell. On the
one with the redemption fee, you would be charged 4 percent of the price
you sold the fund for ($25,000)—a total of $1,000. On the fund with the
deferred sales charge, you would be charged 4 percent of the price you
paid for the fund ($10,000)—a total of $400.

Many back-end funds gradually forgive these charges over time if you hold onto the fund. A back-end fund of this kind might have a five-year forgiveness schedule specifying that you would be assessed 5 percent if you sold out in the first year, 4 percent in the second year, 3 percent in the third year, 2 percent in the fourth year, 1 percent in the fifth year, and nothing after that.

Sales charges, however, represent just part of the cost of owning a mutual fund. Mutual funds also charge annual operational fees, and those fees vary widely. Due to the economy of scale, the larger funds tend to charge lower fees than the smaller funds. For example, the United Services Good and Bad Times Fund, which has only $26 million in total assets, has a total expense ratio of 1.5 percent, while the huge $1.3 billion IDS Stock Fund has an expense ratio of only 0.54 percent. That 1 percent difference in fees each year would add up to a substantial amount over a period of years. Typically, though, mutual funds charge an annual management fee of about 0.5 percent and an operational fee of about 0.5 percent, for a total annual charge of 1 percent.

You may also be subject to other fees. Certain mutual funds charge what is known as a 12b–1 fee to cover advertising and promotional expenses. Under law, they are allowed to charge up to 1.25 percent of their net asset value annually (over and above normal operational fees). As a rough rule of thumb, a 12b–1 fee of less than 0.3 percent should not influence your investment decision. But if this fee goes much higher, you may want to consider a different fund. A 12b–1 fee of 1 percent or more is, by all measures, excessive.

Part or all of the 12b–1 fee often goes to the broker who sells the fund. The Putnam High Income Government Trust, for instance, pays the broker 0.25 percent of the net assets annually. If your broker sold you shares in the fund totaling $100,000, the broker would receive $250 a year. A 0.25 percent annual 12b–1 fee is considered rather modest and would not have much impact on your investment results. By contrast, Investment Portfolios, Inc., managed by Kemper Financial Services, charges the maximum annual 12b–1 fee of 1.25 percent, with 0.25 percent going to the broker and the remaining 1 percent allocated for advertising and promotional costs.

Complicating the fee picture even further are a couple of other twists—albeit favorable twists. There are several ways to get reduced commissions with front-end load funds. The first way is basic quantity discounts—called "break points." Typical break points are $10,000, $25,000, $50,000 and $100,000. The commission percentage goes down as you hit each break point.

The fees of mutual funds can also vary through "rights of accumulation." With some funds (and families of funds), as you add to your holdings, you can qualify for reduced sales charges as you pass each break point. On one fund, for instance, you're charged 8.5 percent if you invest $5,000, 7.75 percent when you hit $10,000 and 6.25 percent when you reach $25,000.

TABLE 12–1   How To Estimate the Cost of Buying and Owning a Mutual Fund

Step	Example
1. Estimate the number of years you expect to hold the fund or stay within the family of funds.	You expect to own the ABC Fund for ten years.
2. Divide the sales fee (front-end or back-end) by the number of years you plan to hold the fund.	The front-end sales charge is 6%; 6% divided by 10 equals 0.6%.
3. Add in the annual expenses, including 12b–1 fee.	The annual management fee is 0.5%, the operational fee is 0.5%, and there is a 0.25% 12b–1 fee, for a total of 1.25% in annual expenses.
	The 0.6% of prorated sales charges plus the 1.25% of annual expenses equals the total annual cost of 1.85%. That represents the real annual cost of buying and owning this mutual fund.

Yet another discounting method, referred to as "letter of intent," allows you to invest in a fund over a 13-month period and get the lowest possible commission based on your total purchases. For instance, if you plan to buy $25,000 worth of a fund during a 13-month period in installments of $2,000 a month, you would be charged the discounted commission based on the $25,000 break point right from the start.

One important point about load funds: the amount of the load has nothing to do with performance. The same holds true for operational and 12b–1 charges. All things being equal, you should try to pay as little as possible in mutual fund fees.

THE BEST FUNDS FOR FAST TIMES

While mutual funds offer many advantages for the modest investor, they are no panacea. Like all investments, mutual funds have drawbacks. Despite their diversity and professional management, many mutual funds have proven as vulnerable to downturns in the market as individual stocks and bonds. Just the same, for investors who take the initiative to choose a fund carefully—either on their own or through their broker—mutual funds may be the best investment alternative available. Nobel Prize-winning economist Paul Samuelson has said, "Anyone with a portfolio of under $100,000 is unlikely to do as well investing his own money as he can do in a mutual fund."

But if you invest in a mutual fund, don't count on stellar returns. That's not the reason to buy mutual funds. The real draw is convenience. Mutual funds make it easy to prepare your taxes (you get one simple statement at the end of the year), easy to reinvest dividends and easy to invest new money with automatic investment programs. And who knows? With a little skill and a little luck in your selection process, maybe you'll be among the 28 percent who outperform the market. After all, *you deserve a break today.*

Tracking the progress of your mutual fund—like following any investment—can be a science in itself. Knowing how to read the financial tables and learning to understand the jargon of the investment business can add not only to your ability as an investor but also to your overall investment comfort level. In the next chapter, you'll learn how to monitor your investments and how to communicate more effectively with your broker through the language of investing.

CHAPTER THIRTEEN _____

Investmentspeak

Mastering the basic concepts of investing is no small undertaking. You're dealing with scores of investment products (common stocks, preferred stocks, convertibles, commodities, annuities, debentures, options, futures, bonds, trusts and so on), each with its own market, its own cycles, its own labyrinth of complex trading strategies.

Worse yet, even after you've learned the basics, you still have the language barrier to crack. Ask your broker a simple question (for instance, "Why do you recommend this stock?") and you expect a simple answer. Instead, too often, you get "investmentspeak":

"I'll tell you why I like it," your broker might say. "Its P/E is down around 12, it's trading at just over book, the fundamentals look solid, and it's paying $7^1/_2$ on a current basis. I'd say it's the best widow-and-orphan pick on the Big Board. The way we've got it charted, it's trading now right at support. It closed up $^1/_8$ this afternoon at $20^1/_4$, and we don't see any resistance until around 25. I say we go long a thousand shares and put in a stop-loss at $18^1/_2$."

(Translation: "It's a good company, it pays a good dividend, and at $20.25 a share, you can buy it right now at a bargain.")

For financial professionals, the language of investing—call it "investmentspeak"—serves as a convenient verbal shorthand for communicating with others in the business. The curse of that language, however, is that those who learn to speak it fluently often have a hard time crossing back over the line to express themselves in layperson's terms. That's why it is important for you to learn the investment vernacular and to learn how brokers think and gather information. Learn to speak their language, and you'll not only be a better client but a better investor as well.

The language of investing is replete with colorful clichés, rich slang and clever euphemisms. When your broker says, "The market can't make up its mind," for instance, what he really means is, "I have no idea where the market's headed next." A "temporary setback," more often than not, means a long-term or permanent setback. A market "correction" means that the market has dropped, and a "jittery," "sluggish," "soft" or "tired" market means that stocks are going down.

And when your broker tells you that your stock is "oversold," brace yourself for the worst. What he means is that the stock has taken a sharp, unexpected drop. In short, it's "heading south."

Giving Orders

The most confusing decision for many new investors is not what stocks to buy but what type of order to place. Should they place a market order, limit order, stop order, stop-loss order or stop-limit order?

- In most cases, the order will be a "market order," which is simply an order to buy or sell a security at the best available price.
- A "limit order" is a buy or sell order that can only be executed at a specific price or better. A limit order to sell sets a minimum sales price; if the stock is trading at 20 and you think it could go up a couple of dollars before it peaks, you can put in a limit order to sell it if it reaches 22. A limit order to buy sets a maximum purchase price; if the stock is trading at 20 and you think it would be a good value if it dropped a couple of dollars, you can put in a limit order to buy it if it drops to 18.

Unless you want your limit order canceled at the end of that day, you should designate it "GTC"—"Good 'til canceled." Your broker will write "GTC" right on the order ticket.

- A "stop order" is an order to buy or sell securities once the market price reaches or passes a price specified by the investor, known as the "stop price." One type of stop order is known as a "stop-loss order," which is an order to sell a stock if it drops to a specified price. Investors sometimes use stop-loss orders to protect profits they've made on a stock.

    Example: You buy EFG Transit at 20. It goes up to 26, and you think it may start dropping back down. To ensure that you'll still make a good profit on the stock, you might wish to put in a stop-loss order at 25. This means that as soon as the stock trades at 25, your order becomes a market order to sell it at 25 (or the best possible price at the time).

- A "stop-limit order" is a combination of a stop order and a limit order. It is an order to buy or sell a security at a specified price or better, but only after the stop price has been reached or passed.

COCKTAIL CHATTER

There are certain "must" terms that you would do well to commit to memory if you want to be a hit not only with your broker but on the social circuit as well. Dropping just the right line at the right time can help any social climber blend in with the best of the blue bloods.

- *Blue chips.* The securities of strong, well-established companies that have demonstrated their ability to pay dividends in good times and bad. IBM, General Motors and General Electric are examples of blue chips.

  Next time you're schmoozing with chums at the club, you might use this line:

  "Blue chips? They used to be too blasé for my taste. But now, of course, with the Dow leading the rally, we're in a classic blue-chip market and I've got a portfolio full of them."

- *Support level.* The lowest price that a declining stock is expected to reach before moving back up. When a stock reaches its support level, investors are likely to start buying it, thus pushing its price back up. Sometimes stocks drop through their support level and keep dropping or "free-falling." Such stocks are often referred to as "air pocket" stocks. For your next party or social engagement, we suggest this line:

  "It's a pity Father didn't heed my advice. I told him his Megatech stock was heading for a free fall, but he just kept loading up on it as it dropped right through support."

- *Resistance level.* The highest price that investors are likely to pay for a stock. When a stock reaches its resistance level, many investors are likely to sell out and take a profit. Sometimes when stocks "break through," or go above, the resistance level, they "break out" and continue to climb in price. Suggested comment:

  "My investment strategy, you ask? Why very simply, I buy at support and sell at resistance. That's always worked marvelously for me."

- *Buying long.* "Buying long" or "going long" simply means buying stock. "Buying *long* 100 shares" is exactly the same as "buying 100 shares." A "long position" simply refers to ownership of a security. Once again, the "long" is silent. "Holding a *long* position" in IBM stock is the same as "holding" IBM stock. Suggested comment:

  "I closed out my long positions as soon as the market started heading south. For now, I've got my money parked in CDs."

- *Selling short.* "Selling short" is selling a security you don't own (or consummating any sale by the delivery of a security borrowed by, or for the account of, the seller). Essentially, what you do when you sell short is borrow shares of a stock when you think its price is likely to decline, sell the shares and replace the borrowed shares later (at a profit if the price does drop). Suggested comment:

Selling Short

If you think a stock is ready to take a fall, you can profit from that decline by selling the stock short. Example: An investor who thinks the price of ABC Corporation stock will drop might "sell short" 100 shares. Here is how the process would work:

• *Scenario:* ABC Corporation stock is trading at $15. The investor borrows 100 shares through his or her broker and sells those shares at the market price—$1,500.
• *Outcome A:* The stock drops to $10. The investor buys 100 shares at $1,000 and turns them over to the broker to replace the 100 borrowed shares. In other words, the investor has sold borrowed shares for $1,500, bought replacement shares for $1,000 and earned $500 in the process.
• *Outcome B:* The stock rises to $20. The investor buys 100 shares at $2,000 to replace the 100 borrowed shares. In other words, the investor has sold borrowed shares for $1,500, bought replacement shares for $2,000 and lost $500 in the process.

Obviously, the strategy with short selling is to pick stocks that you think will drop in price.

"I see Chrysler's down again. My sympathies to Lee. Glad I shorted 5,000 shares last month."

• *Fundamentals.* Refers to the sales, earnings and basic financial condition of a company. Suggested comment:
   "Solid fundamentals? Surely you jest. The company's sales are falling, its inventory is growing, and the only way it managed to show a profit last quarter was by selling off its most profitable division for a onetime gain. I'd hardly call that 'solid fundamentals.' "

• *Point.* Unit of measurement for stocks and bonds. For stock prices, a point represents $1, $1/2$ point represents 50 cents, and $1/8$ point, the smallest quantity used, represents $12 1/2$ cents. For bonds, a point is $10 per $1,000. Suggested comment:
   "I managed to scalp a couple of points in Delta yesterday in a neat little day trade."

• *Street name.* A brokerage account held in "street name" is one in which a customer's securities are held by the brokerage firm. The firm is the "owner of record" or "nominee." The customer is the "beneficial owner." Active investors find it much more convenient to keep their securities in street name than to take physical possession of the certificates. This eliminates the hassle of signing and physically delivering the certificates every time you want to sell a security. It is also safer because you don't have to worry about misplacing the certificates or losing them to theft or fire. Suggested comment:

"I keep everything in street name but my silverware. I mean, why fuss with all those certificates?"

(See Glossary at the end of the book for a more complete listing of related terms.)

GAUGING THE FUTURE

If you want to look ahead to see where the economy—and the market—may be headed, certain economic indicators can help you do that. The National Bureau of Economic Research has identified 28 cyclical economic indicators. By learning which indicators "lead," "lag" and "coincide" with the economy, you can assess in advance the direction the economy may be taking.

- *Coincidental indicators.* If salaries are climbing, production is picking up, retail business is booming and unemployment is dropping, it's not hard to figure out that you're in the midst of an economic expansion. Coincidental indicators mirror or "coincide" with the economy. But no matter how strong the coincidental indicators are, unless the leading indicators are also favorable, the good times may not be around for long.

- *Leading indicators.* If businesses and consumers are ordering more durable goods and taking out more building permits, if production workers are putting in longer hours, if stock prices are climbing and after-tax corporate profits are picking up, then prosperity probably looms ahead. Leading indicators precede or "lead" the economy. They rise or fall prior to movements in the general level of economic activity.

- *Lagging indicators.* If businesses are still holding back on expenses for new plant and equipment, if commercial and industrial loans are on the decrease and the long-term unemployed are still looking for jobs, you've probably just emerged from tough times. Lagging indicators shadow or "lag" the economy. They rise or fall after the economy has shifted.

Key Economic Indicators

- *Leading indicators* (precede shifts in the economy): durable goods orders, new building permits, after-tax corporate profits, stock prices, the average manufacturing workweek
- *Lagging indicators* (follow shifts in the economy): expenditures for new plant and equipment, commercial and industrial loans outstanding, interest rates on short-term business loans, unemployment rate for medium- to long-term unemployed
- *Coincidental indicators* (reflect the economy): personal income, industrial production, retail trade, general unemployment rate

---

The best way to keep an eye on the leading indicators is to watch for the U.S. Commerce Department's Index of Leading Indicators (CLI) release, which is published in most major newspapers toward the end of each month. The CLI, which groups together the leading indicators, offers an excellent gauge of where we're headed and can help you decide what kind of investments you should make.

Other indicators that should also be watched include the following:

• *Consumer price index (CPI)*. The CPI is the standard measure of change in the price of goods and services. If the CPI is rising, the chances are that inflation is rising. It is the most common gauge of inflation, though the inflation indicator that economists use (called the "gross national product deflator") is generally regarded as more accurate.

• *Interest rates*. The prime rate gets a lot of media attention because it's supposed to show what banks charge their best customers. But when banks lend money to corporations, they use the prime only as a guide. Depending on the circumstances, the rates they charge can fall below or above the prime. The prime rate often acts as a lagging indicator. When interest rates are falling, the prime is one of the last rates to drop. A more accurate gauge of current interest rates is the yield on 90-day Treasury bills. Short-term T-bills are sold at auction every week. Investors willing to accept the lowest yields are the first to be awarded T-bills in the competitive bidding process. The auctions set the standard on T-bill rates and offer an accurate indication from one week to the next of whether interest rates are rising or falling.

• *Stock prices*. The most closely watched index, of course, is the Dow Jones Industrial Average. While the Dow is a good gauge of activity in the blue-chip stock market, the best indicator of overall market activity is the Standard & Poor's Composite Index, which reflects the movements of 500 representative stocks—hence its common name, the S&P 500.

READING AN ANNUAL REPORT

It is the story of fortunes earned and spent. Of payables, receivables, deferrables and accruables. For those who are adept at collating, computing and evaluating its many elements, a corporate annual report contains not just reflections of the past but also bodings of the future.

If you own stock or plan to own stock in a particular company, it's worth your while to take a close look at the company's annual report. Compare the company's current performance with its past performance. Does the company seem to be getting bigger, more profitable? How are its newer divisions doing? Are sales up? Inventories down? Are expenses staying in check? Are new products coming on line? Are profit margins on existing products widening? Annual reports carry all of that information—and more. Here are some of the key sections that you should review when reading an annual report:

- *Auditor's letter.* Find this letter near the back of the report with the footnotes and financial tables. If it runs no more than two paragraphs, you can assume that the auditor reviewed the corporation's financials and found them to be "in conformity with generally accepted accounting practices." But if it is longer, take a closer look. This probably means that the auditor uncovered some discrepancy in the financials that was worth noting.

- *Balance sheet.* Also near the back of the report, the balance sheet is a snapshot of the company's present financial condition. You'll find information on assets, receivables, liabilities, inventory and stockholders' equity for the past two years. At a glance, you can see by comparing last year's figures with the figures from the year before whether the company is growing, earning a good return on capital, paring down its inventories or piling up more debt.

- *Income statement* (Also referred to as "earnings statement" "revenue statement," "profit and loss statement" or "statements of operation"). The income statement gives a three-year breakdown of sales, cost of sales, interest income and expense, taxes and other sources of income or expense. Are total earnings rising? Per share earnings? Are expenses being held in check? Did the company have a major jump in interest income, or are there any extraordinary items—sales of fixed assets, one-time tax carry-forwards—that might make for a distorted view of the company's true profitability.

- *Financial highlights.* Near the front of the report, many corporations include a table of financial highlights covering the past five years. That table could include revenues, assets, earnings, earnings per share, dividends paid (if any), stockholders' equity and book value. Not all annual reports have detailed tables of this kind. However, by examining the tables in the back of the report, you can come up with all of the pertinent data you need to evaluate the company's financial condition.

- *From the president.* Most annual reports begin with a message from the president or the CEO, or both. Such messages are often glowing commentaries that tend to dwell on strengths and ignore weaknesses. Try to look beyond the puff. Are the messages mentioning new products or services that sound promising? Has the company surmounted any major hurdles, made any major acquisitions that could lead to accelerated growth or made any significant changes in personnel? What's the tone? Confident? Apologetic? Defensive? Get what you can out of the messages, but don't be taken in by bold promises and "commitments to the future."

- *Footnotes* (or "notes to consolidated financial statements"). You'll see several pages of footnotes in the back that will offer some information on the company's operations regarding such areas as long-term debt, accounts receivable, taxes, benefit plans, stock options, acquisitions, mergers, business segments and discontinued operations.

MAKING SENSE OF THE FINANCIALS

When looking through a company's income statement and balance sheet, you can apply several simple formulas to uncover some key indicators of the company's success:

- *Return on equity.* Are shareholders making more from their investment dollars this year? The formula for determining return on equity is:

    Shareholders' equity (on the balance sheet)
    – Net income (from the income statement)

    Balance divided into net income = Return on equity

    Example: If ABC Corporation has a net income of $10 million and shareholders' equity of $80 million, you would subtract $10 million from $80 million to get $70 million, and then you would divide that into $10 million. The return on equity is 14 percent—a pretty healthy return.

    To put the return on equity into perspective, see how it compares with the previous year's return, how it compares with the return of other companies in the same industry and how it compares with current interest rates on corporate bonds.

- *Gross profit margin on sales.* Has the company been able to widen its margin between costs and revenues, or is competition in its industry forcing it to keep prices down and sale costs up. To calculate the gross profit margin on goods sold, follow this formula:

    Net product sales
    – Cost of goods sold (not including administrative costs)

    Balance = Gross profit margin on sales

    Example: If ABC had sales of $50 million and its cost of goods sold was $30 million, its gross profit margin on sales was $20 million.

- *Gross profit margin ratio.* To go a step further, divide the $20 million profit margin by the $50 million in gross sales and you'll have a very respectable gross profit margin ratio of 40 percent. Again, to get a true reading, compare this ratio to the previous year's gross margin ratio and, if possible, to the gross margin ratios of other companies in the industry.

- *Book value* (per common share). Theoretically, book value tells you what one share of common stock would be worth if all of the company's assets were liquidated and the proceeds returned to the stockholders. To calculate book value:

    Total common shareholders' equity
    – Intangible assets (goodwill, copyrights, patents, etc.)

    Balance ÷ number of shares of stock outstanding = Book value

Traditionally, the book value of a stock has borne some resemblance to its actual trading price. In today's market, however, the link is not as close. But your broker should be able to help you see what insights, if any, a stock's book value will provide.

- *Approximate earnings per share.* How much is the company earning per share of common stock outstanding? To find out:

Net income (available for common stock)
÷ Average outstanding shares of common stock

Approximate earnings per share

Example: If ABC earned $10 million in net earnings and it has issued 10 million shares, its earnings per share are $1.

- *Price-earnings ratio* (P/E ratio). How does the price of the stock compare with its earnings? To calculate the P/E ratio:

Price of the stock
÷ Earnings per share

Price-earnings ratio

Example: If ABC earned $1 a share last year, and its stock is trading at $15, that gives it a P/E of 15.

Generally speaking, P/Es average 10 to 20, although new growing companies may have P/Es that are substantially higher. Many investors believe that the lower the P/E of a stock, the better the value of the stock is. Again, it's all relative to the company's outlook and to the P/Es of other companies in the same industry.

- *Net working capital.* Subtract current liabilities from current assets. With some rare exceptions, a healthy company should show a steady annual increase in working capital.
- *Current ratio.* Divide current assets by current liabilities. This ratio is more applicable to product-oriented rather than to service-oriented companies. A healthy ratio for a company that keeps inventories is about 2 to 1.

If the annual report piques your curiosity, you might also request the company's 10-K report, which offers a drier but far more detailed look at the company's financial situation.

DOLLAR-COST AVERAGING

There is no infallible method for outsmarting the stock market, but an investment system known as "dollar-cost averaging" may be the next best thing.

Dollar-cost averaging, which is commonly used for buying both stocks and mutual fund shares, forces you to buy more shares when the price is at its lowest and fewer shares when the price is at its peak. And unlike many other touted investment strategies, dollar-cost averaging requires no complex calculations or sophisticated timing decisions. All that's required is persistence.

You simply select a good stock (or mutual fund) in which you want to accumulate a position over time, and you buy a predetermined dollar amount of shares on selected dates, regardless of the price of the shares or the general market conditions on those dates.

The success of dollar-cost averaging is based on three assumptions: (1) the long-term trend of stock prices is up; (2) the market movement of most securities is cyclical, and (3) although market prices in general may fall substantially, they will eventually return to their former level (or higher).

With dollar-cost averaging, the price you pay over the long run will, on average, be lower than the overall average price of the shares.

> **Example:** You decide to buy $2,000 worth of ABC stock every two months for a year.

January: The stock is trading at 20 a share. Your $2,000 allotment buys 100 shares.

March: The stock has dropped to 15. You're able to buy 133 shares.

May: The stock has gone back to 20. You buy 100 shares.

July: The stock has moved to 25. You can buy only 80 shares for your $2,000.

September: The stock has gone up further, to 30. You can buy just 66 shares.

November: The stock has dropped back to 25. You buy 80 shares.

For the year: You've paid $12,000 to buy 559 shares at an average price of $22.50. But if you tried to buy 559 shares outright at a price of $22.50, it would cost you $12,577.50. Your actual cost averaged $21.47 per share.

By using dollar-cost averaging, you would have saved more than a dollar per share. The reason? You bought more shares when the price was low and fewer shares when it was high.

In the example given, the breakdown for the year looks like this:

Total expense:	$12,000.00
Average cost per share	
($20 + $15 + $20 + $25 + $30 +	
$25 = $135 divided by 6):	$22.50
Total number of shares:	559
Total value of 559 shares	
@ $22.50/share:	$12,577.50
Savings using dollar-cost	
averaging:	$577.50

While dollar-cost averaging is no guarantee against loss, it has proven to be among the easiest and most successful ways to take advantage of the market's volatility.

OPTIONS TRADING

Test question:

Options trading is a good way to:

a. gamble legally.
b. hedge your investments in certain stocks.
c. make a little extra money on your investments without much risk.
d. lose a lot of money on your investments without much potential for gain.
e. all of the above

Answer: *e*

A relatively small number of investors trade in options, and perhaps that's as it should be. Learning the ins and outs of puts and calls can be more than a little tricky. You can buy a put or sell a call, sell a put or buy a call, establish a spread or put on a straddle. Listed options are traded on only about 400 of the largest stocks plus such financial instruments as the Standard & Poor's 100 Stock Index and the Japanese yen.

- *Buying a call.* In exchange for a premium, a call gives the holder the right to buy 100 shares of a stock at a strike price at any time during a set period. Call options are appropriate for investors who feel that a certain stock is going to go up in value. For instance, if you think that a $50 stock is going to shoot up in the next six months, you could buy a six-month call on the stock. If the stock goes, say, to $60, you could theoretically exercise your option, buy the stock at $50, sell it at the $60 market price and earn a $10-per-share profit (minus the premium). In practice, however, you would simply sell your call, reaping your profit in that way. If the stock drops in value, you let your option expire and your only loss is the price of the premium.

- *Selling a call.* If you have a $50 stock that you've done well on and you suspect that the stock is near its peak, you could squeeze some extra money out of it by selling a call on it. For instance, you might want to sell a $55 call on the stock. Up front, you would receive a premium from the buyer that is yours to keep. If the stock does climb five more points to reach $55 (or ten more points to reach $60, etc.), you would be obligated to sell it for $55 a share—which is fine with you because that was going to be your selling price anyway. If the stock doesn't get that high, you take no action. But either way, you get to keep the premium.

- *Buying a put.* In exchange for a premium, a put gives the holder the right to sell 100 shares of a stock at a set price (known as the "strike price") at any time during a set period. Premiums range from about $100 to about $500 (and sometimes higher), depending on the market. The holding period for such an option can vary from one day to nine months, depending on when the option has been purchased.

You may want to buy a put on a stock that you expect to go down. If you buy a $30 put on a stock and that stock drops to 22, you can buy the stock at 22, then exercise your option and sell the stock at 30, earning $8 per share (minus the premium you paid to buy the put). If the stock goes up or stays the same, you would let the option expire and forfeit your premium.

- *Selling a put.* If you think a $30 stock would be a good buying value at $25, you may want to sell a $25 put on the stock. Up front, you would receive a premium from the put buyer that is yours to keep. If the stock does drop to $25, you would be obligated to buy 100 shares—but for your purposes, that would be fine because you wanted to buy the stock at $25 anyway. If it doesn't drop to $25, you would take no action. Either way, you would get to keep the premium. The one danger with selling puts is that if the stock continues to drop (say to $10), you would be obligated to honor your $25-a-share contract and you'd end up paying $2,500 for stock worth $1,000. One client of Charles Schwab and Co. who was trading in uncovered put options reportedly lost $80 million (his entire fortune and then some) during the week of Black Monday when the market crashed. That's why some options buyers use a "spread." They sell a put for $25 and buy a lower put (at a slightly cheaper premium) at, say, $20 as insurance in case the bottom drops out.

- *The straddle.* On volatile stocks, some investors employ a "straddle" strategy. They buy both a put and a call. On a $50 stock, for instance, an investor might buy a put for three points ($300) and a call for three points ($300), for a total premium cost of $600. If the stock rises or falls more than six points, the investor could make a profit. One profitable scenario would be for the stock to drop six points (the investor then exercises the put option and receives $600) and then bounces back to seven points above the strike price (the investor exercises the call option and pockets another $700).

PROGRAM TRADING

Since the mid-1980s, the stock market has been riding a roller coaster of steep ups and downs that, in point terms at least, make the most volatile swings of earlier eras look like mere dips in the track.

The most dramatic example of the market's new volatility came on Black Monday, October 19, 1987, when the Dow dropped 508 points, the largest one-day drop in history. Many securities experts place the blame for this increased volatility on a small coterie of institutional investors and stock fund managers known as "index traders" or "program traders."

Most of them trade in futures contracts and related stocks of an index such as the Standard and Poor's 500.

To beat the index, these traders often buy or sell futures and stocks when they can get a slight edge on the performance of the index. Normally, a futures contract on a stock index trades at about the same price as the index plus a "fair" premium. But occasionally, the stock index futures price rises substantially above or falls substantially below the current value of the stock index. In other words, a stock index may be trading at $200 while the futures price on the stocks in that index could be as low as $195. On Black Monday, futures prices were as much as 20 percent below stocks—an exorbitant differential.

That's when program traders make their move. They sell their stocks at a profit and load up on the lower-priced futures—sending the market into a sudden tailspin.

On the other hand, when stock prices fall below futures prices, program traders sell their futures contracts at a profit and reinvest in the lower-priced stocks, earning an attractive spread on the transactions. This rapid sell-off of futures and subsequent reinvestment in stocks (all of which is executed at lightning speeds by computers) can send the market soaring.

Although the average investor has no real opportunity to participate in program trading, an alert investor can take advantage of the situation. Stocks that are affected by program trading sometimes fall well below or rise above their fair market value. By buying stocks after program traders have driven prices down, you can sometimes get a bargain on the stocks. Many investors made a killing by buying depressed stocks on the days following Black Monday. Conversely, you may be able to sell your stocks at a better price after program traders have driven up the market.

READING *THE WALL STREET JOURNAL*

Every day a new stack of memos, reports and publications materializes on most brokers' desks. To cover the most important material and still have time to do their jobs, brokers must read selectively and efficiently. At the top of the reading list day in and day out is the bible of the investment business, *The Wall Street Journal.* The *Journal* is must reading for brokers who hope to converse intelligently not only with their peers but with their clients as well. It generally runs about 40 to 60 pages, brimming with important investment information and in-depth articles. To save time, brokers have developed a ten-step method of reading the *Journal* that enables them to cover most of its essential elements in a matter of minutes.

   1. Under "What's News—," on the front page, start with the left-hand column, entitled "Business and Finance." There you'll get a quick overview of the major business news—court cases, legislation, economic trends, market highlights, corporate developments, interest rate changes and so on. The column covers about 15 topics, generally with a one-sentence paragraph on each topic. Often you can just skim the bold-faced lead-ins to get a feel for the important news. Time: 30 seconds to one minute.

2. Also under "What's News—," read the right-hand column, entitled "World-Wide." That contains longer paragraphs on 10 to 15 topics. By reading the bold-faced lead-ins to each paragraph, you can quickly bring yourself up-to-date on the major U.S. and world news. Time: One to two minutes.

3. Read "Today's Contents" at the bottom of page one. This offers one-sentence summaries of the major stories inside the paper, with page numbers in case you want to read up on the details. Time: 10 to 30 seconds.

4. Turn to the next-to-last page (second section) and read "Abreast of the Market," which discusses developments in the stock market on the previous day. Time: One to three minutes.

5. On the same page, move down to the "Heard on the Street" column. This usually provides an analysis of either a single stock or an industry group. Time: One to three minutes.

Having completed the first five steps, you have finished all of the absolute "must read" sections—and you've done it in less than ten minutes. (Actual time elapsed: $4^1/_2$ to $9^1/_2$ minutes.)

6. If you still have some time, you may want to work your way from back to front in the second section, combing through the stock, bond, options or mutual fund tables to see how your own investments are doing. You might also glance at some of the smaller articles and at the "Digest of Earnings Reports," which gives a capsule summary of the newly released quarterly or annual earnings reports of publicly traded companies. As you thumb through the paper, you will also see some specialty columns (futures, currency, world stocks, mutual funds) that may be of interest to you.

7. Turn back to page one and read the article on the far left, which is usually a hard-hitting news article of national or world importance.

8. Also on page one, read the article on the far right which is also a hard news story of national or world importance.

9. Move to the second column from the right, which focuses on a different subject each day of the week. On Monday, "Outlook" typically offers a forecast of economic news; on Tuesday, "Labor Letter" discusses news regarding workers, employee benefits, factories, unions, labor laws and other matters related to the work force; on Wednesday, "Tax Report" covers a broad range of tax-related matters; on Thursday, "Business Bulletin" generally provides a potpourri of new briefs on a wide range of business developments; and on Friday, "Washington Wire" discusses the important, timely legislative issues.

10. If you're active in the stock market, you might want to review the "Stock Market Data Bank" on the second-to-last page, a detailed table

of stock market information from the previous day, including fluctuations and trading volume in the major exchanges, the most active issues and the biggest gainers and losers.

If you still have a few minutes, turn to the front page of the second section, where you can often find excellent in-depth articles and columns on a variety of business-related topics. And if you are a connoisseur of fine prose, we recommend that you return to page one, third column from the right, where there is always an exceptional feature article—generally of a nonbusiness or soft business bent—on topics ranging from the intriguing to the bizarre.

KERNELS OF WISDOM

"Buy low, sell high" is probably the most often used maxim in the investment business. But there are scores of lesser-known maxims that cleverly express some of the deep secrets of the investment trade. These maxims offer advice (sometimes contradictory), convey information or merely describe a situation. Here are some favorites.

Advice

"Don't fall in love with a stock." (Translation: If you become emotionally attached to a stock, you tend to lose your objectivity as to when to buy or sell.)

"Don't fight the tape." (If your stock is dropping in price, wait until it bottoms out and starts moving back up before you buy. If your stock is moving up, wait until it tops out before you sell.)

"Cut your losses and let your profits run." (Sell declining stocks (generally when they drop 10 to 15 percent), but hold onto rising stocks as long as they continue to climb.)

"I never buy at the bottom, and I always sell too soon." (If you try to buy a declining stock at its cheapest price, you may buy too soon and pay too much. Let it bottom out and move up a bit before investing. Conversely, it's safer to sell a rising stock and take a profit when you think the stock is close to the top. In other words, "Fight the tape and don't let your profits run.")

"Don't follow the crowd." (This is the battle cry of those who call themselves contrarians. They buy when everyone else is selling and sell when everyone else is buying. That is, they buy at depressed prices and sell at inflated prices.)

"Buy your straw hats in January."

"Buy your fur coats in July."

"Buy on weakness; sell on strength." (If the price of an investment is moving up, wait until it dips before you buy; if it is moving down, wait until it bounces back up before you sell.)

"Buy on the rumor, sell on the news." (Rumors tend to push prices up [or down]. By the time a rumor becomes news, the price will already have adjusted to it, which makes this a good time to sell and take your profits [or to buy at a discount].)

"Don't put all your eggs in one basket." (Diversify, or you risk losing everything with one unexpected turn of luck.)

"Put all your eggs in one basket, and watch that basket." (Don't over-diversify. Seek out a special investment opportunity, research it thoroughly and commit a significant amount of money to it. Then follow it closely so that you are ready to sell if it begins to falter.)

"Never invest more in a stock than you can afford to lose."

"Never answer a margin call." (If you're asked to meet a margin call— for more collateral—on a declining stock you own, don't deposit more cash. Have your broker liquidate some shares of your stock to cover the call. That way, you can never lose more than you invest.)

"Bulls make money and bears make money, but pigs get swine flu." (You can make money going long, you can make money going short, but if you get too greedy, you're bound to lose big.)

Informational Adages

"What everyone else knows isn't worth knowing." (If everyone has the same information on an investment, the chances are that the market has already adjusted to reflect that information.)

"If too many people agree with you, you must be wrong." (As the theory goes, when everyone thinks the market is headed one way, it's bound to go the opposite way. The following four clichés support that premise.)

"Pessimism is always rampant just before the market hits bottom."

"The public is always wrong at the top and at the bottom of the market." When the market nears the bottom and investors should be buying, many lose hope and sell their stocks. Conversely, when the market nears the top, many investors are buying when they should be selling.)

"When everyone is bearish, the market must go up because there are no sellers left."

"When everyone is bullish, the market must go down because there are no buyers left."

"The market always does what it should but not when it should." (For instance, rising interest rates will affect the market, but that may not happen immediately.)

"The market never discounts the same thing twice." (The market reacts only once to negative information regarding a stock. Repeated exposure to the same information will not cause the stock to drop again.

"The market always gives you a second chance." (When the market goes up, it rarely goes straight up. It usually rises, then falls back, rises, then falls again, giving investors a second chance to invest at an attractive level.)

"Every time a trade takes place on the floor of the exchange, someone is making a mistake." (If the stock goes up after the transaction, the seller has erred by selling too soon. If it goes down, the buyer has erred by buying too soon.)

"As January goes, so goes the year." (If the stock market is up in January, there's a good chance that it will continue to rise throughout the year.)

"It's the summer rally." (The market often picks up the week before July 4 in a burst of patriotism and optimism.)

"You can't lose money taking a profit." (This is usually said by brokers when they have sold a stock for a small profit that went higher after they sold it.)

"Nobody loves a bear." (When you sell securities, you cause their prices to fall, which obviously doesn't sit well with investors who are still holding them.)

"Stocks fall faster than they rise." (If, for instance, the Dow drops 150 points in a week, even in a good market it might take three weeks to regain the lost ground.)

"The market is people." (The market is driven not on the winds of cold, hard fact, but on the whims of human emotion—fear, greed, herd hysteria. The spoils go to those who can best predict how the investment masses will respond to new variables in the market.)

"Money is thicker than blood." (If a broker loses money for a client, even a client who is a good friend, the relationship will be jeopardized.)

"Two things make you smart—bull markets and whiskey. The more of each you consume, the more brilliant you become."

Descriptive Phrases

"It's a buyers' panic." (Common refrain when the market jumps after a long lull. Once prices begin moving up, large investors will often frantically pour their money into the market.)

"The market is climbing a wall of worry." (Stock prices are continuing to rise despite some overriding fear.)

"The market has strong leadership." (Refers to a market rally led by blue-chip stocks, such as IBM, General Motors, Eastman Kodak and AT&T.)

"The stock is moving into strong hands." (A stock is being sold by short-term speculators and bought by long-term investors.)

"The market has run into heavy weather." (The stock has stopped moving up in price.)

"The market has gone south." (The market has declined.)

"Squeezing the shorts." (When stock prices are rising, investors who sold short face the prospect of buying back their stocks at higher prices, thus incurring heavy losses.)

"There are more sellers than buyers." (Standard refrain of brokers when asked why the market went down.)

"It will tend to fluctuate." (The only sure answer to investing's eternal question, "What's the market going to do next?")

READING YOUR STATEMENT

The regular statement that you receive from your brokerage firm offers you a complete overview of your investment status. Statements vary from one firm to another, but most statements provide the following information:

1. The name and address of the brokerage firm
2. The name of the broker and his or her phone number
3. Your name, address and account number and often your social security number or taxpayer identification number
4. The stock, bond and other investment positions you hold—anything you hold in street name—and whether you have long or short positions in those securities.
5. The name and quantity of each security (and in some cases the unit price and the total value of each security).
6. Any cash balance or money market funds in your account.

Statements often also show the date of your transactions, your annual income to date and the due dates for money or certificate deliveries.

FOLLOWING YOUR INVESTMENTS

Keeping track of your investments is easy once you learn to read the securities quotation tables in the business section of your daily newspaper (and *The Wall Street Journal*). On the following pages, 217-220, are simple guides for reading these tables:

Reading the New York Stock Exchange Tables

NEW YORK STOCK EXCHANGE COMPOSITE TRANSACTIONS

Wednesday, October 28, 1987

Quotations include trades on the Midwest, Pacific, Philadelphia, Boston and Cincinnati stock exchanges and reported by the National Association of Securities Dealers and Instinet

52 Weeks High	Low	Stock	Div.	Yld %	P-E Ratio	Sales 100s	High	Low	Close	Net Chg.	52 Weeks High	Low	Stock	Div.	Yld %	P-E Ratio	Sales 100s	High	Low	Close	Net Chg.
49	31⅜	AllgPw	2.92	7.9	9	4950	37½	36¾	37	− ½	28⅜	18⅛	BeldnH	.40	2.2	10	37	18½	18¼	18½	− ¼
105⅞	52	Allegis	1.00	1.4	37	17162	76	69¾	73	+ 2	75¼	35⅜	BellHwl	.62	1.5	7	1529	44¼	42⅜	42½	− 2
19⅜	10¼	AllenG	.56	5.9	...	144	10½d	9½	9½	− 1½	79¾	60½	BellAtl	3.84	5.4	12	4235	72¼	69½	71	− 1½
24⅞	15	Allen pf	1.75	10.6	...	7	16½d	14¼	16½	+ 1½	33⅜	23½	BCE g	2.40	...	7	1595	27⅜	26½	27⅜	+ ⅛
44	15¼	AlldPd	...		7	749	17¼	15⅝	16⅝	− ¼	23⅜	13¾	Bellln s	.28	2.1	21	66	13⅝d	13⅜	13⅜	− ½
49¼	27	AldSgnl	1.80	5.3	10	16279	34½	33½	34	− ¼	44¼	29⅛	BellSo s	2.20	6.2	11	7271	36½	35¼	35¾	− ¾

Columns 1 and 2 (52 Weeks/High Low): Shows the trading range of the stock for the past 52 weeks. The first stock, Allegheny Power, has traded at a high of 49 and a low of 31³/₈.

Column 3 (Stock): Gives the abbreviated name of the stock.

Column 4 (Div.): Gives the annual dividend rate. Allegheny Power pays a dividend of $2.92.

Column 5 (Yld/%): Reports the current yield of the stock. Allegheny Power has a yield of 7.9 percent. The yield is determined by dividing the closing price of the stock into the dividend.

Column 6 (P-E Ratio): Shows the price-to-earnings ratio of the stock (the market price divided by actual or indicated earnings per share). Allegheny Power has a price–earnings ratio of 9.

Column 7 (Sales/100s): Gives the number of shares sold for the day in hundreds. Some 495,000 shares of Allegheny Power changed hands.

Columns 8, 9 and 10 (High Low Close): Give the high trading price for the day, the low trading price for the day and the price of the stock when the market closed. Allegheny Power traded at a high of 37¹/₂ ($37.50) and a low of 36³/₄ ($36.75), closing the day at 37.

Column 11 (Net Chg.): Gives the net change between the previous day's closing price and the reported day's closing price. Allegheny Power was down ¹/₂ point (50 cents).

Reading the Mutual Fund Tables

MUTUAL FUND QUOTATIONS

Thursday, May 7, 1987

Price ranges for investment companies, as quoted by the National Association of Securities Dealers. NAV stands for net asset value per share; the offering includes net asset value plus maximum sales charge, if any.

| | Offer NAV | | | | Offer NAV | |
	NAV	Price Chg.			NAV	Price Chg.
Paramt	15.61	16.70+ .28	GovtP	r	(z) (z)	...
Perenni	19.11	20.44 ...	TF Bd	r	9.63 N.L.+	.01
Franklin Group:			Value	r	10.37 N.L.−	.06
AGE Fd	3.62	3.77 ...	Mathers		18.70 N.L.+	.11
Cal Ins	10.73	11.18+ .03	Meeschr C		(z) (z)	...
Cal TxFr	6.87	7.16+ .01	Merit PA		11.63 N.L.+	.05
Corp Csh	9.05	N.L.− .01	**Merrill Lynch:**			
D N T C	13.10	13.65− .05	Basc Val		19.84 21.22+	.05
Equity	7.52	7.83 ...	CalTxE	r	10.89 N.L.−	.01
Fed TxF	11.04	11.50+ .06	Captl Fd		28.26 30.22+	.11
Gold Fnd	15.71	16.36− .19	Corp Dv		10.79 11.01	...

Column 1: If a mutual fund is part of a family or group of mutual funds, look for it under the bold-faced name of the group. Under the group name will be the names (or abbreviations) of funds within the group. Our sample fund is the Franklin Group Gold Fund.

Column 2 (NAV): Gives the net asset value of a share (the amount received when the investment is redeemed). This is also the bid price. Gold Fund's NAV is $15.71.

Column 3 (Offer Price): Reflects the asking price on a share of the fund—including the net asset value and the maximum sales charge. Gold Fund's offer price is $16.36. The difference between the NAV and the offer price is the sales charge. Gold Fund has a maximum sales charge of 4 percent of the current price (65 cents per share). An "N.L." in this column means "no-load"—there is no sales charge, and therefore the offer price is the same as the net asset value.

Column 4 (NAV Chg.): Shows the change in the net asset value of a share since the last trading date. Gold Fund is down 19 cents.

Reading the Corporate Bond Tables

NEW YORK EXCHANGE BONDS

Wednesday, October 28, 1987

CORPORATION BONDS
Volume, $43,490,000

Bonds	Cur Yld	Vol	High	Low	Close	Net Chg.
AVX 8¼12	cv	192	82	75	80	− 1
AbbtL 11s93	10.4	10	106	106	106	+ 1
Advst 9s08	cv	24	80½	80½	80½	− 10½
AetnLf 8⅛07	9.2	26	87⅞	85⅞	87⅞	+ 1⅞
AHoist 5½93	cv	6	75	75	75	...
AmMed 9½01	cv	120	88	87½	88	+ ½
AmMed 8¼08	cv	33	77	77	77	...
ASmel 4⅝88	4.9	2	94 29/32	94 29/32	94 29/32	...
ATT 3⅞90r	4.3	50	89¾	89¾	89¾	...
ATT 8¾00	9.5	479	95	92⅛	92½	− ½
ATT 7s01	8.9	55	79¼	78	78¾	− ¼
ATT 7⅛03	9.1	142	78⅜	77⅞	78	− ¼
ATT 8.80s05	9.8	287	91¼	90¼	90¼	− ⅞
ATT 8⅝s07	9.7	196	89	88	88¾	− ¼
ATT 8⅝26	10.1	213	86	85¾	85¾	− ⅝
Amoco 6s91	6.6	6	91	91	91	+ ½
Amoco 6s98	8.0	5	75⅛	75⅛	75⅛	...

Bonds	Cur Yld	Vol	High	Low	Close	Net Chg.
Chvrn 8¾96	9.1	10	95¾	95¾	95¾	+ ¾
ChckFul 7s12	cv	15	71¾	71¾	71¾	− ¼
Chrysl 8⅞95	9.6	1	92⅛	92⅛	92⅛	+ ¼
Chryslr 8s98	9.3	10	86	86	86	...
Chryslr 12¾92	11.9	430	109½	107½	107½	− 1½
ChryF 8.35s91	8.9	4	93½	93½	93½	+ ½
ChryF 7.7s92	8.6	9	89⅝	89⅜	89⅝	− 1⅝
CmwE 8¼07	10.9	15	77	76	76	+ 2¾
CmwE 9⅛08	10.7	28	86½	85½	85½	− 1½
CmwE 11⅛10	10.9	3	102	102	102	+ 1½
CmwE 17½88	16.1	24	108½	108½	108½	+ ¼
CmwE 14¼92	13.7	40	104 7/32	104	104 7/32	...
CmwE 15⅜12	13.6	4	112 13/16	112 13/16	112 13/16	+ 5/32
CmwE 12⅛13	11.7	10	103½	103½	103½	...
CmwE 11¾15	11.4	10	103	103	103	+ 1
Compq 5¼12	cv	58	110	105	110	+ 3
ConEd 9⅜00	9.9	40	95½	94½	94½	− 1
ConEd 7.9s01	9.4	49	84	83¼	84	+ ¼
ConEd 8.4s03	9.8	50	86	86	86	− 1
ConEd 9⅛04	9.9	47	92⅜	92	92⅜	− ¼

Corporate bonds are quoted as a percentage of their face amount (or par value), usually in denominations of $1,000. The prices are listed at one-tenth of face value. A $1,000 bond is quoted at 100, a $950 dollar bond at 95, and so on. Fluctuations in bond prices are usually given in eighths, quarters and halves of points, as with stocks. On a bond trading at 98½, the price is $985 (98.5 × 10 = 985)

Column 1: Tells you that the bonds were issued by AT&T, pay 8⅝ percent interest and will mature in 2007.

Column 2: Says that the current yield is 9.7. The current yield is determined by dividing the coupon yield (8.625) by the current market price.

Column 3: Volume of bonds traded. One hundred and ninety-six bonds ($196,000 worth) changed hands on the New York Exchange.

Columns 4, 5 and 6: Shows that AT&T had a high of 89 and a low of 88 ($880) and closed at 88¾.

Column 7: Shows that the bond was down ¼ point ($2.50) from the previous day's close.

NASDAQ National Market

NASDAQ OVER-THE-COUNTER MARKETS
NATIONAL MARKET ISSUES
4:00 p.m. Eastern Time Prices

Thursday, May 7, 1987

365-day High Low				Sales (hds)	High	Low	Last	Net Chg.	365-day High Low					Sales (hds)	High	Low	Last	Net Chg.
16	10½	Cobanco	.20h	1.6 39	4	12¾	12¾	12¾ ...	13½	1⅜	ECI	Telecom		... 241	5⅞	5½	5¾	...
2¾	1 7-16	Cobb	Resourc	.. 65	386	2⅝	2½	2 19-32 + 7-32	6½	3⅞	Edgecomb	Cp		... 22	5½	5¼	5¼	...
26½	14	Cobe	Lab	.. 17	182	23¾	23½	23¾ − ¼	12¼	7½	Edison	Contrl		.. 19 400	9¼	9	9¼ + ⅛
56	26½	CocaBtCn	.88a	2.7 ..	99	33½	32¾	32¾ − ¼	11⅞	6½	EIL	Instrm	5k	.. 15	2	7¾	7¾	7¾ + ⅜
5⅞	3	CoCa	Mines	...	84	5⅞	5⅝	5⅝ − ⅛	9¼	5¾	EIP	Micro	.12	1.7 66	36	7¼	6¾	7¼ ...
15¾	7¼	Codenoll	Tech	...	10	8½	8	8½ ...	8	3⅜	El	Chico	Corp	... 229	5¼ 5 1-16	5¼ + ⅛
36	11⅝	Coeur	d'Aln	2i	... 249	31¼	30¾	30⅞ + ¼	26¼	7½	Elan			... 102	23¼	22½	22¾ − ½
3¾	11-16	Cogenic	Enrg	... ..	58	1⅜	1¼	1¼ ...	11⅜	6¼	ElbitCm	.75d	7.3 ..	65	10½	10¼	10¼ − ⅜

Like stock tables for listed securities, the NASDAQ table shows the high and low for the most recent year; the name of the stock and the dividend; the volume of sales; the day's high, low and last sales price, and the net change from the closing sale on the preceding business day.

CHAPTER FOURTEEN _____

The Final Exam: Rating Your Broker

Several years ago, the New York Stock Exchange conducted an in-depth survey of investor attitudes. One question posed on the survey was, "Why are you doing business with your current broker?" Surprisingly, the number one reason had nothing to do with investment results. It was simply that investors liked their broker. Good service ranked second, and investment results fell a distant third. "Most experienced investors just want a broker who is pleasant to talk with who will write up their orders," says Jim Buehler of Roney & Co. "They usually already know what they want to buy."

However, a study of investor attitudes conducted by an independent research firm shed a different light on the matter. Investors gave their brokers a much higher satisfaction rating during bull markets, when their investments were presumably performing well, then they did during bear markets, when their investments were likely to be on the decline. "Nonperformance," says David Thompson of Prudential-Bache, "is the number one reason clients leave their brokers."

How should you evaluate your broker? What is the single most important factor in gauging your broker's effectiveness?

"Service," claims Donnis Casey of A. G. Edwards. "I think that would be the number one thing."

"The key is chemistry—rapport," says Gary Cohen of E. F. Hutton. "If there is no chemistry, there is no relationship between client and broker."

"Trust. That's absolutely the first criterion," contends Betsy Buckley of Dain Bosworth. "You have to have confidence in both their professional judgment and their ethics."

"Performance," says Lyn Hensle of Morgan Olmstead. "I would evaluate a broker based on performance."

"Investors look for honesty above all," asserts Scott Horrall of Thomson McKinnon. "That's even more important than performance."

The fact is that the success of your relationship with your broker is based, not on a single criterion, but on a wide range of criteria. "You can look at the actual numbers of the performance," says Buckley, "but a better criterion might be, 'How well am I sleeping at night?' "

Most investors, says Perrin Long of Lipper Analytical Services, know instinctively whether their broker is a good fit. "As long as you're comfortable with your broker and your broker is providing you with what you feel you need, whether it's financial or psychological, that's all that really matters. But if you're not comfortable with your broker, you should look for another broker."

What follows is an informal quiz designed to help you assess the effectiveness of your broker. Is your broker knowledgeable in the investment areas that are important to you? Does your broker understand your objectives and your threshold for risk? Do you trust and like your broker? Is your broker helping you achieve your investment goals?

Here are the rules: After reading through each category, you decide how your broker rates. Scores—which are awarded on a graduating scale with zero as the lowest rating—are based solely on your perceptions of your broker's performance. Is your broker doing an excellent, average or less than adequate job of serving your needs? You may already know the answer to that question. If not, you'll soon find out.

1. TRUST (20 POINTS)

In the simplest terms, if you don't trust your broker, the exam ends here. Your broker automatically fails. Begin your search immediately for another broker.

"I have to be able to trust my broker," says Bob Cohn, training manager of Drexel Burnham, "trust that he won't advance himself at my expense." One investor says that he distrusts his broker so much that when his broker gives him a price quote on a stock, he'll often call another broker just to make sure the quote was accurate. If you consistently find that you don't believe what your broker is telling you, that you think he or she is holding things back, overstating the potential of investment recommendations or deceiving you in any way, you should get out of that relationship and find a broker you can trust.

There are, however, varying levels of trust, just as there are varying levels of honesty. Who, for instance, has never rolled through a four-way stop, never stretched things on an income tax return, never exaggerated, never lied by omission? What you should expect in a broker is someone you feel you can believe and can trust to keep your best interests at heart. Here are some questions that you should ask yourself to assess the overall integrity of your broker:

- Does your broker have your best interests at heart? Keep in mind, of course, that a broker who doesn't also have his or her own interests at heart wouldn't be in business for long. Keep in mind also that nearly all brokers will put the best possible face on what they're selling. But you should feel confident that your broker is genuinely concerned about your success as an investor and is not going to mislead you or exaggerate claims.

- Does your broker resist making unnecessary transactions? Has your broker ever talked you out of a trade? Perhaps you wanted to sell a stock that you thought was headed down, or to buy one that you thought looked hot, but your broker persuaded you to hold off. That takes integrity—to turn down a quick commission in order to put the client's interests first. "If a client calls up and wants to buy something I don't think he should buy, I just try to tell it like it is," says Don Tidlund of E. F. Hutton. "I might say, 'You want to buy that; we just had a research report that said it looks like it's topped out.' I tell our young brokers, 'Don't go for the commissions. Just tell it straight. If you're honest with them, you'll get more business in the long run. Don't go for the quick buck.' "

- Does your broker level with you about bad news? "When your broker loses money for you, how does he deal with you?" asks Joe Baxter of Smith Barney. "Does he call you up and admit that he blew it?" You want a broker who will offer a frank assessment of the situation when the investments he or she recommends are not working out.

- Does your broker steer you away from questionable investments? "I've had times when I called my broker to ask about some high-yielding bonds," says one investor, "and my broker convinced me not to buy them. He said, 'Yeah, they have a high yield, but they also have a high degree of risk. Let me tell you the problems with those bonds.' Other times, I've called to ask about an investment and my broker would say, 'That investment may be all right, but I have to tell you I don't know very much about it and I don't feel comfortable putting you into it.' "

- Does your broker admit mistakes? Has your broker ever called to admit having been wrong about an investment he or she recommended? Maybe the yield was lower than the one your broker had quoted, or the company's earnings were lower, or a bond your broker recommended turned out to have a call provision that he or she hadn't been aware of. All brokers make mistakes. Good brokers aren't afraid to own up to those mistakes.

If your broker is impeccably honest (admits mistakes freely, steers you away from questionable investments even if this means turning down a commission, is not afraid to call you with bad news and generally keeps your best interests at heart, award him or her the maximum score of 20 points for trust. Again, remember that scores are awarded on a graduated scale (in this case, from 20 points for the highest rating to 0 for the lowest rating).

2. RAPPORT (20 POINTS)

Call it chemistry; call it compatibility; call it camaraderie—rapport is vital to a satisfactory broker-client relationship. Without rapport, no broker-client relationship can last for long. "If the chemistry between you and your broker is not there, it's just a matter of time before your relationship will disintegrate," says Hutton's Cohen.

How do you know whether you have rapport with your broker? You should know instinctively. "It's like a doctor," says Tom Asher of Robinson-Humphrey. "You don't necessarily know what it is you like about him. All you know is you feel comfortable and confident with him. He puts you at ease. He asks questions that no one ever asked you before. It's the same with brokers."

As Adrian Banky of the Securities Industry Association puts it, "People are people. Why deal with someone you don't like?" Do you hesitate to call your broker when you need advice? Is your broker happy to hear from you when you do call? Do you feel a certain bond between yourself and your broker? Rapport means that you are both on the same wavelength: your broker doesn't patronize you or talk over your head. You like and enjoy doing business with this person. You're not put off by his or her mannerisms, jokes or political or religious commentary.

Award a maximum of 20 points for rapport.

3. SERVICE (15 POINTS)

"Is the broker responsive to your needs?" asks Banky. "Are your calls returned? Do you receive the material that you request?"

There are some other questions that you should also ask yourself in evaluating the caliber of service your broker is providing. Does your broker call you with investment ideas when you have money to invest? Is your broker accessible when you need him or her? Does your broker phone you with important news about your investments? Does your broker call you to tell you when to sell? Does your broker see that your problems are solved and your questions answered? Does your broker call you to tell you at what price your trades are executed? Does your broker conduct an annual review of your investments for you? Does your broker send you written research and news clips when appropriate? "The biggest part of the game," contends Tidlund, "is service. Big accounts leave because of bad service—not because of bad performance. I know brokers who only work two or three hours a day. They're never around; you can't reach them when you need them. Clients expect good service, and they deserve it."

Award a maximum of 15 points for service.

Rating Yourself

Despite reports to the contrary, the customer is not always right. The manner in which clients respond to their brokers can make a significant difference in the success of the broker-client relationship. Here's a quick quiz to help you find out how you rate as a client. (Scores are determined on a graduated scale from 10 to 0, with 10 representing full agreement with the corresponding statement and 0 representing complete disagreement.)

	10 Points Agree Completely	5 Points	0 Points Disagree Completely
1. I'm always completely open and honest with my broker.	___	___	___
2. I never use a discounter to buy or sell investments that my broker recommends.	___	___	___
3. I use the sales assistant as often as possible.	___	___	___
4. I never say "I told you so" or complain when an occasional investment declines in value.	___	___	___
5. I don't expect the moon—just reasonable returns commensurate with the state of the market and my tolerance for risk.	___	___	___
6. I always accept my broker's phone calls (or return them immediately).	___	___	___
7. I'm quick to follow my broker's recommendations.	___	___	___
8. I send my broker as many referrals as possible.	___	___	___
9. I never bother my broker for quotes or other information unless I'm prepared to act on that information.	___	___	___
10. I always thank my broker when he or she makes me money.	___	___	___
TOTAL	___	___	___

Rating system:

Under 70 points. Unsatisfactory. Consider yourself lucky your broker hasn't fired you yet.

70–79 points. Average.

80–89 points. Good.

90–100 points. Excellent. Your broker finds you a pleasure to work with, and the chances are that he or she returns the favor in service and results.

4. UNDERSTANDING (15 POINTS)

Understanding begins with listening. "Does your broker listen to what is important to you?" asks Cohen. "Does he take the time to find out what your needs are? That's crucial."

Does your broker ask good questions? Does he or she listen to your concerns and respond accordingly? Does he or she take the time to find out your needs, your objectives, your risk threshold? "A good broker won't recommend an investment to a client until he knows what the client's objective is," says Kathy Soule of Merrill Lynch.

Adds D'Arcy Fox of A. G. Edwards: "Most clients aren't very good about expressing their needs. It takes real skill to flush out that sort of information. We put great emphasis on training our brokers to ask the right questions in a variety of ways in order to get the investor to express his needs and objectives more clearly."

Award a maximum of 15 points for understanding.

5. INVESTMENT KNOWLEDGE (15 POINTS)

You want a broker who is well versed in the investment areas that are important to you. If you're interested in stocks, you want a broker who not only keeps a close watch on the day-to-day movement of the market but can also give you an opinion on where the market is headed. If you're interested in small over-the-counter stocks, you want a broker who specializes in that area. If you're interested in bonds, you want a broker who deals regularly in bonds and has an opinion on the direction of interest rates and of the bond market. You may find that you need two or three brokers if you have several areas of interest. But you don't want to be trading options with a broker who spends most of his or her time selling mutual funds. "I've had people call me who wanted to 'do puts on the OEX,' " says Dain Bosworth's Buckley. "I can certainly do puts on the OEX, but I'm not a good person for that. I say, 'I think you'd rather do that with another broker.' You want a broker who is either in the same areas you think you're going to be in or someone who is willing to learn about those areas and who you feel is going to be successful in those areas of interest."

When you pay a full-service commission, the premise is that you will receive expert advice on your investments. "The broker has to be able to understand those aspects of the market he talks about," says Drexel's Cohn, "or at least understand them better than the client does." If you find that you have to do most of your research yourself and that your broker is not able to offer satisfactory answers to most of your questions, you should get another broker.

Award a maximum of 15 points for investment knowledge.

6. RESULTS (15 POINTS)

This is the bottom line, the true dollars-and-cents value of your broker. "The successful broker is almost obsessed with helping his clients invest successfully," says Phil Clark of Roney & Co. "He will dig and work and do extraordinary things to help his clients meet their investment objectives."

Look at how your investments have done overall. How much money has your broker made for you? "I would track performance on a quarterly basis and expect an annual portfolio review," says Morgan Olmstead's Hensle.

There are brokers who make a big production of moving clients in and out of promising investments, talking up the winners and downplaying the losers. Don't be deceived by the sizzle. "Is your broker sticking to your initial objectives?" asks Bill Koriath of Prudential-Bache. "If you want long-term investments—you just want to buy something and forget about it—and your broker calls you a week later and says, 'I think we should redo the whole thing,' I would be very suspicious."

If possible, determine the total value of all the investments you currently have with your broker, along with all the money you've received either in income or in sales of past investments, and subtract from that the total amount of money you've invested with your broker. The difference is the amount of money your broker has made (or lost) for you.

Once you've determined your total profit, you should ask yourself this question: "Is this better than I would have done with a bank savings account or a money market account?" If the answer is no, you need another broker.

A more revealing question is: "Am I achieving my investment objective?" Try to be fair here. If your objective is to earn 8 percent in tax-free income each year and your broker has put you into a municipal bond that does just that, then you should be pleased with your results—even if the stock market has gone up 30 percent. Your broker has helped you achieve your stated objective, and that is as much as you can reasonably expect from him.

On the other hand, if you invest all your money in blue-chip stocks and your portfolio has gone up only 8 percent while the Dow Jones Industrial Average has climbed 30 percent, then you have reason for concern. If the market is down and your stocks are down with it, that's not necessarily the fault of your broker. But if your stocks are down consistently (even when the Dow is up), you may need a new broker.

Award a maximum of 15 points for results.

7. EXTRA CREDITS (5 POINTS)

Some brokers take extra pains to keep their clients satisfied. It could be a small courtesy such as mailing out copies of articles that relate to the clients' investments or giving clients a break on their commissions. Lee Kopp of Dain Bosworth says that when a stock he recommends does poorly, he often offers to liquidate the client's position in that stock with no commission. "I often feel worse about the stock than the client does," says Kopp. "This is just my way of telling the client I'm sorry."

Jim Vieburg of Piper Jaffray says that after he sells out a client's position in a stock, he often calls the client later if the stock increases in price. Says Vieburg, "I'll tell the client, 'I want you to know the stock is up. We might have sold a little too soon, but hindsight is 20–20. I still feel comfortable that we did the right thing, given the information we had." His reason for calling, he says, is to offer a little reassurance to investors who may be suffering "seller's remorse."

Other brokers make more ostentatious gestures. Dale Grubb of Shearson Lehman says that he and his partner sometimes sponsor seminars to bring their clients up-to-date on new investments or changes in the tax law. One recent seminar on the new federal tax act drew 300 investors. Grubb and his partner not only conducted the seminar; they also picked up the tab for a three-course meal and an open bar for all 300 attendees.

Award a maximum of five bonus points for extra effort.

Now add up the scores:

		Points Awarded
Trust	(0–20)	_____
Rapport	(0–20)	_____
Service	(0–15)	_____
Understanding	(0–15)	_____
Investment knowledge	(0–15)	_____
Results	(0–15)	_____
Extra credit	(0–5)	_____
Total	(0–105)	_____

Here's how your broker rates:

Under 70 points. Unsatisfactory. You can do better. Begin your search for a broker who will be more tuned in to your specific needs.

70 to 79 points. "C." Average. Your broker is doing an adequate job of handling your account.

80 to 89 points. "B." Good. You should be pleased with your broker. Your innvestments are apparently in fine hands.

90 to 100 points. "A." Excellent. Send your broker a bottle of champagne. Then buy one for yourself. You have reason to celebrate. You have what other investors constantly strive for—a competent, compatible, reliable broker who has proven capable of keeping your investment program on a *winning* track.

APPENDIX —————————————————————————

A DIRECTORY OF THE 100 LARGEST BROKERAGE FIRMS BASED ON NUMBER OF BROKERS

ARKANSAS

Little Rock:

Stephens, Inc.
114 East Capitol Avenue
P.O. Box 3507
Little Rock, AR 72203
(501) 374-4361

CALIFORNIA

Los Angeles:

Bateman Eichler, Hill Richards, Inc.
Parent: Batehill, Inc., wholly owned
subsidiary of Kemper Financial
Companies, Inc.
700 South Flower Street
Los Angeles, CA 90017
(213) 625-3545

Crowell, Weedon & Co.
One Wilshire Building, Suite 2800
Los Angeles, CA 90017
(213) 620-1850

Wedbush Securities, Inc.
Parent: Wedbush Corporation
615 South Flower Street
Los Angeles, CA 90017
(213) 620-1750

San Francisco:

Sutro & Co., Inc.
Parent: Sutro Group, 100% owned by
John Hancock Freedom Securities,
Inc.
201 California Street
San Francisco, CA 94111
(415) 445-8500

COLORADO

Denver:

Boettcher & Co., Inc.
Parent: Boettcher Investment
Corporation, 100% owned by
Kemper Financial Companies, Inc.
828 17th Street
Denver, CO 80202
(303) 628-8000

CONNECTICUT

East Hartford:

**North American Investment
Corporation**
Parent: North American Holding
Corporation
800 Connecticut Boulevard
East Hartford, CT 06108
(203) 528-9021

Hartford:
Advest, Inc.
Parent: Advest Group, Inc.
280 Trumbull Street
Hartford, CT 06103
(203) 525-1421

DISTRICT OF COLUMBIA
Washington:
Ferris & Co., Inc.
1720 Eye Street, NW
Washington, DC 20006
(202) 429-3500
Johnston, Lemon & Co., Inc.
1101 Vermont Avenue, NW
Washington, DC 20005
(202) 842-5500

FLORIDA
St. Petersburg:
Raymond James & Associates, Inc.
Parent: Raymond James Financial, Inc.
1400 66th Street, North
P.O. Box 12749
St. Petersburg, FL 33733
(813) 578-3800

GEORGIA
Atlanta:
Robinson-Humphrey Company, Inc.
Parent: Shearson Lehman Brothers,
Inc., wholly owned subsidiary of
American Express Company
Atlanta Financial Center
3333 Peachtree Road, NE
Atlanta, GA 30326
(404) 266-6000
Savannah:
**Johnson, Lane, Space, Smith & Co.,
Inc.**
101 East Bay Street
P.O. Box 607
Savannah, GA 31402
(912) 236-7101

ILLINOIS
Aurora:
Oberweis Securities, Inc.
841 North Lake Street
Aurora, IL 60506
(312) 897-7100
Chicago:
Clayton Brown & Associates, Inc.
300 West Washington Street
Chicago, IL 60606
(312) 641-3300
Chicago Corporation
Parent: Chicorp, Inc.
208 South LaSalle Street
Chicago, IL 60604
(312) 855-7600
Midland Doherty, Inc.
Parent: Midland Doherty, Ltd.
120 South LaSalle Street
Chicago, IL 60603
(312) 236-9734
John Nuveen & Co., Inc.
Parent: St. Paul Fire and Marine
Insurance Company
333 West Wacker Drive
Chicago, IL 60606
(312) 917-7700

IOWA
Des Moines:
R. G. Dickinson & Co.
Parent: Statesman Group, Inc., 100%
owned by Statesman Financial
Services
200 Des Moines Building
Des Moines, IA 50306-9111
(515) 247-8100

KENTUCKY
Louisville:
J. J. B. Hilliard/W. L. Lyons, Inc.
Parent: Hilliard-Lyons, Inc.
545 South Third Street
Louisville, KY 40202
(502) 588-8400

LOUISIANA
New Orleans:
Howard, Weil, Labouisse, Friedrichs
    Corporation, Inc.
Parent: Howard Weil Financial
1100 Poydras Street, Suite 900
New Orleans, LA 70163-0900
(504) 582-2500

MARYLAND
Baltimore:
Alex. Brown & Sons, Inc.
Parent: Alex. Brown, Inc.
135 East Baltimore Street
Baltimore, MD 21202
(301) 727-1700
Legg Mason Wood Walker, Inc.
Parent: Legg Mason, Inc.
Seven East Redwood Street
Baltimore, MD 21202
(301) 539-3400

MASSACHUSETTS
Boston:
Fidelity Brokerage Services, Inc.
Parent: FMR Corporation
161 Devonshire Street
Boston, MA 02110
(617) 570-7000
Moseley Securities Corporation
Parent: Moseley Holding Corporation,
    39% owned by AMWAL
    American Investments, Ltd.
60 State Street
Boston, MA 02109
(617) 367-2400

MICHIGAN
Detroit:
First of Michigan Corporation
Parent: First of Michigan Capital
    Corporation, 22.2% owned by
    DST Systems, Inc.; DST Securi-
    ties, Inc.
100 Renaissance Center, 26th Floor
Detroit, MI 48243
(313) 259-2600

Roney & Co.
One Griswold Street
Detroit, MI 48226
(313) 963-6700
Southfield:
First Heritage Corporation
26877 Northwestern Highway
P.O. Box 5077
Southfield, MI 48086
(313) 353-4740

MINNESOTA
Minneapolis:
Craig-Hallum, Inc.
Parent: Craig-Hallum Corporation
701 Fourth Avenue South, Tenth Floor
Minneapolis, MN 55415-1655
(612) 332-1212
Dain Bosworth, Inc.
Parent: Inter-Regional Financial Group,
    Inc.
100 Dain Tower
Minneapolis, MN 55402
(612) 371-2711
John G. Kinnard & Co., Inc.
Parent: Kinnard Investments, Inc.
1700 Northstar Center
Minneapolis, MN 55402
(612) 370-2700
Piper, Jaffray & Hopwood, Inc.
Parent: Piper Jaffray, Inc., 25.25%
    owned by Hartford Fire Insurance
    Company
Piper Jaffray Tower, 222 South
    Ninth St.
P.O. Box 28
Minneapolis, MN 55440
(612) 342-6000

MISSOURI
Kansas City:
B. C. Christopher Securities Company
Parent: B. C. Christopher & Co., 85%
    owned by Central Life Assurance
    Company
4800 Main Street, Suite 100
Kansas City, MO 64112
(816) 932-7000

BMA Financial Services, Inc.,
    80% owned by Business Men's
    Assurance Company of America
1830 City Center Square
1100 Main Street
Kansas City, MO 64105
(816) 471-4710
St. Louis:
A. G. Edwards & Sons, Inc.
Parent: A. G. Edwards, Inc.
One North Jefferson
St. Louis, MO 63103
(314) 289-3000
Edward D. Jones & Co.
201 Progress Parkway
St. Louis, MO 63403
(314) 851-2000
Newhard, Cook & Co., Inc.
1600 South Brentwood Boulevard
St. Louis, MO 63144-0717
(314) 968-5901
R. Rowland & Co., Inc.
Parent: Rowland Group, Inc.
720 Olive Street
St. Louis, MO 63101
(314) 342-2800
Stifel, Nicolaus & Co., Inc.
Parent: Stifel Financial Corporation
500 North Broadway
St. Louis, MO 63102
(314) 342-2000

MONTANA
Great Falls:
D. A. Davidson & Co., Inc.
Parent: DADCO
Davidson Building
Eight Third Street, North
Great Falls, MT 59401
(406) 727-4200

NEW YORK
Albany:
First Albany Corporation
Parent: First Albany Companies, Inc.
41 State Street
P.O. Box 52
Albany, NY 12201
(518) 447-8500

New York:
Bear, Stearns & Co., Inc.
Parent: Bear Stearns Companies, Inc.
55 Water Street
New York, NY 10041
(212) 952-5000

Brown Brothers Harriman & Co.
59 Wall Street
New York, NY 10005
(212) 483-1818

Cowen & Co.
One Battery Park Place
New York, NY 10004
(212) 483-0700

Dean Witter Reynolds, Inc.
Parent: Dean Witter Financial Services,
    Inc., wholly owned subsidiary of
    Sears, Roebuck & Co. and a mem-
    ber of the Dean Witter Financial
    Services Group
130 Liberty Street
New York, NY 10006
(212) 524-2222

Dillon, Read & Co., Inc.
Parent: Travelers Corporation
535 Madison Avenue
New York, NY 10022
(212) 906-7000

Dominick & Dominick, Inc.
Parent: Dominick International
    Corporation
90 Broad Street
New York, NY 10004
(212) 558-8800

**Donaldson, Lufkin & Jenrette Securities
    Corporation**
Parent: Donaldson, Lufkin & Jenrette,
    Inc., 100% owned by Equitable
    Life Assurance Society of the
    United States
140 Broadway
New York, NY 10005
(212) 504-3000

Drexel Burnham Lambert, Inc.
Parent: Drexel Burnham Lambert
    Group, Inc.
60 Broad Street
New York, NY 10004
(212) 480-6000

Fahnestock & Co., Inc.
Parent: Nesbitt Thomson Securities,
    Inc.
110 Wall Street
New York, NY 10005
(212) 668-8000

First Boston Corporation
Parent: First Boston, Inc.
Park Avenue Plaza
New York, NY 10055
(212) 909-2000

Goldman, Sachs & Co.
85 Broad Street
New York, NY 10004
(212) 902-1000

Gruntal & Co., Inc.
Parent: Gruntal Financial Corporation
14 Wall Street
New York, NY 10005
(212) 267-8800

E. F. Hutton & Co., Inc.
Parent: E. F. Hutton Group, Inc.
31 West 52nd Street
New York, NY 10019
(212) 969-5300

Josephthal & Co., Inc.
Parent: Josephthal Holding
    Corporation
120 Broadway
New York, NY 10271
(212) 577-3000

Kidder, Peabody & Co., Inc.
Parent: Kidder, Peabody Group, Inc.,
    80% owned by General Electric
    Financial Services, Inc.
10 Hanover Square
New York, NY 10005
(212) 510-3000

Ladenburg, Thalmann & Co., Inc.
540 Madison Avenue
New York, NY 10022
(212) 940-0100

Laidlaw Adams & Peck, Inc.,
    51% owned by Kuhns Brothers &
    Laidlaw, Inc.
275 Madison Avenue
New York, NY 10016
(212) 949-5300

Mabon, Nugent & Co.
115 Broadway
New York, NY 10006
(212) 732-2820

**Merrill Lynch, Pierce, Fenner &
    Smith, Inc.**
Parent: Merrill Lynch & Co., Inc.
One Liberty Plaza
165 Broadway
New York, NY 10080
(212) 637-7455

MKI Securities Corporation
Parent: MKI Investments, Inc., wholly
    owned subsidiary of International
    City Holding PLC
61 Broadway
New York, NY 10006
(212) 425-2288

Moore & Schley, Cameron & Co.
45 Broadway
New York, NY 10006
(212) 483-1800

Morgan Stanley & Co., Inc.
Parent: Morgan Stanley Group, Inc.
1251 Avenue of the Americas
New York, NY 10020
(212) 703-4000

Nomura Securities International, Inc.
Parent: Nomura Securities Company,
    Ltd.
180 Maiden Lane
New York, NY 10038
(212) 208-9300

Oppenheimer & Co., Inc.
Parent: Oppenheimer Group, Inc.,
    100% owned by Oppenheimer
    Holdings, Inc.
Oppenheimer Tower
World Financial Center
New York, NY 10281
(212) 667-7000

PaineWebber, Inc.
Parent: PaineWebber Group, Inc.
1285 Avenue of the Americas
New York, NY 10019
(212) 713-2000

Prudential-Bache Securities, Inc.
Parent: Prudential Securities Group,
    Inc., indirect wholly owned sub-
    sidiary of the Prudential Insurance
    Company of America
One Seaport Plaza
199 Water Street
New York, NY 10292
(212) 214-1000

**L. F. Rothschild, Unterberg, Towbin,
    Inc.**
Parent: L. F. Rothschild, Unterberg,
    Towbin Holdings, Inc.
55 Water Street
New York, NY 10041
(212) 412-1000

Salomon Brothers, Inc.
Parent: Salomon, Inc.
One New York Plaza
New York, NY 10004
(212) 747-7000

Shearson Lehman Brothers, Inc.
Parent: American Express Company
American Express Tower
World Financial Center
New York, NY 10285
(212) 298-2000

**Smith Barney, Harris Upham & Co.,
    Inc.**
Parent: Smith Barney, Inc.
1345 Avenue of the Americas
New York, NY 10105
(212) 698-6000

Thomson McKinnon Securities, Inc.
Parent: Thomson McKinnon, Inc.,
    23% owned by Hartford Accident
    and Indemnity Company
One New York Plaza
New York, NY 10004
(212) 482-7000

Tucker, Anthony & R. L. Day, Inc.
Parent: John Hancock Mutual Life
    Insurance Company
120 Broadway
New York, NY 10271
(212) 618-7400

Wertheim Schroder & Co., Inc.
Parent: Wertheim Schroder Holdings,
    Inc.
200 Park Avenue
New York, NY 10166
(212) 578-0200

NORTH CAROLINA
Charlotte:
Interstate Securities Corporation
Parent: Interstate Securities, Inc.
2700 NCNB Plaza
101 South Tryon Street
Charlotte, NC 28280
(704) 379-9000
Raleigh:
Carolina Securities Corporation
127 West Hargett Street
P.O. Box 1071
Raleigh, NC 27602
(919) 832-3711

OHIO
Cleveland:
McDonald & Co. Securities, Inc.
Parent: McDonald & Co. Investments,
    Inc.
2100 Society Building
Cleveland, OH 44114
(216) 443-2300
Prescott, Ball & Turben, Inc.
Parent: Kemper Financial Companies,
    Inc., 80% owned by Kemper
    Corporation

1331 Euclid Avenue
Cleveland, OH 44115
(216) 574-7300
Columbus:
Ohio Company
155 East Broad Street
Columbus, OH 43215
(614) 464-6811

PENNSYLVANIA
Philadelphia:
Butcher & Singer, Inc.
Parent: Butcher and Co., Inc.
211 South Broad Street
Philadelphia, PA 19107-5324
(215) 985-5000
Hopper Soliday & Co., Inc.
1401 Walnut Street
Philadelphia, PA 19102
(215) 972-5400
Janney Montgomery Scott, Inc.
Parent: Penn Mutual Life Insurance
    Company
Five Penn Center Plaza
Philadelphia, PA 19103
(215) 665-6000
W. H. Newbold's Son & Co., Inc.,
    100% owned by Provident Mutual
    Life Insurance Company of Phila-
    delphia
1500 Walnut Street
Philadelphia, PA 19102
(215) 893-8000
Pittsburgh:
Parker/Hunter, Inc.
600 Grant Street
Pittsburgh, PA 15219
(412) 562-8000

TENNESSEE
Memphis:
Morgan, Keegan & Co., Inc.
Parent: Morgan Keegan, Inc.
Morgan Keegan Tower
50 Front Street
Memphis, TN 38103
(901) 524-4100

UMIC, Inc.
Parent: UMIC Securities Corporation
850 Ridge Lake Boulevard
Memphis, TN 38119
(901) 766-0600
Nashville:
J. C. Bradford & Co.
330 Commerce Street
Nashville, TN 37201-1809
(615) 748-9000

TEXAS
Dallas:
Eppler, Guerin & Turner, Inc.
Parent: EGT Financial Corp., wholly
    owned subsidiary of Principal
    Financial Group, Inc.
2001 Bryan Tower, 23rd Floor
Dallas, TX 75201
(214) 880-9000
Rauscher Pierce Refsnes, Inc.
Parent: Inter-Regional Financial
    Group, Inc.
2500 RPR Tower
Plaza of the Americas Building
Dallas, TX 75201
(214) 978-0111

VIRGINIA
Richmond:
Scott & Stringfellow, Inc.
Parent: Scott & Stringfellow Financial,
    Inc.
Mutual Building
P.O. Box 1575
Richmond, VA 23213
(804) 643-1811
Wheat, First Securities, Inc.
Parent: WFS Financial Corporation,
    25% owned by Hartford Life
    Insurance Company
707 East Main Street
P.O. Box 1357
Richmond, VA 23211
(804) 649-2311

WASHINGTON
Seattle:
Interpacific Investors Securities, Inc.,
    99% owned by Alaska Northwest
1111 Norton Building
801 Second Avenue
Seattle, WA 98104
(206) 623-2784

Spokane:
Murphey Favre, Inc.
Parent: Washington Mutual Savings
    Bank
West 601 Riverside Avenue, Ninth
    Floor
Spokane, WA 99201
(509) 624-4101

WISCONSIN
Milwaukee:
Robert W. Baird & Co., Inc.
Parent: Regis Group, Inc., 75% owned
    by Northwestern Mutual Life
    Insurance Company
777 East Wisconsin Avenue
Milwaukee, WI 53202
(414) 765-3500

Blunt Ellis & Loewi, Inc.
Parent: Financial Companies, Inc.
225 East Mason Street
Milwaukee, WI 53202
(414) 347-3400

Milwaukee Company
Parent: Milwaukee Financial
    Group, Inc.
250 East Wisconsin Avenue
Milwaukee, WI 53202
(414) 347-7000

BRITISH COLUMBIA
Vancouver:
Pemberton Houston Willoughby Bell
    Gouinlock, Inc.
Parent: Pemberton Houston
    Willoughby Investment Corpora-
    tion
2400 Park Place
666 Burrard Street
Vancouver, British Columbia V6C 3C7
    Canada
(604) 688-8411

ONTARIO
Toronto:
Nesbitt Thomson Deacon, Inc.
Parent: Nesbitt Thomson, Inc.
Sun Life Tower, Sun Life Centre,
    Suite 1900
Toronto, Ontario M5H 3W2 Canada
(416) 586-3600

Walwyn Stodgell Cochran Murray,
    Ltd.
Parent: Walwyn, Inc.
70 University Avenue, Suite 800
Toronto, Ontario M5J 2M5 Canada
(416) 591-6000

QUEBEC
Montreal:
Levesque, Beaubien, Inc.
Parent: Levesque, Beaubien & Co., Inc.
1155 Metcalfe Street, Fifth Floor
Montreal, Quebec H3B 4S9 Canada
(514) 879-2222

CONTACTING THE SEC

U. S. Securities and Exchange Commission, Washington, DC 20549

For	Call
Complaints	Consumer Affairs (202) 272-7440
Filings by registered companies	Public Reference (202) 272-7450
General information	Public Affairs (202) 272-2650

CONTACTING SECURITIES INDUSTRY ORGANIZATIONS REGARDING AN ARBITRATION

American Stock Exchange, Inc.
86 Trinity Place
New York, NY 10006
(212) 306-1000

Boston Stock Exchange, Inc.
One Boston Place
Boston, MA 02108
(617) 723-9500

Chicago Board Options Exchange, Inc.
LaSalle at Van Buren
Chicago, IL 60605
(312) 786-5600

Cincinnati Stock Exchange, Inc.
205 Dixie Terminal Building
Cincinnati, OH 45202
(513) 621-1410

Midwest Stock Exchange, Inc.
120 South LaSalle Street
Chicago, IL 60603
(312) 368-2222

Municipal Securities Rulemaking Board
1150 Connecticut Avenue, NW,
Suite 507
Washington, DC 20036
(202) 223-9347

National Association of Securities Dealers, Inc.
Two World Trade Center, 98th Floor
New York, NY 10048
(212) 839-6251

New York Stock Exchange, Inc.
11 Wall Street
New York, NY 10006
(212) 623-3000

Pacific Stock Exchange, Inc.
618 South Spring Street
Los Angeles, CA 90014
(213) 614-8400

Philadelphia Stock Exchange, Inc.
1900 Market Street
Philadelphia, PA 19103
(215) 496-5000

GLOSSARY _____

A

accrued interest Interest that is added to the buyer's price of a bond. This interest has accrued since the last interest payment was made. Exceptions are income bonds and bonds in default. (*See:* flat; income bond.)

ADR American Depository Receipt

advance-decline line A ratio measuring the number of stocks that have advanced versus the number that have declined. By plotting this ratio over a period of days and weeks, analysts can spot a trend in the overall strength or weakness in the market.

agent An investment banker who assumes no financial risk in an underwriting but simply distributes as much of the offering as is feasible and turns back unsold shares.

aggressive policy Investing with the idea of getting the maximum return on a portfolio by timing purchases and sales to coincide with expected market movements and by varying the structure of the portfolio in line with these expected market movements.

American Depository Receipt (ADR) A negotiable receipt for a given number of shares of stock in a foreign corporation. ADRs are traded in the American securities markets just as stock is traded.

American Stock Exchange (AMEX) The second largest stock exchange in the United States.

annuity A contract between an insurance company and an individual. Such a contract generally guarantees lifetime income to the person on whose life it is based in return for either a lump sum or a periodic payment to the insurance company. (*See:* deferred annuity; fixed annuity; variable annuity.)

arbitrage   Simultaneously effecting sales and purchases in the same securities to take advantage of the price difference in separate markets.

asset   Anything that an individual or a corporation owns.

B

balance sheet   A report of a company's financial condition at a specific time.

basis point   One basis point equals 0.01 percent or 0.0001 or $1/100$ of one cent. Basis points are used primarily to describe changes in yields on bonds, notes and other fixed-income securities. If the yield on a bond issue moves from 7 percent to 7.15 percent, the yield has increased 15 basis points.

bearish   Expecting an investment to perform poorly.

bear market   A market in which securities prices are falling or are expected to fall.

bid   The price someone is willing to pay for a security at a specific time.

Big Board   Nickname for the New York Stock Exchange.

blue-chip stocks   The securities of normally strong, well-established companies that have demonstrated their ability to pay dividends in good times and bad. IBM, General Motors, 3M and General Electric are examples of blue chips. The Dow Jones Industrial Average is comprised primarily of major blue-chip stocks.

blue-sky   To qualify a securities offering in a particular state.

bond swap   A technique used by investors in municipal bonds that involves the sale of a bond or bonds at a loss and the simultaneous purchase of entirely different bonds in a like amount with comparable coupons and maturities.

book value per share   Net tangible assets per share of common stock, determined by deducting all liabilities from the company's tangible assets and then dividing this amount by the number of shares of common stock outstanding. (*See* Chapter 13, page 206.)

bottom fishing   Investing in securities when you believe that the decline in the market has nearly ended and that the prices of the securities are at their bottom.

bottom out   A securities market is said to bottom out when it has declined to the point where demand begins to exceed supply and a rise in prices is beginning.

breakout   A stock that is either declining through a "support" level or rising through a "resistance" level. (*See:* resistance; support; Chapter 13, page 201.)

break point   The dollar level of an investment in a mutual fund at which a purchaser qualifies for a reduction in sales charges on a quantity purchase.

broker   A securities firm (or individual) that acts as an agent for a customer and charges the customer a commission for its services.

bullish   Expecting an investment to perform well.

bull market   A market in which the prices of securities are moving higher or are expected to move higher.

buying power   The dollar amount of the securities that a client can purchase using only the balance in the account.

C

call loan rate   The rate of interest a bank charges a brokerage firm. Usually brokerage firms charge a minimum of $1/2$ to 1 percent over the call rate published daily in *The Wall Street Journal*.

call option   The right to buy 100 shares of a security at a specified price by a specific date in exchange for a premium. (See Chapter 13, page 209.)

call protection   The time period during which a bond cannot be redeemed by the issuer.

call provision   The written agreement between an issuing corporation and its bondholders that gives the corporation the option to redeem the bonds at a specified price before their maturity date and also specifies the conditions of the redemption.

CBOE   Chicago Board Options Exchange.

CBOT   Chicago Board of Trade.

CD   Negotiable certificate of deposit.

churning   Excessive trading in a customer's account. The term suggests that the registered representative ignores the objectives and interests of the clients and seeks only to increase commissions. (See Chapter 8, page 127.)

close   The price of a security as of the last transaction for that security on a particular day.

COMEX   Commodity Exchange of New York, where futures on gold, silver and other precious metals are traded.

commercial paper   An unsecured short-term promissory note issued by well-known businesses chiefly for financing accounts receivable. It is usually issued at a prevailing discount with maturities ranging from a few days to 270 days.

common stock   An equity security that represents ownership in a corporation. This is the first security a corporation issues to raise capital. (*See:* equity.)

consumer price index (CPI)   A measure of inflation or deflation based on price changes in consumer goods and services.

conversion parity   The state of having two securities (one of which can be converted into the other) of equal dollar value.

convertible bond   A debt security (usually in the form of a debenture) that can be converted (exchanged) into the common stock of the issuing corporation. (*See:* debenture.)

coupon yield   The interest rate stated on the face of a bond.

current yield   The annual interest return on a security (coupon yield) divided by the current market price of the security.

D

daisy chain   A manipulative device whereby a group of persons buys a particular security at successively higher prices to create a false appearance of trading in the stock, thereby defrauding investors.

dealer   The role of a brokerage firm when it acts as a principal in a particular trade. A firm is acting as a principal when it buys or sells a security for its own account and at its own risk and charges the customer a markup or markdown. (*Syn.:* principal.)

debenture   A debt obligation backed by the general credit of the issuing corporation. (*See:* convertible bond.)

defensive policy   Investing in a way that minimizes the risk of losing principal. (*Ant.:* aggressive policy.)

deferred annuity   An annuity contract that guarantees principal and future income, installment payments, or a lump-sum payment to be made or begun at some agreed-upon time in the future. (*See:* annuity.)

discount rate   The interest rate charged member banks that borrow from the Federal Reserve.

discretionary account   An account in which the principal (beneficial owner) has given the broker authority to make transactions in the account at the broker's discretion. (see Chapter 11, page 178.)

dividend   A distribution of the earnings of a corporation (in the form of cash, stock or property.)

dividend payout ratio   A ratio used to analyze a company's policy of paying cash dividends. This ratio is calculated by dividing the dividends paid on common stock by the net income available for common stock.

dividend yield   The annual percentage of return that an investor receives on either common or preferred stock. The yield is based on the amount of the dividend divided by the current market price of the stock.

dollar-cost averaging   A system of buying fixed dollar amounts of securities (usually mutual funds) at regular fixed intervals, regardless of the price of shares. This method of purchasing shares gives the investor assurance of an average cost that is generally lower than the average price of all prices at which the securities were purchased. (See Chapter 13, page 207.)

Dow   Refers to the Dow Jones Industrial Average.

Dow Jones Industrial Average (DJIA or Dow)   The most widely used market indicator. It is based on the prices of 30 large and actively traded blue-chip industrial stocks. It is quoted in points rather than dollars, and these points are determined by adding up the prices of the 30 stocks comprised by the indicator and then applying a multiplier formula.

due diligence   An investigation necessary to ensure that all material information pertinent to an issue has been disclosed to the public.

E

earnings per share (EPS)   The net income available for common stock divided by the number of shares of common stock outstanding.

efficient market theory   A theory based on the assumption that the market is perfectly efficient. The theory postulates that as new information becomes known, it is reflected immediately in the price of the stock and that stock prices therefore represent "fair" prices.

equipment trust certificate   A debt obligation backed by equipment.

equity   Ownership interest of common and preferred stockholders in a corporation; also, the client's net worth in a margin account; also, what is owned less what is owed.

ex-dividend date   The date on or after which the seller of a security is not entitled to receive any distribution previously declared.

exercise   To implement the rights of an option. For example, a call holder exercises a call by implementing the right to buy 100 shares of the underlying stock at the agreed-upon exercise price.

exercise price   The price per share at which the holder of an option may buy (in the case of a call option) or sell (in the case of a put option) the underlying stock. (*Syn.:* strike price.)

F

face value   par value.

Fed   Federal Reserve System.

Federal National Mortgage Association (FNMA) (also known as **Fannie Mae**)   A publicly held corporation that buys government-guaranteed mortgages and conventional mortgages when mortgage money is in short supply and sells them when the demand for mortgage money slacks off.

fixed annuity   An annuity contract in which the insurance company makes fixed (or guaranteed) dollar payments to the annuitant for the term of the contract (usually until death). (*See:* annuity.)

flat   Bonds traded without accrued interest; also, a term used to describe a market that is neither rising nor falling.

fundamentals   The sales, earnings and basic financial condition of a company.

futures contract   An agreement that gives the buyer the right to buy or sell a particular commodity or financial instrument at a specified price on a specific date.

G

general obligation bond (GO)   A type of municipal bond that is backed by the full faith, credit and taxing power of the issuer for payment of interest and principal.

gilt-edged security   Any security of exceptional quality, very likely to pay interest or dividends; more often refers to bonds rather than stocks.

Ginnie Mae   Government National Mortgage Association.

GO   General obligation bond.

good-till-canceled order (GTC)   An order to buy or sell a security that is left in force until executed. However, such orders are automatically canceled on the last business day of April and October.

Government National Mortgage Association (also called **Ginnie Mae**)   A corporation owned by the U.S. government that invests in mortgages for government-subsidized housing and in other mortgages that carry greater risk than private firms could afford.

H

hedge   Investing to reduce the risk of a position in a security, normally by taking an offsetting position in a related security.

hot issue   An issue that sells at a premium over the public offering price on the first day of trading.

house maintenance call   A brokerage firm's demand that a client deposit money or securities when the client's equity falls below the brokerage firm's minimum maintenance level in a margin account.

I

income bond   A debt obligation that promises to repay bond principal in full at maturity and to pay interest only if there are adequate earnings.

index option   An option on a particular index such as the Standard & Poor's 500 index. Buying a Standard & Poor's 500 index option would be a good way to profit from a rising market.

index trader   One who trades in index options such as the Standard & Poor's 100 or the Major Market Index.

individual retirement account (IRA)   A qualified tax-deferred retirement plan for employed individuals.

initial public offering   The original sale of a company's securities to the public.

inside information   Material information that has not yet been made generally available to the public.

insider   Anyone who has nonpublic knowledge (material information) about a corporation. Insiders include directors, officers and stockholders who own more than ten percent of any class of equity security of a corporation.

in-street-name account   An account in which the customer's securities are held in the name of the brokerage firm.

investment banking   The business of underwriting issues of securities, of buying or selling securities as a dealer or of buying and selling securities on the order and for the benefit of others as a broker.

issuer   The corporation or municipality that offers its securities for sale.

J

joint account   An account in which two or more individuals act as cotenants or co-owners of the account. The account owners may be joint tenants in common or "joint tenants with rights of survivorship," in which a deceased tenant's fractional interest in the account is retained by the surviving tenant(s).

junk bonds   Bonds that are rated double-B or lower. These are often referred to as "high-yield bonds."

K

Keogh Plan   A qualified tax-deferred retirement plan for persons who are self-employed and unincorporated or who earn extra income aside from their regular employment through personal services.

L

limit order   An order that is to be executed only at a specific price or better. A limit order to sell sets a minimum sales price. A limit order to buy sets a maximum purchase price. (See Chapter 13, page 200.)

limited partnership   A form of business organization in which one or more of the partners is liable only to the extent of the amount of dollars each partner has invested. Limited partners are not involved in management decisions but do enjoy direct flow-through of income and expenses.

listed option   An option that can be bought and sold on a national securities exchange in a continuous secondary market.

listed securities   Securities that are traded on a national securities exchange such as the New York Stock Exchange.

long position   The ownership of shares of a particular stock.

M

Major Market Index   A stock index based on 20 major blue-chip stocks that is traded on the American Stock Exchange. The symbol is MMI.

margin account   An account in which a brokerage firm lends a client part of the price of the securities purchased by the client.

margin call A demand for a client to deposit money or securities when a purchase has been made in a margin account.

markdown The difference between the current bid price among other dealers and the actual price that a dealer pays to a customer.

market order An order to buy or sell a security that is to be executed at the best available price.

markup The difference between the current offering price among other dealers and the actual price that a dealer charges its customers.

M1 A definition of the money supply that includes all coins, currency and demand deposits.

money market The segment of the securities market that deals in short-term (less than one year) debt issues.

mortgage bonds Debt obligations secured by a property pledge. These are liens or mortgages against the issuing corporation's properties and real estate assets.

M2 A definition of the money supply that includes all coins, currency and demand deposits; time deposits, and savings deposits.

municipal bond A debt security issued by a municipality to raise capital to finance its capital expenditures. These expenditures can include highway construction, public works, school buildings, etc.

mutual fund A type of investment company that has outstanding or offers for sale securities that it has issued. These securities are redeemable on demand by the fund at their current net asset value. All owners of the fund share in its gains or losses.

N

NASDAQ (pronounced "nazdak") National Association of Securities Dealers Automated Quotations system.

National Association of Securities Dealers (NASD) The association empowered by the SEC to supervise over-the-counter brokers and dealers that are members.

National Association of Securities Dealers Automated Quotations system (NASDAQ) A National Association of Securities Dealers subsidiary that owns and operates a computerized communications system that stores up-to-the-second price quotations from a nationwide network of dealers for more than 3,000 over-the-counter stocks.

NAV Net asset value.

negotiable certificate of deposit A negotiable certificate that evidences a time deposit of funds with a bank. It is an unsecured promissory note normally issued in $100,000 denominations.

net change The difference between the closing price on the trading day reported and the previous day's closing price.

new issue   A stock or bond being offered to the public for the first time by a public or previously private corporation. (*See:* public offering.)

New York Stock Exchange (NYSE)   The largest and oldest stock exchange in the United States. Address: 11 Wall Street, New York, NY 10005.

no-load fund   A mutual fund whose shares are sold without having a sales charge added to the net asset value. (See Chapter 12, page 185.)

numbered account   An account titled with something other than a client's name, such as a number, symbol or special title.

NYSE   New York Stock Exchange.

O

odd-lot   An order for less than the normal unit of trading, which is usually 100 shares.

OEX   Symbol and nickname for the Standard & Poor's 100 stock index.

offer   The price at which a person is willing to sell a particular security.

offering price   With reference to mutual funds, the price an investor will pay per share. The offering price is the net asset value plus a sales charge (for funds that have a sales charge).

option   A security that gives the buyer the right to buy (or sell) a quantity of stock at a specified price within a specified period of time.

outstanding stock   Issued stock in the hands of the public minus issued stock that has been reacquired by the corporation.

P

par value   An arbitrary dollar value assigned to each share of stock at the time of issuance; also, the face value (principal) amount of a bond.

P/E   Price-earnings ratio.

point   In the U.S. stock market, a point is equal to $1; in the U.S. bond market, it is equal to 1 percent of par and worth $10 per $1,000.

position   A net long or short inventory in a security established by either an individual or a dealer.

preferred stock   An equity security that represents ownership in a corporation. It has a fixed dividend, has dividend preference over common stock and generally carries no voting right.

preliminary prospectus   The first prospectus issued on a forthcoming offering. This prospectus includes all of the essential facts except the underwriting spread, the final offering price and the date shares will be delivered. (*Syn.:* red herring.)

premium   A bond that sells above par (above 100 percent of $1,000); that is, the purchase price of the bond is greater than its par value. Also, the selling price of an option.

price-earnings ratio   The ratio of the current market value of a stock divided by the annual earnings per share. (See Chapter 13, page 207.)

primary distribution   An offering of newly issued securities, the proceeds of which go to the company. (*Syn.:* primary offering.)

prime rate   The interest rate that commercial banks charge their most creditworthy customers.

principal   A firm that is actively engaged in the buying and reselling of securities; also, an investor's capital; also, the face or par value of a bond.

prospectus   The legal document that must be given to every investor who purchases registered securities in an offering. This document describes the company and the details of the particular offering.

proxy   The written power of attorney by which a stockholder authorizes someone else to vote in the stockholder's absence.

public offering   The sale of a corporation's securities to the investment public, usually conducted by an investment banker or a group or syndicate of investment bankers.

put   The right to sell a specific number of shares of stock at a stated price within a specified time.

R

redemption notice   An announcement that a company or municipality is redeeming, or recalling, a certain issue of bonds.

red herring   Preliminary prospectus.

registered representative   A salesperson who is licensed and employed by a securities firm to handle securities transactions.

Regulation A offering   An offering of securities that is not registered, on the condition that no more than $1.5 million worth of securities will be offered during a 12-month period.

REIT   Real estate investment trust.

resistance   A term used in technical analysis to describe the top of a stock's trading range. (See Chapter 13, page 201.)

restricted account   A margin account in which the equity is less than the initial margin amount required by the Federal Reserve Board.

S

S&P 500   Standard & Poor's 500; also, the option traded on the Chicago Board Options Exchange based on the S&P 500 stock index.

S&P 100   The option traded on the Chicago Board Options Exchange based on the Standard & Poor's 100 stock index.

SEC   Securities and Exchange Commission.

secondary distribution   An offering of previously issued securities, usually owned by a major stockholder such as a company founder. Such an offering does not increase the number of shares outstanding.

secondary market   The market in which previously issued securities are traded.

secondary offering   A redistribution of a block of stock. The proceeds of such an offering go to the party that owned the stock, not to the corporation whose stock is being offered.

Securities and Exchange Commission (SEC)   A government body created by Congress to protect investors. (See Chapter 8, page 134.)

Securities Investor Protection Corporation (SIPC) (pronounced "Si-pick")   A nonprofit membership corporation created by Congress to protect clients of brokerage firms that are forced into bankruptcy. It insures each client's account for up to $500,000. Many brokerage firms also offer several million dollars of additional insurance through a private insurance carrier.

settlement date   The date on which a transaction must be settled (cash is exchanged for securities).

short sale   The sale of a security that the seller does not own or any sale consummated by the delivery of a security borrowed by, or for the account of, the seller. (See Chapter 13, page 202.)

SIPC   Securities Investor Protection Corporation.

special miscellaneous account (SMA)   A separate account operated in conjunction with a general margin account. Funds are credited to the SMA on a memo basis, and the SMA is used much like a line of credit with a bank.

spot   The cash price or current delivery price of a commodity. Gold, oil and other commodities can be bought on the "spot market."

spread   In reference to a quotation, the spread is the difference between the bid and the offer.

Standard & Poor's 500 (S&P 500)   A market indicator composed of 400 industrial stocks, 20 transportation stocks, 40 financial stocks and 40 public utility stocks.

stop-limit order   A stop order that becomes a limit order once the market price reaches or passes the specific price stated in the stop order. (See Chapter 13, page 200.)

stop order   An order to buy or sell securities once the market price reaches or passes a specified price. (See Chapter 13, page 200.)

street name   Refers to securities that are owned by a client but, for reasons of convenience, are held by the brokerage firm in its own name. (See Chapter 13, page 202.)

support   A term used in technical analysis to describe the bottom of a stock's trading range. (See Chapter 13, page 201.)

T

T-bill   U.S. Treasury bill.

technical analysis   A method of securities analysis that concentrates on the supply and demand of the stock market, a particular industry group or an individual stock.

tender offer   An offer to buy securities for cash, for other securities or for both.

10-K report   A version of an annual report with more detailed financial information that all U.S. corporations are required to file with the SEC.

trade confirmation   A bill or comparison of a trade that is sent to a customer on or before the first business day following the trade date.

trade date   The date on which a transaction occurred.

Treasury bill *(T-bill)*   Non-interest-bearing discount securities issued by the U.S. Treasury to finance the national debt. Most Treasury bills are issued with maturities of three months, six months or one year and are sold in units of $10,000 to $1 million at a discount from face value.

trend line   The line that traces a stock's movement by connecting the reaction lows in an upward trend or the rally highs in a downward trend.

U

UIT   Unit investment trust.

uncovered call writer   An investor who writes a call without owning the underlying security. *(See:* call option.)

underwriter   In reference to securities, an investment banker (or group or syndicate) that agrees to purchase a new issue of securities from an issuer and to distribute it to investors at a profit.

unit investment trust (UIT)   An investment vehicle with a portfolio of stocks or bonds. Investors can buy both "fixed" (no portfolio changes are made) and "nonfixed" (portfolio changes are permissible) redeemable UIT securities.

V

variable annuity   A type of annuity contract in which the insurance company makes variable dollar payments for the term of the contract. *(See:* annuity.)

volatility   The degree to which a security is subject to sudden and unpredictable price changes.

W

warrant   A certificate giving the holder the right to purchase securities at a stipulated price. This certificate is usually a long-term instrument affording the investor the option of buying shares at a later date (presumably when the shares are worth more) at the subscription price, subject to the warrant's expiration date.

wash sale   The purchase of the same security within 30 days of realizing a capital loss in that security.

widow-and-orphan security   A stock that is considered safe and pays high dividends. Utility stocks are often referred to as widow-and-orphan stocks.

window dressing   A mutual fund that makes portfolio adjustments at the end of a quarter to sell stocks that have performed badly and to buy stocks that have performed well, so that when the quarterly report is issued, it will appear that the mutual fund manager has invested in the right stocks during the previous quarter.

wire house   Generally refers to the largest national and international brokerage firms.

Y

yield   The rate of return on an investment, generally expressed as a percentage of the current price.

yield to maturity   The rate of return on an investment that accounts for the cash difference between a bond's acquisition cost and its maturity proceeds.

INDEX

A

AAII Journal, 168
A, B, and C accounts, 105-06
Account and monthly statement,
    181-82
Accrued interest, def., 239
Advance-decline line, def., 239
Advertisements, as source of suspects,
    97-98
Advest, Inc., 45, 230
Aetna Life and Casualty, 167
A.G. Edwards & Sons, Inc., 41, 63-64,
    65, 105, 182, 232
    profile of, 63-64
Agent, def., 239
Aggressive growth funds, 189
Aggressive policy, def., 239
Air pocket stocks, 201
Alex Brown & Sons, Inc., 44, 231
Allen, Woody, 122
American Association of Individual
    Investors (AAII), 168
American Can, 66
American Depository Receipt (ADR),
    def., 239
American Express, 62
American Stock Exchange (AMEX),
    def., 239

Analysts, 29-32
    major areas of research, 31-32
Annual report, reading, 204-06
Annuity, def., 239
Approximate earnings per share, 207
Arbitrage, def., 240
Arbitration, 138-42, 238
    securities industry organizations to
    contact, 238
Asher, Tom, 12, 46, 76-77, 81, 86, 120,
    132, 145, 148, 152, 157, 163-64,
    224
Ashland, 167
Asset, def., 240
Asset management account, 182
Assets, determining, 70
AT & T, 98
Auditor's letter, 205
Automatic calling machines, 95-96

B

Back-end sales charge, 195
Balance sheet, 205, 240
Ball, George, 62
Banaszak, Pete, 4-5
Banky, Adrian, 33, 150, 224
Barrons, 20, 97, 167, 187

Baruch, Bernard, 27
Basil, Henry, 19, 21-22, 26, 27, 28, 98,
   110-11, 114-15, 118
Basis point, def., 240
Bateman Eichler, Hill Richards, Inc.,
   229
Baxter, Joe, 81, 106, 118, 223
B.C. Christopher Securities Company,
   231
Bearish, def., 240
Bear markets, 14-15, 146, 173, 240
Bear Stearns & Co., Inc., 51, 52, 67,
   232
Bergstrom, William, 184, 185, 195
Bertelsen, Rab, 166, 183, 187, 188
Best Mailing Lists and Printing
   Corporation, 97
Better Investing, 168
Bid, def., 240
Big Board, def., 240
Biotech field, 21-22
Black Monday, 4, 24, 175, 184, 210,
   211
Blinder-Robinson, 50
Blount, Bill, 110, 117, 119, 133, 158,
   178
Blue chips, 201, 240
Blue-sky, def., 240
Blunt Ellis & Loewi, Inc., 236
Blyth Eastman Dillon, 63
BMA Financial Services, Inc., 232
Boettcher & Co., Inc., 229
Bond funds, 189
Bond swap, def., 240
Book value, 206-07, 240
Bottom fishing, def., 240
Bottom out, def., 240
Bradford, Kim, 94
Branch office approach to finding
   stockbroker, 75-77, 87
Breakout, def., 240
Break points, 196
Broker, def., 240
Broker-client relationship, 72, 109-20
Broker partnerships, 178-79
Brokerage firms
   design of, 7-8

NASD, 48-49, 50
NYSE national, 41-44
NYSE regional, 44-48
   selection of, 40-68
   special services, 182
Brokers; *see* Stockbrokers
Brown Brothers Harriman & Co., 232
Buckley, Betsy, 10, 17, 23, 34, 80-81,
   93, 106, 110, 119, 149, 178, 221,
   222, 226
Buehler, Jim, 9, 10, 14, 20, 29, 94, 104,
   221
Bullish, def., 241
Bull markets, 25, 150, 173, 184, 241
"Business Report", 20
Business Week, 20, 97, 168, 187
Butcher & Singer, Inc., 235
Buying a call, 209
Buying a put, 209-10
Buying long, 201
Buying power, def., 241

C

California Microwave, 21
Call loan rate, 174, 241
Call option, def., 241
Call protection, def., 241
Call provision, def., 241
Calvert Social Investment Fund, 191
Cardiac Pacemaker, 49
Carolina Securities Corporation, 234
Casey, Donnis, 8, 53, 124, 142, 146,
   148, 221
Cash Management Account, 58, 182
"Center of influence", 19
Changing brokers, 152-54
Charles Schwab & Co., 41, 157, 210
Chicago Corporation, 230
Choosing a stockbroker, 39-68, 69-88
   determining your objectives, 69-72
   four-stage process, 40
   suspects, seeking out, 72-77
Churning, 125, 127-28, 241
City Securities, 41

Clark, Phil, 12-13, 45, 46, 147, 148, 227
Clayton Brown & Associates, 230
Client referrals, 14
Close, def., 241
Closed-end funds, 191-93
Cohen, Gary, 150, 221, 224
Cohn, Bob, 41, 147, 222
Coincidental indicators, 203
Cold calls, 8, 12, 13-14, 91, 94-96, 99-101, 108
responding to, 108
Cole, Merrilee, 17, 179
Command Account, 182
COMEX, def., 241
Commercial paper, def., 241
Commission-free stocks, 166-67
Commissions, 15-16, 22-23
Commodities, 62, 129-31
violations, 129-31
Common stock, def., 241
Compliance, 122, 124, 134, 140
Comprehensive personalized financial plans, 55
Compulsory commission rate schedule, 158
Computer-aided financial plans, 55
Computer printout financial plan, 177
Computerized forecasting techniques, 31
"Computerized Investing", 169
Confidence schemes, 141
Consumer education, 42
Consumer price index (CPI), 204, 241
Control Data, 25, 133
Conversion parity, def., 241
Convertible bond, def., 241
Coupon yield, def., 242
Covered call options, 130
Cowen & Co., 30, 232
Craig Hallum, Inc., 41, 49, 231
Crash of 1929, 173
Crash of October, 1987, 4, 15, 173; *see also* Black Monday
Crowell, Weedon, & Co., 229
Current Investment Strategy, 177
Current ratio, 207

Current yield, def., 242
Cyclical economic indicators, 203
Cyrus J. Lawrence, 30

D

D.A. Davidson & Co., Inc., 232
Dain Bosworth, Inc., 231
Daisy chain, def., 242
Davis, Britt, 54
Dealer, def., 242
Dean Witter Reynolds, 11, 30, 41, 52, 59-60, 194, 232
profile of, 59-60
Debenture, def., 242
Defensive policy, def., 242
Deferred annuity, def., 242
Deluxe financial plan, 178
Dillon, Read & Co., Inc., 232
Discount brokers, 57, 118, 157-70
Discount buying, 157-70
Discount rate, def., 242
Discounts, from full-service brokers, 171-72
Discretionary accounts, 178, 242
Dishonorable stockbrokers, 4-5
Dismissing brokers, 145-52
Diversity of investments, 5-6
Dividend, def., 242
Dividend payout ratio, def., 242
Dividend yield, def., 242
Dollar-cost averaging, 207-09, 242
Dominick & Dominick, Inc., 232
Donaldson, Lufkin & Jenrette Securities Corporation, 30, 51, 53, 65, 232
Door-to-door, in prospecting, 98-99
Dow Jones Industrial Average, 14, 150, 191, 204, 210, 242
Dow Theory Forecasts, 169
Drexel Burnham Lambert, Inc., 30, 41, 67-68, 233
profile of, 67-68
Dubbels, Lory, 180
Due diligence, def., 243
Dunwoody, Bob, 40, 57, 80, 114

E

Earnings per share (EPS), def., 243
Eberstadt Fleming, 30
Edward D. Jones, 52, 57, 68, 232
Efficient market theory, def., 243
E.F. Hutton, 3, 11, 30, 34, 41, 53, 57,
    60-61, 98, 233
    profile of, 60-61
Eli Lilly, 49
Eppler, Guerin & Turner, Inc., 235
Equipment trust certificate, def., 243
Equity, def., 243
Ethical funds, 190-91
Ex-dividend date, def., 243
Exercise, def., 243
Exercise price, def., 243

F

Face value, def., 243
Fahnestock & Co., Inc., 233
Families of funds, 194-95
Farrell Report, 177
Federal National Mortgage Association
    (FNMA) (Fannie Mae), def., 243
Female stockbrokers, 17-18
Ferris & Co., Inc., 230
Fidelity Brokerage Services, Inc., 231
Fidelity Investments, 41, 159, 164, 165,
    194
Fidelity Magellan, 194
Financial highlights, reading, 205
Financial planners, finding, 56-57
Financial planning firms, 53-57, 61
Financial planning services, from
    stockbrokers, 177-78
Financial plans, 53-57
Financial Services Corporation, 41, 53
Financial statements, understanding,
    206-07
Financial World, 59, 66, 68
Firing brokers, 145-52
First Albany Corporation, 232
First All-American Analyst, 30
First Boston Corporation, 30, 51, 233
First Heritage Corporation, 231
First of Michigan Corporation, 231
Fixed annuity, def., 243

Flat, def., 243
Fleitman, Ed, 48, 49
Footnotes, reading on annual report,
    205-06
Forbes, 20, 97, 167, 168, 187
Fortune, 20, 97, 167, 168
14/71 Rule, 104-06
44 Wall Street Equity Fund, 184
Fox, D'Arcy, 40, 85, 105, 133, 142,
    145, 226
Free-falling, 201
"From the president" notice, reading,
    205
Fundamentals, 202, 243
Futures contract, def., 243

G

Gemini Capital Fund, 192, 193
Genentech Corporation, 21-22
General Electric, 66, 67
General obligation bond (GO), def.,
    244
General Telephone, 28
Gerber, Ed, 167
Gilt-edged security, def., 244
Ginnie Maes, 63
Goldman, Sachs & Co., 30, 40, 50, 51,
    64, 233
Government National Mortgage
    Association (Ginnie Maes), 244
Government securities funds, 190
Granville, Joe, 170
Granville Market Letter, 170
Gross commissions, 15-16; *see also*
    Commissions
Gross profit margin ratio, 206
Growth and income funds, 188-89
Growth Stock Outlook, 169
Grubb, Dale, 13, 14, 33, 79, 100, 101,
    109, 116, 146-47, 178, 228
Gruntal & Co., 233
GTC, 200, 244

H

Haas Securities, 164, 165
Hartford Accident and Indemnity

Company, 65
Hartwell Leverage Fund, 184
Hedge, def., 244
Heiam, Al, 11, 15, 23, 24, 28, 82, 86, 105, 113
Hensle, Lyn, 45, 221, 227
Henley, Shawn, 94, 100
Honesty, with broker, 112
Hopper Soliday & Co., Inc., 235
Horrall, Scott, 8, 10, 19, 23, 94, 99, 103, 104, 222
Hot issue, def., 244
House maintnenance call, def., 244
Houseman, John, 65
Howard, Weil, Labouisse, Friedrichs, Inc., 231
Hudson, Tom, 4, 16, 40, 73, 82, 116, 145
Hulbert, Mark, 4, 169-70
Hulbert Financial Digest, 4, 169
Hunt brothers, 62

International securities, 58
Interpacific Investors Securities, Inc., 236
Interstate Securities Corporation, 234
Interviewing a stockbroker, 78-86
Investment banking, def., 245
Investment clubs, 168-69
Investment objective, determining, 71, 93
Investment Portfolios, Inc., 196
Investment profile, 71
Investment seminars, 73-74, 98
Investments
    effects of emotions on, 23-26
    packaged, 52
    types of, 34, 183
Investmentspeak, 199-220
Investor complaints to SEC, 125
first time, profile, 78
Investor's Daily, 20, 97, 167, 168
Issuer, def., 245

I

IDS Financial Services, 41, 53, 54, 194
IDS Stock Fund, 196
Incentives to sell, 106-08
Income bond, 244
Income statement, 205
Index funds, 191
Index option, def., 244
Index traders, 210-11, 244
Individual retirement account (IRA), def., 244
Inertia Dynamics, 29
Influence of national NYSE firms, 41
Initial public offering, def., 244
Inside information, def., 244
Insider, def., 245
Insider trading scandal, 67, 68
Insitutional firms, 50-53
Institutional Investor, 30, 58, 67
Institutional securities, 58
In-street-name account, def., 245
Interest rates, as economic indicators, 204
Integrated Resources, 53
International funds, 190

J

Janney Montgomery Scott, Inc., 235
Japan Fund, 193
J.C. Bradford & Co., 235
J.J.B. Hilliard/W.L. Lyons, Inc., 230
John G. Kinnard & Co., Inc., 231
John Nuveen & Co., Inc., 230
Johnson, Judy, 4, 43, 45, 127, 132, 152
Johnson, Lane, Space, Smith & Co., 230
Johnston, Lemon & Co., Inc., 230
Joint account, def., 245
Josephthal & Co., Inc., 233
Junk bonds, 67, 189, 245

K

Kane, Arthur, 176
Kemper Financial Services, 194, 195
Keogh Plan, def., 245
Key economic indicators, 203-04
Kidder, Peabody & Co., Inc., 30, 41, 66-67, 233
    profile of, 66-67

Kopp, Lee, 3, 12, 14, 21, 23, 29, 35, 57, 80, 113, 114, 117, 129, 134, 163, 177, 228
Korea Fund, 192
Koriath, Bill, 9, 13, 34, 93, 111, 117-18, 148, 149, 151, 227

L

Landenburg, Thalmann & Co., Inc., 233
Lagging indicators, 203
Laidlaw Adams & Peck, Inc., 233
Language of investment, 199-220
Leading indicators, 203
Lefton, Dr. Robert, 9, 10, 11, 20, 123
Legg Mason Wood Walker, Inc. 231
L.F. Rothschild, Unterberg, Towbin, Inc., 30, 51, 53, 234
Legal action against broker, 137-38
Lehman closed-end fund, 193
Lehman Brothers, 61
Letter of intent, 197
Levesque, Beaubien, Inc., 236
Liabilities, determining, 70
Limited partnership, def., 245
Limit order, 200, 245
Lipper Analytical Services, 187, 188
Lipper Indexes, 187
Listed option, def., 245
Listed securities, def., 245
Load funds, 195
Long, Perrin, 11, 45, 57, 64, 65, 68, 123, 130, 131, 222
Longman Financial Services Institute, 126
Long position, def., 245
Lorain County Investment Club, 168
Low-load funds, 195

M

McDonald & Co. Securities, Inc., 234
McDonald's, 167
McKinney, Bill, 53, 54, 55, 98
McTaggart, Jack, 126, 142
Mabon, Nugent, & Co., 233

"Magnetic meatballism", 76-77
Major Market Index, def., 246
Malo, Norman, 53, 54, 55, 57
Management training programs, 61
Margin accounts, 14, 24, 122, 173-75, 246
Margin calls, 175-76, 246
Markdown, def., 246
Market Logic 169
Market newsletters, 169-70
Market order, 200, 246
Markup, def., 246
Maximizer, 187
Mentor Corporation, 189
Merrill, Charles, 189
Merrill, Charles, 58
Merrill Lynch Pierce, Fenner & Smith, Inc., 3, 11, 30, 41, 52, 57, 58-59, 162, 177, 182, 194, 233
profile of, 58-59
Midland Doherty, Inc., 230
Milwaukee Company, 236
Misappropriation, 131-32
Misrepresentation, 125-26
Mitchell Hutchins, 63
MKI Securities Coproation, 233
M1, def., 246
Money, 20, 97, 166, 167, 168, 187, 188
"Moneyline", 20
Money management, 61
Money market funds, 191, 246
Montgomery Securities, 30
Moore & Schley, Cameron & Co., 233
Morgan, Keegan & Co., Inc., 235
Morgan Olmstead, 40
Morgan Stanley & Co., 30, 40, 51, 53, 233
Mortgage bonds, def., 246
Moseley Securities Corporation, 231
M2, def., 246
Municipal bonds, 41, 46, 246
Murphey Favre, Inc., 236
Musicland, 66
Mutual Fund Forecaster, 187
Mutual funds, 58, 183-98, 218, 246
benefits, 184
compared to Standard & Poor's 500, 184-85

estimating cost of buying, 197
of mutual funds, 191

N

Naked calls, 130
NAIC; *see* National Association of
Investors Corporation
NASD; *see* National Association of
Securities Dealers
NASDAQ National Market, 220
National Association of Investors
Corporation (NAIC), 168
National Association of Securities
Dealers (NASD), 48-49, 50, 107,
246
arbitration, 148, 140
filing complaints with, 134-35
National Association of Securities
Dealers Automated Quotation
System (NASDAQ), def., 246
National Bureau of Economic
Research, 203
Nationals; *see* New York Stock
Exchange; national firms
Need approach sales pitch, 101-102
Negotiable certificate of deposit, def.,
247
Neighborhood cross-reference
directories, as source of
suspects, 97
Neimann, Paul, 137-38, 141
Nesbill Thomson Deacon, Inc., 236
Net change, def., 247
Net working capital, 207
Net worth, determining, 70
New issue, def., 247
New York Exchange Bonds, 219-20
New York Stock Exchange (NYSE), 16,
19, 41-48, 57-68, 217, 221, 247
brokers, compared to NASD
brokers, 48
filing complaints with, 134-35
national firms, 41-44, 57-68
regional firms, 44-48
Newhard, Cook & Co., Inc., 232
Newspapers, as source of suspects, 97

Niagara Shares, 193
90-second sale, 102-04
Nippon Life, 62
No-load funds, 185, 195, 247
Nomura Securities International, Inc.,
233
North American Investment
Corporation, 229
Numbered account, def., 247
NYSE; *see* New York Stock Exchange

O

Oberweis Securities, Inc., 230
Obituaries, as source of suspects, 97
Odd-lot, def., 247
OEX, def., 247
Offer, def., 247
Offering price, def., 247
Ohio Company, 235
*100 Best Companies in America to
Work For,* 64
Onetime transactions, and discount
brokers, 162
Operational problems, 143-154
Oppenheimer & Co., Inc., 30, 51, 234
Option, def., 247
Options disclosure statement, 130, 131
Options trading, 209-10
Options violations, 129-31
Outstanding stock, def., 247
Over-the-counter stocks, 41, 62

P

Packaged investments, 41
PaineWebber, 3, 11, 30, 34, 41, 57, 63,
104, 105, 182, 234
discounts, 163
profile of, 63
Parker/Hunter, Inc., 235
Par value, def., 247
Pax World Fund, 190
Pemberton Houston Willoughby Bell
Gouinlock, Inc., 236
Penny stock firms, 50
Periodic investment privileges, 193-94

Personalized computer printout
  financial plan, 177
Piper, Jaffray, & Hopwood, Inc., 45,
  231
Pizza Transit Authority, 49
Point, def., 202, 247
Poor performance, 150-51
Position, def., 247
"Power dialing", 94
Preferred stock, def., 247
Preliminary prospectus, def., 248
Premium, def., 248
Prescott, Ball & Turben, Inc., 234
Pressures of stockbrokers, 107
Price-earnings ratio, 207, 248
Primary distribution, def., 248
Prime rate, def., 248
Primerica Corporation, 66
Principal, def., 248
Problems with stockbrokers, 143-54
Product approach sales pitch, 99-101
Program traders, 210-211
Prospects, 13
Prospectus, def., 248
Proxy, def., 248
Prudential-Bache Securities, Inc., 11,
  30, 57, 62-63, 182, 194, 234
  profile of, 62, 63
Prudential Insurance Company, 63
Psychological Associates, 9, 11, 123
Public corporations, shareholders of,
  84, 85
Public offering, def., 248
Put, def., 248
Putnam High Income Government
  Trust, 196

Real estate limited partnerships, 24
Recommendations, unsuitable, 126-27
Redemption notice, def., 248
Red herring, def., 248
Regan, Donald, 182
Registered representative, def., 248
Registered Representative, 14, 20
Regulation A offering, def., 248
Reinvestment of dividends from mutual
  funds, 194
Rejection, and stockbrokers, 12-14
Relationship between broker and client,
  72, 109-20, 143-54
Rented lists, for acquring suspects, 97
Research analysts, 29-32
Research departments, 30, 41, 46, 119,
  176-77
  rankings, 30
Research Highlights, 177
Reserve Management Account, 182
Resisteance level, 201, 248
Restricted account, def., 248
Return on equity, 206
R.G. Dickinson & Co., 230
Rights of accumulation, 196
Risk disclosure booklets, 130
"Risk threshold", 70, 93
Ritterreiser, Robert P., 60-61
Robert W. Baird & Co., Inc., 236
Robinson-Humphrey Company, Inc.,
  40, 230
Roney & Co., 231
Rose & Co., 164, 165
R. Rowland & Co., 232
Ruby, Allen, 5-6

Q-R

Quaker Oats, 167
Qualfying suspects, 92-93, 96
Quick & Reilly, 164, 165
Rating your broker, 221-28
Rating yourself as a client, 225
Rauscher Pierce Refsnes, Inc., 235
Raymond James & Associates, Inc.,
  230
RCM Corporation, 107

S

S&P 100, def., 249
St. Jude Medical, 49
St. Paul Companies, 167
Salaries, noncommissioned, 15
Sales assistants, 179-81
Sales methods by brokers, 91-108
Salomon Brothers, 30, 50, 61, 66,
  234
Samuelson, Paul, 197
Sanford C. Bernstein, 30

Schwab, Charles, 157, 159, 160,
    161-62, 164-65
Scott & Stringfellow, Inc., 235
Sears Financial Centers, 60
Sears Roebuck, 41, 59
Secondary distribution, def., 249
Secondary market, def., 249
Secondary offering, def., 249
Sector funds, 190
Securities and Exchange Commission,
    50, 67, 122, 125, 158, 237, 249
    advice for investors, 141
    filing complaints with, 134-35
    number of complaints to, 139-40
    offices of, 136-37
    and options complaints, 130-31
Securities attorneys, finding, 137
Securities Industry Organizations, and
    arbitrations, 238
Securities Investor Protection
    Corporation (SIPC), def., 249
Securities violations, 123
Selecting a stockbroker, 39-68, 69-88
    four-stage process, 40
Selling a call, 209
Selling long, 201
Selling a put, 210
Selling short, 201-02
Selling your stock, 26-28
Services of stockbrokers, 4, 34-35
Settlement date, def., 249
Shareholders of public corporations,
    84, 85
Shearson/American Express v.
    McMahom, 138
Shearson Lehman Brothers, Inc., 11,
    30, 41, 61-62, 194, 234
    profile of, 61-62
Short sale, def., 249
Siegel, Martin, 66, 67
Single premium deferred annuities, 34
Sliding scale pay, 17
Smith Barney, Harris Upham & Co.,
    Inc., 30, 41, 65-66, 106, 234
    profile of, 65-66
Solot, Lee, 9, 76, 81-82
Soule, Kathy, 13, 18, 19, 81, 92, 99,
    101, 117, 177, 226
Special miscellaneous account (SMA),

    def., 249
Specialty funds, 190
Spot, def., 249
Spread, def., 249
Standard & Poor's 500 Index, 150, 188,
    191, 204, 211, 249
Standard & Poor's Outlook 169
Standard & Poor's Stock Guide 177
Statements, reading, 216
Steadman American Industry Fund,
    188
Stephens, Inc., 229
Stern, Harry, 5
Stifel, Nicolaus & Co., Inc., 232
Stock prices
    as economic indicators, 204
    factors that determine, 32
Stockbrokers
    alternate names of, 3
    backgrounds of, 10-11
    choosing, 39-68, 69-88
    client referrals, 14
    client relationship, 72, 109-20,
        149-50
    commissions, 22-23
    discount, 57, 118, 157-70
    discounts from full service, 171-72
    dishonorable, 4-5, 121, 42
    and down markets, 29
    experienced vs. newer brokers,
        80-82
    extras from, 171-82
    firing of, 145-52
    getting relief from 134-42
    gross commissions, 15-16; *see also*
        Commissions
    hiring of, 8, 123
    information, translations of, 33-34
    interviewing, 77-86
    legal action against, 137-38
    long hours, of, 8
    loss of clients, 145-52
    noncommissioned salaries, 15
    potential, 11
    pressures of, 107-08
    pressures by, 147
    problems with, 143-54
    profile of, 8-10, 12-14, 23-26, 123
    rating your, 221

recommendations, 46, 113-14
referrals, 72-73, 115
sales methods of, 91-108; *see also*
    Cold calls
services of, 4, 34-35, 171-82
sliding scale pay, 17
sources of prospects, 13-14, 92-93,
    96, 97-99
switching firms by brokers, 151
TAPES approach, 79-86
training of, 15
turnover of, 43
typical day of, 19-20
unscrupulous, 121,-42
violations, most common, 128
Stop-limit order, 200, 249
Stop-loss order, 200
Stop orders, 28, 200, 249
Street name, def., 202, 249
Stuart-James, 40-41, 50
Sundeen, John, 40, 122
Support level, 2301, 250
Suspects, seeking out, 72-77, 97-99
Sutro & Co., 44, 229
Switching brokers, 152-54

T

TAPES approach, 79-86
Tax-exempt bond funds, 190
Technical analysis, def., 250
Technical Equities, 5-6
Templeton family of funds, 194
Tender offer, def., 250
10-K report, def., 250
Thompson, David, 10, 19, 20, 34, 81,
    86, 107, 115, 181, 186, 221
Thomson McKinnon Securities, Inc.,
    33, 41, 65, 234
    profile of, 65
Tidlund, Don, 8, 14, 25, 26, 109-10,
    119-20, 180, 223, 224
"Top producers", 4
Total Assets Account, 182
Trade confirmation, def., 250
Trade date, def., 250
Treasury bill (T-bill), def., 250
Trend line, def., 250

Tri-Continental, 193
Tucker, Anthony, & R.L. Day, Inc., 234
12b-1 fee, 196

U

UMIC, Inc., 235
Unauthorized trades, 128-29
Uncovered call writer, def., 250
Underwriter, def., 250
Unit investment trusts, 193, 250
United Business Service 169
United Services Good and Bad Times
    Fund, 196
Universal life, 34, 61
Unscrupulous brokers, 121-42
Unscrupulous clients, 132-33
Unsuitable recommendations, 126-27
U.S. Commerce Department's Index of
    Leading Indicators (CLI), 204

V

Value Line Investment Survey 169, 170
Vanguard Index Trust, 191, 194
Variable annuity, def., 250
Vieburg, Jim, 27, 115, 132-33, 147,
    171, 172, 181, 228
Violations, most common broker, 128
Volatility, def., 251

W

Walt Disney Corporation, 25, 167
Wall Street Journal, 19, 97, 166, 167,
    192, 211-13, 216
"Wall Street Week", 20, 167
Walwyn Stodgell Cochran Murray,
    Ltd., 236
Warrant, def., 251
Wash sale, def., 251
Waterbury, David, 13, 14, 22-23, 25,
    114, 119, 151, 178, 179
Wedbush Securities, Inc., 229
Weiner, Marie, 5
Wertheim Schroder & Co., Inc., 30,
    234

Westbrook, Bonnie, 135
W.H. Newbold's Son & Co., Inc., 235
Wheat, First Securities, Inc., 235
Widow-and-orphan security, def., 251
Williams Securities, 41
Window dressing, def., 251
Wire house, def., 251
Wise, Bill, 183
Wisenberger Investment Companies
    Service, 187
Withdrawal plans, mutual funds, 194
Women stockbrokers, 17-18
Working Assets Money Fund, 191

Y-Z

Yellow pad plan, 177
Yield, def., 251
Yield to maturity, def., 251
Ziegler Thrift Trading, 165
Zuckerberg, Roy, 51
Zweig Forecast, 169